A PLACE BOTH WONDERFUL AND STRANGE

The Extraordinary Untold History of *Twin Peaks*

SCOTT MESLOW

RUNNING PRESS
PHILADELPHIA

Running Press
Hachette Book Group
1290 Avenue of the Americas, New York, NY 10104
www.runningpress.com
@Running_Press

First Edition: February 2026

Published by Running Press, an imprint of Hachette Book Group, Inc.
The Running Press name and logo are trademarks of Hachette Book Group, Inc.

Image credits: Pages 26, 91, 113: Courtesy Richard Hoover;
all other photography courtesy Photofest

Print book cover and interior design by Amanda Richmond

Library of Congress Cataloging-in-Publication Data
Names: Meslow, Scott author
Title: A place both wonderful and strange: the extraordinary untold history of *Twin Peaks*/Scott Meslow.
Description: Philadelphia: Running Press, 2026. | Includes bibliographical references and index. | Summary: "The full history of the cult franchise *Twin Peaks*—the original 1990 series, 1992 film Fire Walk With Me, and the 2017 follow-up series *The Return*—told with new insight from the people who made it, including co-creator Mark Frost, and many more"—Provided by publisher.
Identifiers: LCCN 2025026806 (print) | LCCN 2025026807 (ebook) | ISBN 9798894140391 hardcover | ISBN 9798894140414 epub
Subjects: LCSH: Twin Peaks (Television program: 1990–1991) | Twin Peaks, fire walk with me (Motion picture) | Twin Peaks (Television program: 2017) | Twin Peaks (Wash.: Imaginary place) | LCGFT: Television criticism and reviews | Film criticism
Classification: LCC PN1992.77.T88 M47 2026 (print) | LCC PN1992.77.T88 (ebook) | DDC 791.45/75—dc23/eng/20250721
LC record available at https://lccn.loc.gov/2025026806
LC ebook record available at https://lccn.loc.gov/2025026807

ISBNs: 979-8-89414-039-1 (hardcover), 979-8-89414-041-4 (ebook)

Printed in the United States of America

LSC-C

Printing 1, 2025

FOR PETER

CONTENTS

Foreword by Harley Peyton

It is often better to be lucky than good, and I was very lucky to have an acquaintance who suggested that maybe I'd like to see a screening of the TV pilot he wrote and produced with David Lynch. Like many who saw *Twin Peaks* at the Director's Guild that night, I stepped into the lobby stunned by what I had seen, and quite suddenly, like a door had been opened, inspired by all the things I had no idea a TV show could do. In the stupefied aftermath, I found Mark Frost in the crowd, and after telling him how I felt about his work, I added that while I hadn't written a lot of television, I'd do pretty much anything to get a shot at writing a future episode of his series.

Mark was kind enough to give me that chance. And I stepped into the world that he and David made, was able to meet all those extraordinary characters, was able, in my own modest way, to add a little bit of myself to the world and the characters I met. And that's about giving yourself a present, every day, like it's Christmas. And that's about the way pancake syrup collides with ham. (And yes, it's about a damn fine cup of coffee.) And before I knew it, I had joined the relatively insane enterprise that would shape and dominate my life for the next eighteen months.

That's about writing scripts, that's about working on set, that's about having lunch with Mark every day to talk more about our lives than the show he was creating. It's about the sudden and explosive *Twin Peaks* mania, pre-internet thank god, that took hold. And that's a feeling I'll never forget. Like riding a tiger who is riding a wave and tumbling, wave and tiger, toward shore.

But good things, even impossibly singular things, come to an end. And this one came to an end more quickly than any of us factored. In the aftermath, I moved on to other TV shows, other movies. But *Twin Peaks* always felt like a kind of baptism, the thing that came before all the other things. It was the first subject people asked me about when they discovered I had been there at the time. It taught me an inestimable amount about entering worlds created by others. It taught me how to create my own worlds too. But despite that, despite how important it was, those eighteen months, those days and nights, faded over the years. And the experience was transmuted more into memory.

But then, one afternoon, Mark called because he wanted me to hear the news from him and not a tweet. The thing we hoped for then was finally going to happen. A third season of *Twin Peaks*. But this time I was just another dedicated fan, eagerly waiting for what happened next, and not entirely sure how Mark and David could possibly land this particular plane.

But, oh, they did. And season three stands as the best TV show of the century to my eyes, and a perfect extension of the television show I called home. That was not only unexpected, it was a kind of miracle. And in its way, a fitting capstone to the series as a whole. I'd already said goodbye to *Twin Peaks* once. But now, after this third season, watching Cooper try so hard to change the past toward a circumstance that fit his humanity, listening to Carrie—who is really Laura—screaming with horror at what the world has done, I said goodbye a second time.

During Covid, my family and I moved out of Los Angeles and back to where I've always belonged. First, in a rental on Bainbridge Island. Then, having crossed the bridge toward more affordable land, in a little house deep in the Suquamish Woods. It made sense, then, that after all this time it was finally time for me to visit the annual *Twin Peaks* festival in Snoqualmie. I met Scott Meslow there—we'd already had several phone conversations—and we found ourselves immersed in the happily diverse and wonderfully eccentric family that has grown up around this television show. I genuinely treasured my time there, I'm determined to come back next year too, and not only because I now live approximately forty-five minutes from the Double R Diner's front door.

Not long after the festival, Scott surprised me by asking if I would write a forward to this book. And it's worth noting that in all the years since the eighteen months that changed my life, I've never actually read a book about *Twin Peaks*. The time, the place, the people who built it. And I think in part that's because I wanted to keep the past where it belonged. But also because I wanted to protect my own memories, my own experience, from the predations of opinion, perspective, and subjective history.

Hey. We do what we can to protect the things we love.

But now I've finally read a book about all that and I can say without hesitation that I'm delighted that *A Place Both Wonderful and Strange* is the book I read. And just to be clear, it's a moderately bold act to boast an *Extraordinary and Untold History* below that title. And to be honest, as I turned to the first page, there was a small voice inside me murmuring "Untold, really? We'll see about that." But by the time I arrived at the last page, I realized it was not a boast but rather a promise kept.

A Place Both Wonderful and Strange is many things. First, it's the history the show deserves, starting with the original Lynch/Frost collaboration, the fits and starts, the stories that were never told. And the way all of that ultimately become part of Twin Peak's DNA. And after that, firmly locating the reader inside the *way it all happened*, the book takes us, took me, from that start to its eventual finish. And that's about the first two seasons, it's about

Fire Walk with Me and it's about *The Return* too. The level of detail in the latter is as it should be, meticulous and revealing. And yes, it is factually correct to call it as it is called below the title. An extraordinary and untold history.

But that's not all! (I'm selling now, but I'm also pleased that you're reading this because it means you bought the book.). There is deeply felt analysis here, and that's a tricky venture when it comes to *Twin Peaks*. Because it is all too easy to dive into a pond so deep you never return to the surface. But Meslow—hi Scott!—manages to go deep and find his way back. And that's about the stories we told, it's about the characters and how they moved through them. In this way, the analysis is a perfect complement to the history. And speaking as someone who was there at the time, I enjoyed every word of it.

In the end, *Twin Peaks* has always contained more meaning than any show could possibly harbor. That's a by-product, of course. It's not something you can plan. But it makes *Twin Peaks* a great way to spend an hour (okay, nearly an hour) but also a text open to endless examination. That's the trick, isn't it? To welcome the viewer to a place that is familiar and deeply strange at the same time. To introduce them to characters they will never forget. I was lucky, I was there. And reading this book reminded me of how it felt at the time, how those feelings evolved over the years since. But most of all, *A Place Both Wonderful and Strange* is a kind of sentimental education. Beginning, middle, and end. And as close to the whole story, the history of *Twin Peaks*, as is possible.

I'm grateful for all of that. And while the reader will have their own connections, their own memories, I believe they, *you*, will be grateful too.

Time to turn the page. Time to read.

—Harley Peyton

August 2025

Chapter 1

A WOMAN IN TROUBLE

It began—how else?—over breakfast. In August of 1988, ABC executives Chad Hoffman and Gary Levine invited David Lynch and Mark Frost for a breakfast meeting at Café Plaza, an upscale hotel restaurant in the Century City district of Los Angeles. The cocreators were there to deliver their pitch for a quirky TV murder mystery that could serve as a midseason replacement following that summer's bruising Writers Guild strike. With the aid of a map, which Lynch had helpfully sketched in charcoal for the occasion, Lynch and Frost described a small town left shattered when the corpse of the homecoming queen washes up on the lakeshore.

It wasn't the first time ABC executives had heard a version of this story. Earlier that year, Lynch and Frost had met with Hoffman, the network's vice president of dramatic series development, who had earned a reputation as a forward-thinking executive by championing critical darlings like the Vietnam-set military drama *China Beach* and the yuppie-courting *thirtysomething*, which struck a chord with a cult audience of angsty baby boomers. When Lynch and Frost met with Hoffman to discuss the show that they were then calling *Northwest Passage*, it was, to say the least, mostly unformed: "There's this town and this wind . . . and there's a dead girl and then a whole bunch of stuff happens." Lynch, Frost recalls, punctuated this fuzzy description with enthusiastic jazz hands.

It had been a long path for both Lynch and Frost to reach this point. Then forty-two, Lynch had enjoyed cult success with his surreal debut feature, *Eraserhead*; the attention of the Academy Awards with his follow-up, *The Elephant Man*; an out-and-out flop with his sci-fi adaptation, *Dune*; and a career resuscitation with his psychological thriller, *Blue Velvet*, which explored the dark underbelly of American suburbia. He had never made a TV show before. In that way, he had an ideal partner in Frost, a wunderkind who wrote for *The Six Million Dollar Man* while he was still in college. Frost had cut his teeth in the writers' room for *Hill Street Blues*, a cop drama that was critically adored and daringly ahead of its time for its dense, serialized storytelling, handheld camerawork, and willingness to explore societal ills such as police corruption and institutional racism.

Lynch and Frost's pairing had a whiff of fate to it; after attending a midnight screening of *Eraserhead* in 1979, Frost recalls, he had "the oddest feeling" that he'd work with David Lynch someday. But it wasn't until 1986 that an agent put them in a room together, suggesting their sensibilities might align. "Upon meeting him, I kind of felt like Huck Finn meeting Tom Sawyer," says Frost. "We sort of looked at each other, and there was a twinkle in his eye that I kind of recognized."

Their first collaboration was to be a film adaptation of Anthony Summers' biography *Goddess: The Secret Lives of Marilyn Monroe*, written by Frost, with Lynch slated to direct. Though the book includes the bombshell allegations that John F. Kennedy and Robert F. Kennedy were both intimately involved with Monroe and helped to cover up the circumstances of her death, Frost and Lynch's attraction to the story was more universal. "What really brought us together was a mutual interest in Marilyn Monroe and what she kind of stood for as an American archetype," says Frost. "How she is very much a stand-in for misogyny and the desperate ways in which men have been using women—not only in Hollywood, but in many places, for hundreds of years. She was a tremendously good actor, and she got involved with the wrong people, and it ended up costing her life."

Frost's script, titled *Venus Descending*, generated some heat in Hollywood. "Everybody who read it thought it was really compelling, and David wanted to do it," says Frost. Unfortunately, it was also doomed from the start. "What we *didn't* know was that United Artists, who had optioned the book, had Ethel Kennedy on the board of directors. That did not set you up for success at that particular studio," says Frost. "And so, having nothing to do with whatever the relative merits of the script might have been, the film was spun into turnaround faster than a speeding bullet over the course of a weekend. They asked us to rewrite it once, to see if we could take away any kind of possible reference to the Kennedys—and that, of course, just rendered it toothless."

But if *Venus Descending* was dead in the water, it was, at least, proof of concept that Lynch and Frost might be able to do something special together, and they began developing projects as not as writer and director, but as cowriters—a first for both men. "I'd never written with a partner before, and neither had David," says Frost. "What you quickly realize is that it's quite a bit like a marriage. You've got to have a formula for compromise that will get you out of the corners you sometimes paint yourself into."

The question was what form their collaboration would take. One completed but ultimately unproduced effort was a film script titled *One Saliva Bubble*. It was a comedy about mouth-breathing security guards who accidentally set off a top-secret government project, which sparks, among other chaotic consequences, a series of body swaps in their small Kansas town. "An out-and-out wacko dumb comedy," said Lynch. "Clichés one end to the other." It did earn an enthusiastic endorsement from Paramount script reader Loren Kantor, who was shocked to see a script by a filmmaker as venerated as Lynch coming through the slush pile. "When I finally finished the script I was in love with screenwriting again," he says. "The story had a slapstick feel, a Coen brothers–like rhythm with the silliness of Monty Python." It was, Frost says, heading toward production, and tentatively slated to star Steve Martin and Martin Short, before the funding fell through—one of many casualties when the De Laurentiis Entertainment Group, which had also produced *Blue Velvet*, declared bankruptcy after a string of box-office failures in 1988.

Less fully formed was *The Lemurians*, a series Lynch and Frost pitched unsuccessfully to NBC. Drawing inspiration from the fictional lost continent of Lemuria, the show would have followed government agents investigating extraterrestrial life. (If that sounds like the long-lost ancestor of the *The X-Files*, don't be too sure; Lynch described it, like *One Saliva Bubble*, as a comedy.) "I don't think we ever did more than, like, a four- or five-page outline," says Frost.

Though *The Lemurians* was another project that had stalled out before it had even truly started, Tony Krantz, a notoriously persistent agent shared by Lynch and Frost, continued to nudge them toward focusing on a television collaboration. Frost, who had taken to television like a duck to water, was on board to push the boundaries even beyond what he'd done on *Hill Street Blues*; Lynch, who had never directed television, remained intrigued by what he saw as the medium's unrealized potential. When watching TV, viewers "are in their own homes and nobody's bothering them," Lynch told one interviewer. "They're well placed for entering into a dream." During one exploratory lunch meeting at Nibblers, a cozy, unpretentious diner, Krantz tossed out a vague suggestion: "You should do a show about these people, the customers here."

What he meant, in practice, was a night soap—something akin to twisty, melodramatic weepies such as *Dallas*, *Dynasty*, or *Peyton Place*, which Lynch and Frost screened as inspiration. "That was what ABC asked us to try to do

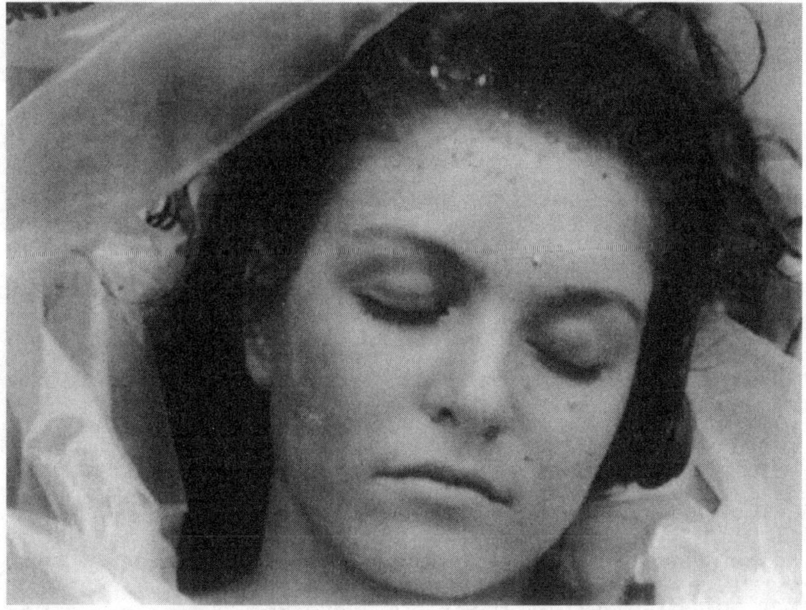

"She's dead. Wrapped in plastic."

for them: a different take on that genre," says Frost. "Which didn't particularly interest either of us other than, 'Okay, here's a template and here's a canvas that we can really fill with anything we want—as long as they can put the rubric of 'nighttime soap' on it. The thing that we added that they *didn't* expect was the murder mystery as a way in."

The project, *Northwest Passage*, felt a bit like a Frankenstein's monster composed of everything that came before it. You can see glimpses of *Venus Descending*'s focus on a beautiful young woman in trouble, *One Saliva Bubble*'s anything-goes approach to quirky characters and worldbuilding, and *The Lemurians'* interest in conspiracy-level cosmologies and the government agents who protect us.

It also pulled deeply from the lives of its two creators. As they crafted the murder mystery at the heart of *Northwest Passage*, Frost didn't just draw on the sturdy experience he'd had on *Hill Street Blues*—he drew from his own hazy childhood memories. On an adolescent visit to upstate New York, his maternal grandmother regaled her grandchildren with the story of a couple of drunk locals who thought they saw a ghost hovering over a nearby pond. When asked *why* they'd believe they'd seen a ghost, Frost's grandmother revealed that a young woman had been found murdered in that pond a decade earlier. "Twenty-year-old Hazel Drew—beautiful, blond, and connected to a number of powerful men—died in that pond one hot July night in 1908. She was a local girl who'd moved to the city, encountered a new way of life, and got caught up in the fast lane," wrote Frost in the introduction to *Murder at Teal's Pond*, a book-length exploration of the case by David Bushman and Mark T. Givens. "The woods freak Mark out. He was not a big fan of the woods or the lake," says Scott Frost, Mark's brother, who went on to write for *Twin Peaks* in its second season.

Lynch had a different way in—one rooted, characteristically, in a vague but intoxicating image. "The first thing I got excited about was the idea of a girl sneaking out of her house at night to meet someone that she didn't know really well, and that they would have an encounter that would change their lives," he said in 1990. He was also, characteristically, thinking about trees, and what they did to people surrounded by them: "I saw a lot of strange things happen in the woods, and it just seemed to me that people only told you ten percent of what they knew and it was up to you to discover the other ninety percent."

But while Lynch and Frost shared a fascination with the concept of a tragically doomed young woman, they also saw her murder as an entry point for their story, not its final destination.

"I wanted to tell a sort of Dickensian story about multiple lives in a contained area that could sort of go on perpetually," says Frost. And if the unexplained murder would be enough to unite a community in shock and grief, it would also offer an entry point to the individual passions and troubles of each resident.

Twin Peaks was a place long before Lynch and Frost had conceived of the many characters who would eventually occupy it. Before writing a word of the pilot, Lynch and Frost talked for weeks, establishing the basics of the town's geography and economy, including details like the presence of a lumber mill. In the crucible of that process, the script "becomes written by a third party," reflects Frost. "The author is someone called Lynch-Frost. I can only describe it as a kind of Vulcan mind-meld." The series was originally to be set in North Dakota, but Frost—who had once spent a weekend in the state—was skeptical. "It's a flat barren place that's very cold and I didn't want to shoot there," he says. He helped to convince Lynch that Washington State was a better fit for the dark story they had in mind. The writing process was "a little like ping-pong," says Frost. "Somebody throws out an idea, and the other person bats it back at you with some sort of spin on it, or they knock it out of the room if it stinks."

During one meal at Du-par's, a diner where they regularly met, Lynch flipped over a place mat and drew a map to help solidify the hazy contours of their imagined town—which is, Frost says, what led to the show's name. "As we talked through all the elements, we started to place where they were on the map as he sketched them," says Frost. "We didn't have a name for the town, but we had these two mountains, White Tail and Blue Pine, on either side. And I said, 'Well, why don't we call it Twin Peaks?' It hit us on the head like a two-by-four. We said, 'Yeah, that works.'" For both writers, the town was becoming real. "We knew where everything was, and it helped us decide what mood each place had, and what could happen there," said Lynch. "Then the characters just introduced themselves to us and walked into the story."

It is startling, even today, how confidently the *Twin Peaks* pilot script introduces its many, many characters. Those who are familiar with the show will find a few jarring differences in the script—and not just because the trees that prove so entrancing to Dale Cooper were originally written as ponderosa pines, not Douglas firs. In this early draft, Sheriff Harry S. Truman is Sheriff Dan Steadman; Deputy Tommy "Hawk" Hill is Deputy Bernie Hill; Ronette Pulaski, who survives the attack that resulted in Laura's death, is Sharon Pulaski; and Josie Packard is an Italian beauty named Giovanna Pasqualini Packard—a nod to Lynch's then-girlfriend Isabella Rossellini, who was tentatively slated to play the character. The Log Lady is conspicuously absent.

But most of the show's beloved characters are there, intact, in all their oddball glory. There's Deputy Andy Brennan (Harry Goaz), weeping over every crime scene he visits; Sheriff's Department receptionist Lucy Moran (Kimmy Robertson), offering needless details about the precise geography of the office; Nadine Hurley, screaming at her husband to hang up the drape runners; and even Donna Hayward's (Lara Flynn Boyle) precocious little sister Harriet (Jessica Wallenfels), reciting mediocre poetry to herself on the night after Laura's body was discovered.

Most of all, there's FBI Special Agent Dale Cooper (Kyle MacLachlan), who arrives in what remains one of the great character introductions in television history. Lynch and Frost spend more than thirty pages giving us an insider's look at Twin Peaks before introducing this outsider with an unbroken, two-minute monologue so intricate and character defining it can only be quoted in its entirety:

> Diane, two fifteen in the afternoon, November fourteenth. Entering town of Twin Peaks. Five miles south of the Canadian border, twelve miles west of the state line. Never seen so many trees in my life. As W. C. Fields would say, I'd rather be here than Philadelphia. It's fifty-four degrees on a beautiful

> sunny afternoon. Weatherman said rain. If you could get paid that kind of money for being wrong sixty percent of the time it'd beat working. Mileage is 79,345, gauge is on reserve, I'm riding on fumes, have to tank up when I get into town, remind me to tell you how much that is. Lunch was $6.31 and I left her a dollar tip, at the . . . Lamplighter Inn, that's on Highway 2 near Lewis Fork. That was a tuna fish sandwich on whole wheat and a slice of cherry pie and coffee. Darn good food. And if you ever get up this way, Diane, that cherry pie is worth a stop. Okay. I'll be looking for a . . . Sheriff Daniel Steadman, he's going to be at the Calhoun Memorial Hospital with that girl they pulled off the mountain. I'll be checking into a motel after we're through there. Sure the Sheriff'll be able to recommend a clean place. Reasonably priced. Forgot to mention. I stopped for coffee and a pit stop about ten thirty, little diner near Bitteroot Lake. Excellent coffee. Forgot to get the receipt, can you believe it? That was seventy-five cents and I left a quarter on the counter. Got to find out what kind of trees these are. They're really something.

Months later, when cameras were rolling on the *Twin Peaks* pilot, some minor details needed to be changed. Cooper arrived in town on a February morning, not a November afternoon; the weather was slightly overcast, not sunny. But even before an actor had been cast to play him, the FBI special agent zips into Twin Peaks almost fully formed: quirky, detail-oriented, and food-obsessed. Even Cooper's famous love for coffee, donuts, and pie are part of his investigative technique—as Lynch once said, the show's hero was a man who understood that a sugar high is useful for keeping ideas flowing. (Lynch knew from experience; in a 1990 *New York Times* profile,

Lynch revealed that his order at Bob's Big Boy, the Los Angeles restaurant he famously frequented every day for seven years, consisted of one chocolate milkshake and as many as seven cups of coffee with sugar.) Perhaps the only difference is that the Cooper on the page, unlike the Cooper on the screen, is habitually whistling "Rhapsody in Blue." As it turns out, not even Gershwin can compete with Angelo Badalamenti's score.

The character's name—an allusion to the famous plane hijacker D. B. Cooper—was "just a little bit of playfulness on my part," says Frost. "I think in the back of my mind, I was thinking, *Well, wouldn't it be great if people just had the tiniest little sliver of doubt in their mind that this guy actually is an FBI agent? Did he jump out of a plane and put on a nice suit?* It's one of many ways that the show could have gone on a very different road."

Cooper has come to Twin Peaks to solve Laura Palmer's (Sheryl Lee) murder. At the time the pilot was written, it was an inherently doomed mission; not even Lynch and Frost knew who had done it. "We didn't want to solve it, at that point," says Frost. "That was a clear decision on our part, creatively. We didn't want to limit ourselves. And we felt if we locked it in too early, that's exactly what we'd end up doing. [If we waited], something that might occur to us that's even more interesting."

Where the cocreators disagreed was whether the murder mystery would *ever* be resolved. "I felt that we would have to do it sooner or later," says Frost. "David, in his kind of wonderful, Peter Pan sort of way, thought, *Well, no, we don't* ever *have to solve it.* And I said, 'Well, that's not how television works. You have to give them something at some point, or they're going to just drift away.'"

But that was a problem for the future. For now, their only job was getting the network to green-light the pilot, and they had chosen the right network. ABC had been lagging behind NBC and CBS for years; they were coming off a particularly dismal season of new programs, and they were in the market for something that might turn heads—even if it failed to attract audiences, or never even aired. It was, recalled senior drama executive Gary Levine, a "golden age" for risk-taking on television. "We're in third place and love taking big swings," he said.

A murder with no solution. A town full of interconnected characters and dark secrets. A pair of creators, individually accomplished but untested together, promising something unlike anything else on television—even if they couldn't quite explain how. "I don't think we even knew what it was," confessed Lynch years later.

It was, ABC decided, a big swing worth taking. They green-lit the pilot. "I remember walking back to my office, thinking, *This is either going to be an incredibly terrific success or it will be very cool and no one will get it. But it will not be boring*," said Hoffman.

LAURA PALMER

"I am dead, yet I live."

Think back on all the time you've spent sitting at home, in front of your TV, watching fictional investigators trying to solve vicious assaults or serial murders.

How many of the victims had names you can remember? When it comes to perpetually popular shows like *CSI*, *Law & Order: SVU*, or *NCIS*—feel free to insert the alphabet-soup crime drama of your choice—television offers a vast, endless graveyard of basically interchangeable corpses. These victims aren't so much characters as props. Their dead bodies are the first clues in the puzzles that the show's cops, detectives, or especially clever viewers have been invited to solve. By the end of the arc—and usually by the end of the hour—their corpses have been yanked off-screen with all the ceremony of *The Gong Show*. They've served their purpose, and the next mystery can begin.

Twin Peaks wouldn't let you forget Laura Palmer. In the first of the Log Lady introductions later added to the series—written and directed by David Lynch, and shown before each episode re-aired on Bravo—Margaret Lanterman offers a succinct analysis of the sprawling narrative that's about to unfold. "It is a story of many, but begins with one—and I knew her," she says. "The one leading to the many is Laura Palmer. Laura is the one." *Laura is the one.* In case you missed it, it's a line she repeats, decades later, in *Twin Peaks: The Return*.

Laura's murder is the engine that kicks *Twin Peaks* into motion. But though she dies before its story even begins, the show returns to Laura over and over again—a locked groove in a record that keeps spinning back to her. We first come to care about Laura through her absence. The impact of her death ripples through the entire town, and not just in the obvious ways. In the pilot alone, we see the raw grief not just through her sobbing parents and friends, but through several characters *Twin Peaks* never even revisits. In a shaky, quivering voice, her homeroom teacher tells the class an announcement will be forthcoming. An unnamed student runs screaming through the high school's courtyard. Over the intercom, the school's principal announces classes will be canceled for the day before breaking into sobs.

But even in the pilot, Laura is also startlingly alive, in a videotape of a picnic that seems to hypnotize anyone who watches it. Soon after, she haunts Agent Cooper in the iconic Red Room dream sequence, dropping cryptic clues before kissing him. She shows up in the flesh just three episodes later in the form of Maddy Ferguson, Laura's brunette cousin—also played by Sheryl Lee—who, inevitably, dons a blond wig and explicitly doubles as Laura before the season is over. Even when the show attempts to branch into a post-"Who killed Laura Palmer?" world, it can't shake her; long after her murder is solved, the closing credits for every episode still roll over Laura's homecoming photo. It's no wonder that her best friend Donna, soliloquizing over Laura's grave in season two, cries, "It's almost like they didn't bury you deep enough!"

It doesn't take long before *Twin Peaks* complicates the image of Laura Palmer, a Meals on Wheels volunteer and homecoming queen. Like Otto Preminger's 1944 noir classic *Laura*—one of the show's more explicit points of reference—we learn about Laura's interesting, sometimes contradictory qualities from those who were entranced by her: some with love, some with lust, some with hate, and some with all three. In the words of Dr. Jacoby—both her psychiatrist and yet another man who was disturbingly and pruriently obsessed with her—"Laura had secrets. And around those secrets, she built the fortress that, in my six months with her, I was not able to penetrate."

What were those secrets? To the shock of those who knew her only superficially, like Sheriff Harry S. Truman, she was both a habitual cocaine user and a teenage sex worker—at seventeen, technically one year over the age of consent in Washington State, but unquestionably lusted over and preyed on by older men (and, occasionally, women). Some, like Ben Horne (Richard Beymer) and Josie Packard (Joan Chen), were people of high social standing in the community; others, like Leo Johnson (Eric Da Re), Jacques Renault (Walter Olkewicz), and Blackie O'Reilly (Victoria Catlin), are criminals and hustlers at the margins of society. And then there are those who Laura herself treats with casual cruelty. Innocents like James Hurley (James Marshall), who she privately mocks as "sweet, but so dumb;" Bobby Briggs (Dana Ashbrook), who tearfully admits that Laura mocked him when he cried after he gave his virginity to her; or Harold Smith (Lenny Von Dohlen), who—as David Lynch's daughter Jennifer writes, channeling Laura's voice, in her tie-in novel, *The Secret Diary of Laura Palmer*—was "basically, because he could not leave his house, *forced* to have sex with [her]."

Crucially, *Twin Peaks* never feels judgmental of Laura, or her peers, who are almost constantly subjected to the dangers faced by any teenage girl who dares to exist in a hostile and violent world. That doesn't excuse the physical and emotional violence Laura inflicts on others; it's simply an acknowledgment of the cycle of abuse that began, if you take *The Secret Diary of Laura Palmer* as canon, in 1984, when Laura was twelve.

It's not for nothing that Sheryl Lee carried *The Secret Diary of Laura Palmer* around like a totem on the set of *Twin Peaks: Fire Walk with Me*, a prequel film that chronicles the last week of Laura's life in excruciating detail. On paper, it would seem impossible for any actress to live up to the idea of Laura Palmer, because the idea of Laura Palmer was, by definition, both personal and diffuse. Every *Twin Peaks* viewer had composed their own version of Laura in their head, built from fleeting images or snippets of dialogue or the filtered, secondhand memories of the show's other characters. But few could speak for Laura Palmer with the knowledge and weight Sheryl Lee brought to the character. "It's almost like I could feel her spirit or life force having more to say," said Lee. "So, when David started talking to me about the possibility of the film, it felt necessary for her to be able to have a voice."

She found it. As the critic Greil Marcus wrote, Lee takes the challenge posed by *Fire Walk with Me* and delivers "the most bottomless female film performance of the latter days of the twentieth century—the most extreme, the most dangerous." Filmmaker Gregg Araki, who cast Lee in his 2014 drama *White Bird in a Blizzard*, went even further, calling her work in *Fire Walk with Me* "one of the greatest performances in the history of cinema."

As hyperbolic as that might sound, it is hard to overstate what Lee accomplishes in *Fire Walk with Me*. In her hands, it's clear that Laura Palmer has survived abuse by becoming a masterful code-switcher. She can shift, apparently at will, between girlish and embittered, innocent and hardened. She's full of pain and rage, but her feelings of isolation and self-loathing are so entrenched that she lashes out at Bobby, James, Harold Smith, and anyone else who tries to help her. When she learns the truth about the man who's been abusing her, her horror is endless. From there, her downward spiral leads her, unwillingly and unfairly, in the only direction this story could conceivably go; Laura's murder, inevitable from the moment *Twin Peaks* was conceived, is no less awful for being preordained in the story Lynch wanted to tell.

Lee's performance in *Fire Walk with Me* came at a personal cost. As Grace Zabriskie, who played Laura's mother, Sarah, put it in an interview with author Brad Dukes: "She gave everything she had, she gave more than she could afford to give, and she spent years coming back." Though she had other roles, in films like the 1994 Beatles biopic *Backbeat* and John

Carpenter's 1998 action-horror flick *Vampires*, there's no question that embodying a character as iconic as Laura Palmer both opened up Lee's acting career and set it in stone.

Fire Walk with Me also gave Lee an unexpected responsibility in her day-to-day life—one that she couldn't have anticipated when she was cast in *Twin Peaks*, and which she never asked for. As the literal face of TV's most famous story of violence and rape, Lee regularly receives correspondence from those who have been victimized in their actual lives. It's a role she has accepted with grace. "I know that there are a lot of sexual abuse survivors and incest survivors and rape survivors and physical abuse survivors out there that were touched by the *Twin Peaks* story," Lee said. "The fact that they're able to voice it and talk about it, means that they're in a place of healing with it. And the fact that they are trusting me enough—I'm a total stranger to them—that they're sharing something so personal, it really moves me."

What role could Laura Palmer possibly have in a TV series set actual decades after her murder? Arriving twenty-five years later, *Twin Peaks: The Return* foregrounds the same trick *Twin Peaks* employed in its closing credits. Even when the show takes us to its farthest-flung locations—New York City, South Dakota, Las Vegas, the Black Lodge—it uses Angelo Badalamenti's theme song and Laura Palmer's face to remind us of the absence at the center of the story. She's still there in the show's first scene; she's still there in its last.

At the time of this publication, *Twin Peaks* has ended three times—each time, apparently, forever. In the finale of the original series, the image that plays over the credits is Laura, reflected in a coffee cup and smiling. In the closing shot of *Fire Walk with Me*, the last image is Laura laughing, apparently in joy, surrounded by her dual protectors: an angel and Agent Cooper. In the ending of *Twin Peaks: The Return*, the final shot is Carrie Paige—a

Laura Palmer double, escorted to Twin Peaks—having a terrible realization about the trauma endured by her shadow self, and screaming, apparently, in both recognition and agony.

A smile, a laugh, a scream. Somewhere, in the nexus between all those emotions, you'll find Laura Palmer.

Chapter 2

WELCOME TO TWIN PEAKS

There's a strange kind of alchemy required when a screenplay goes into preproduction. Up until that point, the only limits on the story had been Lynch and Frost's collective imagination. For all practical purposes, *Twin Peaks* was, at that point, ninety-two pages of screenwriting and one charcoal map. With little more than five minutes and a few keystrokes, they could turn North Dakota into northern Washington, or conjure up a massive luxury hotel nestled between two mountains, at no cost to anybody.

Actually *making* something—as any overburdened, underfunded producer could (and would) tell you—requires a different skill set entirely. Any time a writer introduces a new character, big or small, someone needs to comb through headshots and hold auditions to find the actor who can actually bring that character to life. When you write a scene set at a "massive industrial sawmill" you need, you know, a massive industrial sawmill.

You can imagine the relief when a production crew drove into the neighboring towns of Snoqualmie and North Bend, Washington, and discovered that Twin Peaks was waiting for them. They'd already spent days trying, and failing, to find any filming sites that could match the world Frost and Lynch had dreamed up. "We finally drove into Snoqualmie and

David Lynch on "Ronette's bridge"

North Bend and realized, *Oh, it's all right here,*'" says Frost. "*In fact, it's right here the way we wrote it.* The Double R Diner was just as we described it. The waterfall was just as we wrote it. The Great Northern was almost as if we'd had a dream of what that hotel would look like. It was spooky." They even managed to film footage of the town's sawmill, which had operated since 1914, just before it was dismantled in 1989, capturing images that would go on to appear in the opening credits of every episode of *Twin Peaks*.

It was one of many serendipitous breaks for a production that would, in many ways, be defined by serendipity. That was no accident. David Lynch was a director whose openness to the unexpected was at the core of his talent. It wasn't that he had no plan. When pressed on his process, Lynch had a phrase he was fond of repeating: "Most of filmmaking is common sense."

He was, perhaps surprisingly, skeptical of improvisation. "You follow the script to the letter," he said. "But at the same time, you're always on guard for new things. So, on the day, when everybody comes there, and they're dressed properly, and the set is right, and everything is just exactly right, sometimes things can take off in other directions."

The trick, of course, was assembling the team who understood how Lynch worked. One key early hire was Duwayne Dunham, who Lynch brought on to edit the pilot. "David sent me the script for *Twin Peaks* and with a note saying, 'They're never going to air this thing, but they're going to give us money to shoot it. So why don't we just go up and have some fun and make a movie?'" says Dunham.

Dunham, an assistant editor on all three installments of the original *Star Wars* trilogy, had first worked with Lynch as the editor of *Blue Velvet*, and the two had developed a natural trust and rapport rooted in the unusual amount of creative freedom Lynch had granted. "On *Blue Velvet*, I said to David one day, 'How come you don't ever give me any specific notes on how to do the scenes?' says Dunham. "He said, 'Because if I gave you notes, I would simply be telling you how I would do it. If I *don't* tell you, you use your own instincts, you do it your way, and I might like your way better.'"

Though no one would accuse Lynch of having anything but a singular directional vision, he was wise enough to know when he had found a collaborator talented enough to enhance a project. Decades later, he would hire Dunham once again to edit *Twin Peaks: The Return*.

▲▲

The show's distinctive cinematography is "to David's credit, and to Ron García's, who shot the pilot," says Dunham. "They're up in cold, cold, snowy Washington—and they're not only shooting with coral filters on the camera, but in post we were *adding* red. It gave it a really interesting look: warm but freezing cold."

Populating the town was another problem entirely. "We were thinking of characters. We didn't actively start talking about actors until the thing was written," says Frost. "And we tried to pick not only the right people, and terrific actors, but also people who were fun and good to work with." The show's casting came with an additional wrinkle, though it would be a long time before it actually came into play: Anyone who was cast could, plausibly, later be revealed as the killer of Laura Palmer. They would simply have to load the cast with actors talented enough to convey a previously unseen dark side with total credibility whenever the murderer was revealed.

A key piece of the puzzle was Johanna Ray, a casting director who, like Duwayne Dunham, had begun working with Lynch on *Blue Velvet*. The third wife of legendary tough-guy actor Aldo Ray, she gave up her own young career in acting—as well as her life in England—when Ray asked her to move with him to the United States. Even then, she says, she "always knew" she wanted to be a casting director; though it wasn't until she and Ray divorced that she formally pursued a career in casting, she realized later that she'd always had a unique knack for spotting talent. "When I was married, I spent a lot of time alone watching TV," she says. "In those days, *TV Guide* had a list of every actor in every show that you were watching, so whenever I'd see an actor that I was curious about, I would look him up in *TV Guide*. And it was years later that I realized that all the actors that I'd looked up were the actors who later became stars."

On *Blue Velvet*, Ray learned that—unlike other directors she'd worked with—Lynch both disliked and distrusted traditional auditions, in which prospective actors are fed lines to read from a script. "David really didn't want to meet with actors in the traditional way," says Ray. "He just liked to sit down and talk to them. Basically, David was looking for something within the person—not the actor, but the *person*—to see what hit him and what he found interesting." She soon realized that the actors Lynch was naturally drawn toward had something essential, albeit hard to define, in common: "That mysterious quality, you know, that some people have."

By the time they were casting *Twin Peaks*, Lynch and Ray had further streamlined the process. "All I did was show him pictures," she says. "But a lot of their eight by tens didn't really look like them, or project the quality that they had, so I started taking photos of everyone and showing him. From then onward, whenever we started a new project, David would say, 'Johanna, come up to the house with your photo albums.'"

Given that Lynch's previous two films had starred Kyle MacLachlan—and that it's incredibly easy to imagine Cooper's introductory monologue in the actor's peppy, boyish tone—one might imagine that the *Twin Peaks* pilot had been written with MacLachlan in mind. That's not how Mark Frost remembers it. "We had talked about some names for Cooper, and I believe I was the one who one day just said, 'Well, what about Kyle?' We really didn't think of him until after it was finished," says Frost. Johanna Ray recalls it differently. "I don't know if we even talked about other actors, because that's who David wanted all along, right from the very start," she says.

Lynch had recognized something in MacLachlan from the very beginning. *Dune* wasn't technically the Yakima, Washington–born actor's first film role; as a drama student at the University of Washington, he'd been paid ten dollars as an extra in the 1980 horror film *The Changeling*, which was partially shot on campus. But it wasn't until years later, when a casting agent spotted him performing in Molière's *Tartuffe* at a Seattle theater and brought him in for an audition, that Lynch launched MacLachlan's professional acting career by casting him as Paul Atreides, the messianic figure at the heart of *Dune*.

At their first meeting, Lynch and MacLachlan bonded over their mutual interest in red wine and the Pacific Northwest. But by MacLachlan's own account, his first formal screen test for *Dune*—which required him to deliver one of Paul's rousing speeches directly to a camera—went badly. "I failed a couple of times and I was getting a little frustrated. And I remember David just came up to me, and I said, 'David, I don't really know if I can do this. I'm not sure,'" said MacLachlan. "He said, 'Kyle, I know you can do this. You got this. Just relax, breathe. Take your time.' And he just said all the right things that kind of chilled me down. He recognized immediately what I needed as an actor."

During the production of *Dune*, Lynch gave MacLachlan the screenplay for *Blue Velvet*, suggesting they could make the film as their follow-up. MacLachlan, perhaps unwisely, shared the script with his mother, who was so horrified by the thought of her son starring in the film that MacLachlan originally turned it down, sheepishly returning to Lynch months later and confessing he hadn't been able to get the screenplay out of his head.

Blue Velvet follows Jeffrey Beaumont, a gee-whiz, All-American hero played by MacLachlan, as he's forced to confront the darker aspects of both the world and himself. Among its many virtues, it solidified MacLachlan's role as the closest thing Lynch ever had to an on-screen surrogate. "I saw so much of David in the Kyle character—his walk, his mannerisms," said production designer Jack Fisk, a friend of Lynch's since childhood. To MacLachlan, *Twin Peaks* was essentially a continuation of the work they'd begun in *Blue Velvet*. "I see my character [in *Twin Peaks*] as Jeffrey Beaumont grown-up," he told *The New York Times* in 1990.

Which isn't to say casting MacLachlan was a sure thing. It was, after all, the late 1980s, when TV was still frequently greeted with a kind of reflexive snobbery, and MacLachlan was just beginning to establish a reputation as a film star on the rise. "Kyle was very resistant to doing a series," says Johanna Ray. "We didn't know that we had him until the very last minute. But usually, David ends up getting what he wants."

An early, extreme example of that came on Ray's first day on the show, as they discussed who might play Andy Brennan, the weepy deputy with a heart of gold. "Harry [Goaz] was David's limo driver," says Ray. "I was in a meeting with David and Mark Frost, and David said, 'Well, I know who I want for the deputy sheriff. This guy that drove me to the Roy Orbison concert the other night.' Mark and I went, 'Oh, here we go,'" but they gamely agreed to meet with Goaz, who had exactly zero credits to his name. "And he turned out to be brilliant."

Lynch, famously loyal to his collaborators, filled out the pilot with familiar faces. Everett Marshall, like MacLachlan, came over from *Dune*. *Eraserhead* costars Jack Nance and Charlotte Stewart were cast, respectively, as Pete Martell—the lovably gruff fisherman who discovers Laura's body—and Betty Briggs, mother of Laura's boyfriend, Bobby, who remains determinedly cheerful even as her son falls under suspicion for the murder. Stewart was cast, she says, with less than a minute of discussion. "I got a phone call one day, and it was David Lynch, yelling, 'Hey, Char! You want to go to work?'" she remembers. "I said, 'Sure, okay, great.' And that was it. I didn't know what he was planning." When she learned it was a TV pilot, Stewart was even more befuddled. "I remember thinking, *How can David do a series? He takes so long to shoot*," she says. One actress who didn't come along, despite the original plan, was Isabella Rossellini. "Obviously, David was going out with her at the time," says Frost. "We thought, *Well, she'd be interesting*. But she had a conflict and couldn't do it."

Enter Joan Chen, whose casting necessitated a rewrite from the dark Italian beauty they'd originally conceived. A Chinese actress who had been discovered, at age fourteen, by Jiang Qing—an actress turned producer who was also the wife of Mao Zedong—Chen had won China's prestigious Hundred Flowers Award for Best Actress when she was still a teenager but had only recently established herself as a force in

Hollywood. It was Frost's idea to cast Joan Chen on the strength of her performance in Bernardo Bertolucci's Best Picture–winning epic *The Last Emperor,* and once Lynch met Chen and agreed, Giovanni Packard became Josie Packard.

Casting Harry S. Truman, the town's sheriff and Josie's secret lover, proved more challenging. Truman is essentially the show's second lead, but his sturdy reliability is undeniably less flashy than the eccentric Dale Cooper. David Strathairn, already known for a series of law enforcement roles, was considered. So was Robert Forster, a veteran of crime and war movies. Lynch and Frost adored him, but he bowed out, apologetically, as the production came closer to reality. "Bob came in with a caveat, which is, 'I would love to do this,'" recalls Frost. "'Unfortunately, a friend of mine had asked me to do a pilot. I don't think it's going to go to series, but I can't turn my back on my friend.' It was really impressive, actually."

Josie Packard and Harry S. Truman

In the end, they settled on Canadian actor Michael Ontkean, to the network's delight. "He was under contract at the time, so ABC requested that he play the role," recalls Ray. Also reading for Truman was Ray Wise, who ended up with the role of Leland, the father of the murdered girl. "I got a phone call from my agent saying, 'David wants you to play Leland Palmer,'" says Wise. "And I had to think. *Leland Palmer?* Wait a minute. I've got to go back and look at the script. So I'm looking at the script, and I see: 'Leland Palmer finds out his daughter is dead, and he drops the phone and starts to cry.' 'Leland Palmer goes to the morgue to identify his daughter's body, and he starts to cry.' 'He's up in his daughter's room, where the police are looking for her diary, and he starts to cry.' I said, 'All this guy *does* is cry.'" It was only after a little reflection that he concluded he might enjoy the work required to play a father contending with such an unfathomable loss in an interesting way. "That was going to be the challenge: to show different degrees of grief, and try to make each one very specific and different and, hopefully, interesting to the viewer," says Wise.

Much of the rest of the adult cast was filled out with time-tested performers, who had relatively small roles in the pilot but who, Lynch and Frost knew, would be called to do much more if *Twin Peaks* were picked up to series. Richard Beymer, best known for his starring role in *West Side Story*, was cast as Ben Horne, the town's scheming businessman (though Lynch playfully instructed Beymer and Wise to swap roles during the all-cast reading mandated by ABC executives). The town's oddball psychiatrist, Lawrence Jacoby, was played by Beymer's *West Side Story* costar Russ Tamblyn, who had originally pitched Lynch on working together at a birthday party thrown by Dennis Hopper. Frost didn't need much convincing. "Russ Tamblyn had been one of, without question, one of my favorite screen presences throughout my childhood," says Frost. "There was just nobody else like him." Peggy Lipton, star of the hit cop show *The Mod Squad*, took her first main TV role in fifteen years to play Norma Jennings, the warmhearted proprietor of the Double R Diner. Piper Laurie, one of the more famous names in the cast, took the role of brassy businesswoman Catherine Martell almost on a lark. "I just wanted to work with David Lynch, never expecting they'd get picked up and go to series," she said. Mark Frost even got his father, Warren, into the cast as Doc Hayward, in an especially personal role. "That part was basically an homage to my mother's father, Douglas Calhoun, who was an obstetrician in the state of New York, who I greatly admired and had many of those characteristics," says Frost. Twin Peaks' Calhoun Memorial Hospital was also named in tribute.

But the adult side of the story was only half of what *Twin Peaks* required. The original idea, of course, had been something like a modern *Peyton Place*, which meant a story full of hot-blooded teenagers enmeshed in complicated romantic webs. And telling that part of the story would require an eye for fresh talent.

When it came to filling out the teenage side of *Twin Peaks*' narrative, Johanna Ray tried to cast as wide a net as possible, including one up-and-coming actress who would ultimately join the show much later in its run. "Heather Graham, I would bring in for almost anything," says Ray. "She was someone who was always, like, the top of my list. But I don't think she came in for the pilot, because I don't think she was available at the time." ("If I knew I'd had any chance to be involved in the pilot, I would have one hundred percent dropped anything else I had. I would have *killed* to be in that pilot," says Graham.)

Dana Ashbrook—cast as Bobby Briggs, Laura's boyfriend, football star, and all-around smug bully—eventually reveals a startling number of unexpected dimensions. But he got in the door for a simpler reason: "David liked his look," says Ray. Dana "just came in and blew off the doors when we were looking for Bobby. He was just a live wire," says Frost. After a meeting full of laughing and joking, Ashbrook recalled, Lynch had just one note for him: "You know, Bobby doesn't smile a lot."

The rest of Twin Peaks High was filled in with actors Ray had earmarked, years earlier, for potential stardom. "I'd had my eye on James Marshall and Sherilyn Fenn for a long time. I had met them probably a couple of years before. And they were hopeless. They were terrible," says Ray. "But there was something about both of them. Every once in a while I would bring them in to audition for something to see if there'd been any improvement. And very, very slowly and gradually, there was."

Like most of the young actresses they saw, Sherilyn Fenn read for Donna Hayward. "He brought me in off a picture with a short, platinum-blonde haircut. And I walked in with dark hair," says Fenn. Lynch, Fenn recalls, asked her a lot of questions. "He wanted to know what I thought of the script," says Fenn. "I said, 'Well, everyone's sleeping with everyone.' And he said, 'Well, that's how it is in this world, Sherilyn Fenn!' And I was no longer Sherilyn, for the rest of my time knowing him. I was Sherilyn Fenn." It was after that meeting, Fenn says, that the character of Audrey Horne was truly born. Described as "a delicate, Botticelli-like beauty, with a halo of wavy black hair and dark, haunted eyes" in the original pilot script, Audrey is barely a presence; she appears in just two scenes and doesn't have a single line of dialogue. Lynch, enchanted with Fenn after meeting her, rewrote the character, adding scenes with the actress in mind. "[His daughter Jennifer Lynch] told me later that I'd reminded him of a schoolboy crush—a girl he really liked," says Fenn. The role was small enough that Fenn, unlike most of her costars, wore her own clothing instead of an outfit selected by costumer Patrica Norris. "That was my pink sweater David ruined in the pilot, because he kept making it tighter behind my back," says Fenn.

As James Marshall recalls it, he was one of the last to be cast. "I had really, really bad headshots at the time," says Marshall. "They were very awkward headshots that looked like *Teen Beat* magazine, and it was like David instantly looked at them and said, 'No, absolutely not.' And this went on for months. The only thing that got me was when Johanna finally sat David down and said, 'Look, he's with Dick Clayton. That was James Dean's manager, and you want a James Dean type. He doesn't look like this picture. Please see him.' He goes, 'The only reason I'll say yes is because there's nobody else.' And then when I walked in, he instantly gave me the part. He didn't even read me. He looked at me and went, 'You know, James, this pisses me off, that you have this awful picture, because I'll tell you right now: I want you for the part.' I was so elated. I felt like I was meeting my family."

Mädchen Amick was also considered for Donna Hayward, and while she didn't land the role, Lynch and Frost were so impressed that they decided to rewrite Shelly Johnson, a waitress at the Double R Diner, with her in mind. "We didn't even have Shelly written as a role," says Frost. "She had, like, a one-line part. And then Mädchen came in and we just said, 'Oh my gosh, she's just so perfect for this. Let's beef this up because she's really special.'"

For Shelly's husband, the trucker Leo Johnson—initially, perhaps, the most obvious suspect in Laura's murder—Lynch had his own vision, born out of the pilot's extensive casting process. "My son [Eric Da Re] was working for me at the time," says Ray. "And I said, 'Eric, would you go in please and read the parts that haven't been cast?' And he said no. And I said, 'You have to. I'm sorry, you don't have any choice.' And after the script read, David came to me and said, 'Do I have permission to cast Eric in the role of Leo?'" It was a surprise to Ray, whose son hadn't actively pursued a career as an actor. It also meant she pushed aside two of the actors she'd had in mind for the role of Leo Johnson: "I had Brad Pitt and Michael Madsen," she says. "I totally saw those two in that role."

There were two more absolutely essential roles that would go on to shape the entirety of *Twin Peaks*, though neither actor knew it yet. Laura Palmer, whose death kicks off the narrative, was deemed such a nonessential role that it wasn't even cast in Los Angeles. A local actress, the production reasoned, would do just fine in the role of a waterlogged corpse. "At the time, she was just a body," says Ray. "And Sheryl was the only one who agreed to be naked and wrapped up in plastic in the freezing cold."

The nudity was a sticking point for Phoebe Augustine—a runner-up for the role of Laura who was cast, instead, as Ronette Pulaski, the victim who survives the same attack that leads to Laura's death. (It was also a sticking point for Alfred Schneider, the vice president of policy and standards at ABC, who had concerns about how Lynch would shoot Laura Palmer's corpse, but was satisfied when the director revealed he'd wrap the naked body in plastic and focus on her face.)

Then an actress performing theater in Washington, Sheryl Lee was up for anything that seemed compelling—even the silent, apparently one-off role of a frozen corpse. "For myself, I knew that I needed to go into the deepest state of relaxation—almost like meditation. I knew that I needed to slow my system down because the camera's looking at you, so you don't want to be fidgeting or breathing too fast. I just really worked on my state of being, or nonbeing," said Lee.

The other, even stranger belated addition to the cast was Frank Silva, who was cast, on a whim, in what became the role of BOB, *Twin Peaks*' all-purpose avatar of the evil that men do. It is a story no less remarkable for its familiarity among the *Twin Peaks* faithful. Silva, a set dresser, was moving furniture around in Laura Palmer's bedroom. When a production assistant called out, "Don't get locked in there, Frank!" an image flashed into Lynch's head: Silva crouching menacingly at the foot of Laura's bed.

This is the kind of impulse that nearly any other director would have let pass. Lynch, as was his way, decided to shoot it, without any idea what it meant or if he'd use it. Later that day—shooting a scene in which Laura's sleeping mother, Sarah, played by Grace Zabriskie, suddenly wakes up and screams—Lynch was warned by the camera operator that the shot was unusable because a crew member had been caught in the mirror behind her. It was, of course, Frank Silva, whose ghoulish reflection, while totally unplanned, made the final cut. Lynch's burst of inspiration was so spontaneous that Silva hadn't been through wardrobe; the blue denim jacket, which BOB wears through the rest of the series, is simply what Silva had pulled out of his closet and worn to work that morning.

Similar moments of serendipity, which Lynch liked to call "happy accidents," popped up over the course of filming. Former Directors Guild of America president Lesli Linka Glatter tells a story about a scene in the pilot in which a mounted deer's head sits atop a conference table. ("It fell down," explains the bank teller.) Glatter, tickled by the detail, asked Lynch what it meant; Lynch, in his plainspoken manner, told her that it had been there when he'd arrived to set that morning. A similarly off-kilter, memorable detail comes during Laura's autopsy, which incorporated a flickering light overhead because Lynch saw an actual flickering light on set and liked the effect. "Those are the things I appreciate about David most," says Harley Peyton, a writer (and later a producer) on *Twin Peaks*. "Suddenly, that light starts glitching, and on ninety-nine out of one hundred sets, that becomes 'We've got to fix this.' And no one knows what's wrong, the grips are getting involved, and the actors or director might be getting a little pissy. And David was just like, 'This is great. Let's do it this way.'"

Of course, happy accidents can only happen if everything else has been meticulously planned, and by all accounts it was a high-functioning and enjoyable shoot. "I never saw someone whose vision was as precise right from the beginning as David," said ABC executive Gary Levine. "It was like a giant mosaic in which he knew where every little tile fit before he ever rolled a foot of film." One of the scenes filmed on the very first day of production was the dangling traffic light, cycling between red, yellow, and green, that became one of the show's most memorable visual motifs.

The pilot defies the obvious (or, perhaps, sets up its first red herring) from its opening shot. After a brief image of some ducks on the lake, Lynch slowly pans for the show's first major character introduction: Josie Packard, widow and heir to the town's logging empire, as she applies makeup in the mirror. The story doesn't properly begin until the following scene, when Pete Martell, walking down to the lake for some fishing, discovers Laura's body. Rushing back to the telephone, he calls the sheriff's department, where receptionist Lucy Moran delivers the first bit of comic relief as she overexplains which phone Sheriff Truman should pick up. When Truman finally gets on the line, Pete, breathless, and shaky, delivers the first of *Twin Peaks*' many iconic lines: "She's dead. Wrapped in plastic."

All of this happens in the show's first five minutes. It's a remarkable crash course in everything *Twin Peaks* will deliver: beauty, tragedy, comedy, and devastating loss—all expertly balanced within the same short sequence. *Twin Peaks* had arrived.

In the eighty-five minutes that follow, what the pilot conveys—more than anything—is a true sense of loss. It's one thing to say, as the script does, that Sarah Palmer lets out "a heartrending wail of grief." It's another to watch actress Grace Zabriskie perform it, or to mercifully cut away from it—as Lynch does—only to suddenly cut back to her sobbing one last time. The effect, which forces the audience to sit with Sarah in her naked despair, is almost like a jump scare. The news spreads, from there, like wildfire: through Twin Peaks High School, where Laura's best friend, Donna Hayward, and secret boyfriend, James Hurley, react with shock and pain, and the Great Northern Hotel, where the tragedy throws a wrench into Ben Horne's elaborate business deal with a group of Norwegian investors. In fact, Laura's death brings *both* of Twin Peaks' major industries to a grinding halt. Josie also shuts down the sawmill after Ronette Pulaski, the daughter of an employee, emerges, nearly catatonic after barely surviving the attack that led to Laura's death. Even the material that isn't directly related to Laura's murder is pretty grim: We learn that Laura's boyfriend, Bobby Briggs, and Double R waitress Shelly Johnson are having a barely concealed affair, then witness their terror when they head to Shelly's house for a morning hookup before realizing that Shelly's abusive husband, Leo, has arrived home early.

All of this was by design. "What's startling about it is how real the grief is," says Frost. "The whole first hour is just about the discovery of the death of this young woman, and these very real, very powerful reactions by good actors, showing you how devastated they are. I was kind of stunned when I saw it again. Nothing funny happens for quite a while."

The tone only brightens, appropriately enough, when Agent Cooper drives into town (and not only because Angelo Badalamenti's "Dance of the Dream Man" is playing on the soundtrack—an up-tempo number that tells us, even before we know it, that we'll be following Cooper into his dreams). It's a classic narrative trick: Introducing an outsider to serve as the audience's on-screen surrogate, asking the questions we'll also need answered to comprehend what's going on. To that end, the pilot includes a town hall meeting that doubles as a mechanism for blunt exposition, as Truman literally points out important characters and tells Cooper who they are.

The peppiness is there from the start, but there's also a darkness to MacLachlan's performance in the pilot that largely fades into the background for the rest of the series. During his first day in Twin Peaks, Cooper seems to delight in taunting potential suspects—especially Bobby Briggs, though Cooper is actually certain Bobby is innocent. And he's positively giddy when he discovers a letter, typed on a scrap of paper and slipped under Laura's fingernail, which provides a conclusive link to the murder of another girl named Teresa Banks (about whom we'll learn much more, much later, in Lynch's film *Twin Peaks: Fire Walk with Me*). The contrast in attitudes is especially pronounced coming so soon after the collective grief that has defined the rest of the episode. As Cooper celebrates what he's discovered under Laura's fingernail in one of his many tapes for Diane, he needs to be reminded, by Truman, of the victim's name.

But even as MacLachlan is still working out the intricacies of his performance, you can see he's the right actor, if not the *only* actor, for the role. There's a moment in the pilot script when Cooper reads aloud from Laura's diary: "*Asparagus for dinner again. I hate asparagus. Does this mean I'll never grow up?*" On the page, it slips right by you. As played by MacLachlan, it's quietly heartbreaking—a seasoned FBI agent whose voice catches with emotion, just slightly, as he reads a note from a precocious teenager about growing up and realizes she never will.

The clues amass rapidly from there. Cooper opens Laura's diary and finds a baggie with white powder residue—suspected, and soon confirmed, to be cocaine—along with a final note that reads "*nervous about meeting J tonight.*" Attentive viewers will start running down the list of characters we've already met who could be "J": James Hurley, Leo Johnson, Lawrence Jacoby, or someone even further off the plausible suspect list based on current information, including Josie Packard, Johnny Horne (Robert Davenport), or Norma Jennings. Laura's safety deposit box is opened, revealing at least ten thousand dollars in cash and a porno magazine that connects her with both Ronette Pulaski and Leo Johnson. The murder site, once discovered, turns out to be an abandoned train car in the woods: It contains a note, written in blood, that reads "*FIRE WALK WITH ME*," along with half of a heart-shaped necklace.

Here, at least, the audience has more information than even Dale Cooper. James Hurley has the other half of that heart-shaped necklace, and he and Donna break curfew to bury it. They discover, in the process, that they've actually been falling in love with each other all along (and retroactively make James's insistence that Laura was "the one"—earlier that very day!—seem awfully fickle, albeit plausible. Teenage love, right?). "David loved that scene," says Marshall. "We did it over and over and over. I mean, when I say he did hundreds of takes... I wouldn't be surprised if it *is* hundreds." With a closing scene in which Sarah Palmer awakes from a vision and sees a gloved hand digging the necklace out of the hole where James and Donna buried it, *Twin Peaks* has a crackerjack cliff-hanger to propel audiences into the next episode—assuming, of course, that ABC picked up a full season of *Twin Peaks*.

There was, however, one matter left to resolve. As part of the deal they cut with ABC, Lynch was obligated to shoot a closed ending for the pilot, which would allow the network to sell it as a movie in Europe if it *wasn't* ordered to series. Since Lynch had no idea who had killed Laura Palmer, and no interest in solving the crime, he would need to improvise. "We're having breakfast and pancakes and coffee, and just kind of out of nowhere, David says, 'What would you think about a guy who has a tattoo on his arm, and he hates that tattoo so much that he cuts his arm off to get rid of it?'" says Duwayne Dunham. "And I said, 'I think you've had too much syrup and coffee. I don't know *what* to make of that.' And that's all he said."

After filming on the *Twin Peaks* pilot had wrapped, and Dunham was working on the edit, he received an unscheduled visitor. "Sometime well after midnight, a guy comes to the door with a handcart stacked with film boxes. He says, 'Is this the *Twin Peaks* cutting room?'" recalls Dunham. "He said, 'This is for you,' and I said, 'That's not for me. We're done.' And he said 'They told me to bring it here.' I'm thinking, *What is this?* So I opened a box and started watching, and it was all this strange stuff: BOB lighting candles down in a boiler room, and the one-armed man saying they lived above a convenience store. I watched it all, and when I spoke with David the next day, I said, 'What is this stuff?' And he said, 'That's the closed ending.'"

The European ending, as it's come to be known among fans, is a fascinating glimpse into an alternate reality—one in which the murder of Laura Palmer is (sort of) solved in a tidy two hours. Mike, the one-armed man briefly glimpsed in an elevator earlier in the episode, invites Cooper back to the hospital. There, he spins a strange story about living with BOB above a convenience store, before he saw the face of God and removed his own arm, which bore a tattoo connecting him to the killer. Cooper goes to the basement and finds BOB in the middle of a strange candlelight ritual. BOB explains that the letters under the fingernails were going to spell his proper name, Robert, confirming him as the killer. Mike rushes in and shoots BOB, apparently killing him before dying himself. "Make a wish," says Cooper, and the candles go out.

But there was also one more crucial scene left to be filmed for the European version of the pilot. Back in Los Angeles, Dunham had been with Lynch after a long day of editing as they walked out to the parking lot together to Lynch's maroon Mercedes. "It was pretty warm, and David leaned on the car, and all of a sudden just bolted upright," says Dunham. "He said, 'I've got to go. Don't say anything,' and he bolted in his car and sped away."

As Lynch later revealed in his book *Catching the Big Fish*, an idea had suddenly taken hold of him: a red room in which Agent Cooper was suddenly twenty-five years older; a dancing, backward-talking dwarf who spoke in cryptic riddles; and Laura Palmer—or at least, a girl, played by Sheryl Lee, who looked exactly like Laura Palmer—offering a few more clues before planting a passionate kiss on Cooper's lips.

The Red Room sequence, which would later be repurposed as the closing scene of "Episode 2," is perhaps the show's most iconic—and certainly its most parodied. (Note: When *Twin Peaks* initially aired, the episodes were only numbered, not named, with "Episode 1" being the second episode to air, following the pilot.) Lynch credited the initial spark, like so many of his creative impulses, to his decades-long practice of transcendental meditation. "That's how it starts. The idea tells you to build this Red Room," he wrote. "So you think about it. 'Wait a minute,' you say, 'the walls are red, but they're not hard walls.' Then you think some more. 'They're curtains. And they're not opaque; they're translucent.' Then you put these curtains there. 'But the floor . . . it needs something.' And you go back to the idea and there was something on the floor—it was all there. So you do this thing on the floor. And you start to remember the idea more. You try some things and you make mistakes, but you rearrange, add other stuff, and then it feels the way that idea felt.'"

Despite the bargain the production had made with ABC, this is not, in any sense, a satisfying resolution to the murder mystery. It's not just that the introduction of Mike and BOB raises infinitely more questions than it answers; it's that it retroactively makes the entire pilot an elaborate red herring, full of half-explained characters and aborted storylines that turn out to have nothing to do with the murder's solution. It was as inexplicable as it was mesmerizing—the first full glimpse into the slippery, surreal side that *Twin Peaks* would quietly ramp up over the course of its run. This was as strange as the pilot got, and all to fulfill a fussy little quirk of the contract they'd signed. "Sometimes being forced into a corner is not a bad thing," said Lynch.

Those who had been involved in the production of *Twin Peaks* had known they were making something special—so much so that they doubted it had any chance of resonating with a general TV audience. "Not a person in the cast thought this was going to go further than this one two-hour episode," said MacLachlan. "We shot the pilot thinking, *I don't know what they're going to do with this. Either it's going to be huge or it's just going to flop,*" says James Marshall. "And when we saw it, we all thought, *Oh, this is going to be huge.*"

Upon reviewing the pilot, the executives at ABC weren't as confident. "They weren't really sure if it was going to work, and all the research and test screenings they had said this was going to be a turkey," says Frost. "We were hearing things. The same kind of ugly reviews David would get on *Blue Velvet*. 'It's *sick*,'" recalls Dunham. "I was baffled by it," confessed ABC president Mark Mandala. "I wasn't a big fan," said fellow executive John Sias.

But *Twin Peaks* had one important champion among network executives: Bob Iger, an executive who had recently been promoted to head of ABC Entertainment. After watching the pilot, he recalled thinking, *This is unlike anything I've ever seen and we have to do this.*

Iger had been promoted by Tom Murphy and Dan Burke, two executives whose smaller company, Capital Cities Communications, had shocked the entertainment world by purchasing ABC outright in 1986. When Iger screened the pilot for the executives, Burke was confused but impressed. Murphy, however, disliked it—feeling, Iger recalled, it was too weird and dark for the network.

"I had such respect for Tom, but I also knew this show was important enough to fight for," wrote Iger in his 2019 memoir *The Ride of a Lifetime*. "I felt that network television had become boring and derivative, and we had the chance with *Twin Peaks* to put something on TV that was utterly original." He arranged for a younger, more diverse test audience to view the pilot, and while the numbers improved, they were far from glowing. "The test audiences didn't exactly support putting the show on network television, particularly because it was so different," said Iger. "But it was just that—its being *different*—that motivated us to give it the green light." He ordered seven more episodes months before the pilot had formally aired.

In the lengthy gap between the pilot's completion and its premiere on ABC, the network sought to generate buzz by getting it in front of as many critics and industry tastemakers as possible. It screened at film festivals in Telluride, Palm Springs, and Miami, and served as the opening-night gala for the Vancouver International Film Festival in September of 1989. It was screened for the Television Critics Association during their winter press tour in January of 1990. Those who saw *Twin Peaks*—and recognized it as something special in a medium known for monotony and repetition—buzzed about it, and that buzz manifested in articles that instructed readers they'd be missing out on the most interesting TV show in ages if they didn't tune in when ABC finally aired it.

Digging into the archives, you can feel critics of the era trying, and often struggling, to describe *Twin Peaks* in a way that would even be comprehensible to readers. *The Washington Post*'s Tom Shales called it "*Mayberry RFD* as it might have been written by Franz Kafka and directed by Alfred Hitchcock." *New York Magazine*'s John Leonard called it "*Mary Hartman, Mary Hartman* written by Louis-Ferdinand Celine." *Time*'s Richard Zoglin halfheartedly cited predecessors such as *Colombo* and *Knots Landing* before conceding, more accurately, that it "may be the most hauntingly original work ever done for American TV." These comparisons, which barely scratched the surface of what *Twin Peaks* was up to, didn't surprise its creator. "That's what people do," says Frost. "They try to compare in order to figure out a way to understand what it is that you're doing."

Twin Peaks finally premiered for the general public on April 8, 1990, opposite a new episode of *Murder, She Wrote* on CBS and a rerun of *Married... with Children* on Fox. Concerned that viewers might lack the patience for the series without a helping hand, ABC considered taking a six-figure loss on the pilot by airing it without commercials. (Ultimately, cooler heads prevailed, though it aired with fewer commercial interruptions than the network's norm.) "A lot of people have said *Twin Peaks* is the critic's dream," said Bob Iger at the time. "But is it the viewer's nightmare? I would hope that the answer is that it isn't."

As it turned out, ABC had nothing to worry about. All that buzz had successfully attracted an audience curious to see the groundbreaking TV series they'd been hearing about for months. *Twin Peaks* premiered to a whopping thirty-four million viewers—"almost Super Bowl numbers," says Mark Frost. The gamble had paid off. *Twin Peaks* wasn't just a hit; it was a phenomenon. "So much of the credit you have to give to David [Lynch], and to Mark Frost," said Kyle MacLachlan. "Because I think on the strength of that pilot—which I think is as good as anything, even today, and would stand up as a feature film—they were able to build a very strong vessel, and they launched it, and it was very powerful."

SHERIFF HARRY S. TRUMAN

"I'm beginning to feel a bit like Dr. Watson."

Almost immediately after shaking hands with Sheriff Harry S. Truman for the first time, Dale Cooper gives the ranking peacekeeper of Twin Peaks a gentle but firm warning. "When the Bureau gets called in, the Bureau's in charge. You're going to be working for me," Cooper says. "Sometimes local law enforcement has a problem with that. I hope you understand."

"Like I said, we're glad to have you," says Truman. And the key to his character is that he actually means it. "It was always my intention to create an anti-conflict between the fed and the local," says Mark Frost. "Instead, I said, 'We're going to make them best friends. It's not the cliché that we've seen a hundred times. It's Holmes and Watson.'" For the rest of the series, the bromance between these two law enforcement officers—one solving crimes through dreams and visions, the other offering straightlaced, occasionally skeptical, but always unconditional support—has a unique purity in a show where even the happiest of relationships tend to take twists and turns. By the end of the show's original run, Cooper and Truman enjoyed what was, by far, the most functional relationship in all of *Twin Peaks*.

Originally named Dan Steadman—and changed, as best as Mark Frost can recall, because that name couldn't be cleared legally—the head of the Twin Peaks Sheriff's Department was rechristened Harry S. Truman as a cheeky nod to . . . well, you know. ("Shouldn't be too hard to remember that," quips Cooper, dryly, into his tape recorder.) But if Truman's name (and his mounted "the buck stopped here" deer's head) were inspired by the thirty-third president of the United States, it's the Log Lady who gets the final word on Harry, in *Twin Peaks: The Return*, when she tells Deputy Hawk (Michael Horse) that Truman is a true man.

It's not easy to play second fiddle to a character as indelible as Dale Cooper, and Harry's arc is one of the show's subtler, more internal ones. A lifelong Twin Peaks resident—and the son and younger brother, respectively, of the town's two previous sheriffs—Harry has a vague but powerful sense of the horrors that surround Twin Peaks, and the unconventional methods required to oppose them. "There's a sort of evil out there. Something very, very strange in these old woods," he tells Cooper early in season one. "Call it what you want. A darkness, a presence. It takes many forms, but it's been out there for as long as anyone can remember, and we've always been here to fight it."

But whatever he intuits about what's actually bearing down on Twin Peaks, Harry is not prepared for the surreal (but inarguably effective) investigative techniques Cooper brings to the table. In one early, memorable sequence in which Cooper throws rocks at a glass bottle in an effort to determine the killer's identity, Harry questions him only gently: "The idea for all this came from a dream?" When Cooper confirms that, Harry nods and takes his position, skeptical but willing—as he vowed from the start—to let the FBI agent take charge.

Why is he willing to go along with this? Because he gave his word, and that's what a true man does. Though season two missteps by having the grief-stricken Harry fall, briefly, into a raging alcoholic stupor, the show wisely returns him to his core role as the platonic ideal of someone you'd trust to have your back. Even Harry's deep, dark secrets—a romantic entanglement with a woman who is single and his membership in the secret society called the Bookhouse Boys—are kind of adorable. In the real world, it is not ideal for a town's sheriff to be a member of an extralegal vigilante society, but in the context of *Twin Peaks*, the Bookhouse Boys are unambiguously good, fighting the good fight against drug dealers and the cosmic evil in the woods from the sanctity of their little library.

What Harry sees over the course of *Twin Peaks* pushes him to the brink of his entire conception of how the world works. When the supernatural nature of Laura's killer is revealed, Harry insists that the only explanation is insanity or schizophrenia. "What's the alternative? Ghosts and goblins?" he scoffs. "I've lived in these woods all my life. I've heard some strange things. Seen some too. But this is way off the map. I'm having a hard time believing."

By the season two finale, as Harry watches Cooper slip through the red curtains that have suddenly appeared in the woods, he has little choice but to believe. With no real way to make sense of what's happening, he maintains his post all night, waiting for the opportunity to do something to help his friend.

That opportunity never comes. The last time we see Truman in *Twin Peaks* is at the very end of season two, when he rushes to the bathroom door to make sure Cooper is all right. (Cooper is, uh, not all right.) And while that story would have continued in *Twin Peaks: The Return*, production realities left the rest of Harry's story off-screen. Though he originally planned to return, Michael Ontkean ultimately opted out of *Twin Peaks: The Return* for personal reasons. Of the characters played by living actors who didn't come back, Harry's absence—explained as an illness he's battling out of town—always felt like the biggest loss. Then again, it's possible that *The Return*, with its twenty-five-year time gap, simply wouldn't have made any sense with Truman in it. It's hard to imagine the Harry S. Truman we knew being fooled by the doppelgänger's Cooper disguise for more than a minute, or ever giving up on trying to rescue his friend, no matter the time or cost.

Chapter 3

A WHOLE DAMN TOWN

In the early 1980s, David Lynch made a mistake he swore he'd never make again. Fresh off the success of *The Elephant Man*, which earned him an Academy Award nomination for Best Director at the age of thirty-five, he decided to tackle a big-screen adaptation of a beloved sci-fi novel long thought unfilmable: Frank Herbert's *Dune*.

Dune was a box-office bomb. It was also, as Lynch himself later put it, both a "failure" and a "huge gigantic sadness" in his life. It wasn't just that Lynch had made a mistake by signing a contract that explicitly stated he would not have final cut on the film. It's that he *knew*—even as he signed it—that he was making a mistake. Though he worked with producer Dino De Laurentiis to trim his three-hour cut of the movie down to the simpler, two-hour version they expected, he never got over his regret for agreeing to compromise his vision. "Why would anyone make a film, work for three years, on something that wasn't yours? Why do that? Why? I died the death, and it was all my fault," he reflected in 2024. It was a hard lesson to learn, but one Lynch would carry for the rest of his career: Whatever the reason, never give up your creative control.

And now, six years later, here was *Twin Peaks*: a massive hit that—owing to the practical realities of television production—Lynch literally *couldn't* control. It wasn't just that he had an equal partner in Mark Frost. More writers and directors would need to be recruited to help shoulder the burden of an entire season of television. ABC executives would weigh in with notes on scripts and episodes. And Lynch was already in preproduction for his next film, *Wild at Heart*, which would necessitate a lengthy absence from the soundstage in Van Nuys, California, where most of the key *Twin Peaks* locations—including the Double R Diner and the Great Northern—had been reconstructed. Even this compromise, which was completely normal for a network TV production, seemed to frustrate Lynch. "As far as I'm concerned, the only thing in the entire first two seasons that's really *Twin Peaks* is the pilot," he later said. "That had everything to do with the fact that we were shooting on location. The place itself is so important."

While Lynch and Frost are credited as cowriters on the first three episodes of *Twin Peaks*, Lynch spent relatively little time working on the show's first season. He returned to direct "Episode 2," which was filmed out of sequence, after much of the rest of the season had been shot, to accommodate the production schedule for *Wild at Heart*. Having a rotating lineup of directors was, and is, the norm for television—but Lynch's absence did leave *Twin Peaks* without the directorial perspective everyone agreed was one of the show's key strengths. "Nothing about the script struck me as being astoundingly brilliant," says Scott Frost. "You know, it seemed pretty meat-and-potatoes, in a sense. It got fully realized in the shooting in a way that I didn't see coming, frankly. And that's what David could do, you know? He had that ability to just get to the core of things in a way that was hard to see on the page. Once everybody saw the pilot, there was no doubt: *Oh, wow, this is one of the best things I've ever seen on television*." Lynch's pilot had set the template. It was time to find other directors who could follow in his footsteps.

Fortunately, the production didn't need to look far for someone who was intimately familiar with Lynch's work. Having edited the *Twin Peaks* pilot, Duwayne Dunham understood the show as well as anyone, and he was interested in trying his hand at directing. Lynch, already looking ahead to his next movie, cut him a deal: If Dunham agree to edit *Wild at Heart*, he could also direct "Episode 1." Dunham agreed, landing his first-ever directing job. "I asked David, 'Have you got any advice for me?'" recalls Dunham. "He said, 'Yeah. When the car shows up in the morning to pick you up, get in. When it takes you to the set, get out.'"

It's safe to say Dunham's job was slightly more complicated than that. As the first director not named David Lynch to helm an episode of *Twin Peaks*, it would be his responsibility to demonstrate what a "normal" episode—or, at least, as normal as *Twin Peaks* got—would look like on a week-to-week basis. The first trick *Twin Peaks*' new writers and directors would need to learn, he discovered, was that *Twin Peaks* had a pace unlike anything else on television. "Usually, it's one page of script for one minute of screen time," says Dunham. "It took a couple of scripts before the writers got it down, but the ideal length of a *Twin Peaks* script was thirty-four pages. *Twin Peaks* has a whole different kind of movement to it. It's at a much slower pace."

If *Twin Peaks* was notable for its languorous, dreamy pace, its first season also unfolds as a propulsive murder mystery. Frost's time on *Hill Street Blues*, and the procedural story structure he had learned and internalized, served the show well: The clues and red herrings are scattered together, ensuring that Laura's murder is never far from the center of the show's narrative thrust. An autopsy reveals a series of leads to follow up on, including the brands of twine Laura was bound with and the number of sexual partners she had on the night of her murder. Shelly finds a bloody shirt in Leo's laundry. Dr. Jacoby is revealed as the mystery man who dug up the half-heart necklace that James and Donna buried.

But while these clues pushed the mystery forward, they weren't the ones that made *Twin Peaks* stand apart. The aspect of the show that drove the most watercooler chatter—and that made it unique from any other murder mystery on television—were the clues that dipped into the surreal. The Log Lady, telling Cooper that her log had seen something that night. Cooper, drawing the entire Sheriff's Department into a hunt for the killer that involves throwing rocks at bottles—a "certain deductive technique, involving mind-body coordination operating hand in hand with the deepest levels of intuition," which he says he learned from a dream. Sheryl Lee, emerging in a brunette wig and glasses, to play Laura's cousin Maddy Ferguson—her name an obvious reference to Alfred Hitchcock's *Vertigo*, which put *Twin Peaks* in direct conversation with another mystery classic about dual lives and doubling.

Most of all, there was the Red Room, in which every single detail presented raises questions with no obvious answers. Why does the girl who looks exactly like Laura Palmer respond to a question about her identity with a non sequitur about her arms bending back? What is the Man from

"My log has something to tell you."

Another Place (Michael J. Anderson) talking about when he says "that gum you like is going to come back in style"? Where is he from that there's "always music in the air"?

Already, *Twin Peaks* was struggling with a tension: The show needed to keep moving the mystery forward to keep the audience hooked, but it also couldn't advance the plot so much that the murder was resolved, because no one had any good ideas yet for what a post–Laura Palmer *Twin Peaks* might look like.

This problem required the show's writers to bend the narrative in some frustrating ways. One early, vexing example comes when Harley Peyton, who Frost recruited to write for Twin Peaks after meeting him in a fantasy-baseball league, is forced to resolve the previous episode's cliff-hanger. At the end of "Episode 2," Cooper, waking up from his Red Room dream, calls Truman and tells him he knows who killed Laura Palmer. "No, it *can* wait till morning," says Cooper, still snapping his fingers to the song from the dream, as Harry squawks excitedly over the phone. When Truman and Lucy meet Cooper for breakfast the following day, he describes the dream in detail before revealing, anticlimactically, that he can't remember who killed Laura. But even in this deflating moment, Cooper ends up delivering a prophetic piece of dialogue. The dream was full of cryptic clues; the murderer would be found, he said, as soon as the true meaning behind all those bizarre lines and symbols could be uncovered. "Our job is simple," he tells Harry. "Break the code, solve the crime."

For a certain subset of highly engaged *Twin Peaks* fans, this dictum was treated as gospel. On alt.tv.twin-peaks—a nascent Internet discussion group where devotees gathered weekly to discuss the latest episode—the show was treated as an elaborate puzzle box to be solved, and no possible clue was too esoteric to be interrogated and debated. These discussions, facilitated by the Internet, were supercharged by VCRs. Even as *Twin Peaks*' viewership declined, it remained the most videotaped show on network television, with some 830,000 viewers recording each episode so they could pause, rewind, and fast-forward to ensure they hadn't missed a single detail. One fan described going through a BOB scene frame by frame to see if another character's face had been superimposed on him for even a single second; others spotted shadows in the backgrounds of certain scenes, or other minor continuity errors, that they interpreted as deliberate clues, which pointed toward the true solution for anyone clever and devoted enough to spot them. This phenomenon, basically brand-new, amused and puzzled even those who reported on television for a living. In ratings, *Twin Peaks* "routinely gets beat by NBC's perennial hit *Cheers*," noted *Newsweek* at the time. "But once people begin watching, addiction usually follows. Then, madness."

The confluence of video and Internet technology—when combined with a TV show that seemed to warrant closer scrutiny—would play out more deliberately in shows like ABC's *Lost* or Apple TV+'s *Severance*, where eagle-eyed fans were rewarded for their attention with blink-and-you'll-miss-it easter eggs. It's no accident that *Lost* cocreator Damon Lindelof describes *Twin Peaks* as "the greatest piece of art ever to be broadcast on a television screen," or that *Severance* showrunner Ben Stiller says "nothing that's out there on television and takes chances exists without [David Lynch]."

But if *Twin Peaks* diehards were correctly intuiting where genre TV would go in the years that followed, they were also ahead of what *Twin Peaks* was actually doing. Why, to cite one of many examples, is Hawk asked to wear oven mitts while he's holding the bucket of rocks for Cooper to throw at the bottle? "They said, 'Go pick that bucket up. And put these oven mitts on,'" says Michael Horse. "And I said, 'What the fuck does this mean?' And they said, 'Nothing. We just thought it'd be funny to see Hawk in oven mitts.'"

It's not that the myriad of strange details in *Twin Peaks* were meaningless. It's that they had value on their own terms, and not as discrete pieces that, when combined, would offer a completed puzzle. The various directors who worked on *Twin Peaks* were trusted to figure out the show's unique rhythms while putting their own stamp on the material, and they often took that license, inventing flourishes that felt congruent within the world Lynch and Frost had created. "It felt like you were making a feature film or quasi–feature film. There was an enormous amount of freedom," said director Tina Rathborne. "I had absolutely no idea what the plot was about," said Tim Hunter, who helmed one midseason episode. "I mean, there's so much plot in it. *Twin Peaks* is just full of plot. Almost every scene is an expository plot scene, and that's kind of miraculous, in a way, to have a show that had so much plot on the one hand, but the plot actually mattering so little because the subtext of the scenes is almost everything in *Twin Peaks*."

Reveling in their freedom, the show's directors embedded strange, never-explained background details, suffusing the town with an almost subliminal feeling of the uncanny. "*Twin Peaks* was the show where actually you could ask somebody to get you a llama—go out and get you a llama—and they would actually do it without blinking," said Tim Hunter. (This idea became one of *Twin Peaks*' other "happy accidents," when the llama in question paused during filming to snort in Kyle MacLachlan's face; MacLachlan, to his credit, didn't break, and the take made the final cut.) In Hunter's episode, two extras appear, playing tennis at night in full winter gear. In Lesli Linka Glatter's episodes, the Great Northern is always populated with extras who have arrived for an extremely specific convention, including cheerleading, square dancing, and tuba playing. "It's just there whether anyone notices or not," she said.

The writers, too, were encouraged to explore. "There wasn't a writer's room in the way that there are now, traditionally, in television shows. We were basically all freelance writers in that first season," says Peyton. "Mark would sit down with you and walk you through the story. Mark provided the framework, but you were given a huge amount of leeway for what you did within that frame." That was, says fellow writer Robert Engels, "the whole idea: There's nothing normal about Twin Peaks. You could just go out to get a coffee and *something* would happen."

As Lynch and Frost had always intended, the first season of *Twin Peaks* busies itself with plenty of stories that are almost entirely disconnected from Laura Palmer's murder. The show spends ample time on a convoluted subplot about the fate of the Packard sawmill, which balloons into a conspiracy of double crosses between Catherine Martell, Ben Horne, and Josie Packard, with Leo Johnson and Hank Jennings (Chris Mulkey) carrying out the dirty work of blackmail and arson. It's a subplot that would have been right at home in *Dallas*, *Dynasty*, or the other night soaps *Twin Peaks* was supposedly riffing on ironically—and yet it's played almost completely straight. The teen drama, which spirals into a melodramatic love triangle between James, Donna, and Maddy, would have been right at home in *Peyton Place*. "You forget that, 'Oh, David Lynch is just a person. He was addicted to soap operas for a long time.' That's part of what *Twin Peaks* was," says James Marshall.

Still, the structural principle Lynch and Frost had devised remained sturdy: Whenever it felt like *Twin Peaks* might be going down a fruitless detour, a new development in the murder mystery pulled things back on track. It also led to what Peyton recalls as "*Twin Peaks* at its best": the brief life and violent death of a bird named Waldo. "It starts out as, *Well, this is just weird*," says Peyton. "And it's also sort of funny. And then it's also tragic."

Let's back up. By now, Cooper and Truman have put together a partial time line of Laura's whereabouts on the night of her murder. After sneaking out of her house that night, she met up with James Hurley before ditching him to join Leo Johnson, Ronette Pulaski, and Jacques Renault—a sleazy Canadian card-and-drug dealer—for a BDSM-inflected sex party. Tied up in Jacques's cabin, she has sex with both men before Waldo, Jacques's pet mynah bird, alights on Laura's shoulder and begins pecking. When Cooper and Truman find Jacques's now-abandoned cabin, they discover Waldo ("Where we're from, the birds sing a pretty song," said the Man from Another Place) and a spinning record ("and there's always music in the air," the Man from Another Place also said).

With Leo and Jacques dodging the law and Ronette in a coma, Waldo emerges as the key witness in Laura's murder, parroting a few disturbing phrases from the evening of Laura's murder in its singsong chirp. "*Hurting me, hurting me. Stop it, stop it. Leo, no, Leo, no.*" It's enough to put Waldo under police protection—which isn't enough to stop Leo from assassinating the bird through a window, spattering its blood all over the doughnuts on the table below. "That was just, like, a great thrill," said Caleb Deschanel, who directed the episode. "To take one of the sort of key archetypal elements of this show and then, you know, use it in a way that, I mean, it's both—it's both very funny and very horrific at the same time, which was really sort of the essence of this show."

Or, in a word, the Waldo subplot was *Lynchian*—a shorthand for a specific tone and style that would be defined a few years later, by the writer David Foster Wallace, as "a particular kind of irony where the very macabre and the very mundane combine in such a way as to reveal the former's perpetual containment within the latter." But while Lynch was regularly discussing *Twin Peaks* (and signing off on scripts) with Mark Frost, his absence was noted—especially by the cast that had been so painstakingly assembled. "I think a lot of the cast was upset when David went and did *Wild at Heart*. It's like, Willy Wonka can't be imitated," says James Marshall. "When David came on the set, it was like the owner coming home and being able to do whatever he wants," said Dana Ashbrook. "In his mind, it was a roiling vortex of ideas. Always, always, always," says Ray Wise. "He came up with the strangest ideas, at the most opportune times, that worked."

What was the "Lynchian" touch that only Lynch himself could deliver? When asked, each of the show's actors—almost without fail—can recall at least one strange, abstract piece of direction from Lynch that helped shape their performance across the entirety of the series. "One of his directions was, 'Russ, do it again. But this time, just forget the lines and just think about ghosts,'" says Russ Tamblyn. "I remember, in the pilot, I did a very long scene that we had to shoot thirty or forty times," said Lara Flynn Boyle. "David came up to me and said quietly, in my ear: 'Think of how gently a deer has to move in the snow . . .' It was strange direction. But that's what I thought of, and it worked." Before filming one Double R Diner scene, Sheryl Lee recalled, Lynch told her and Boyle that it was summer in the 1950s and they were drinking milkshakes. The scene, set in 1989, took place on a rainy day, and the characters were drinking coffee. "Now, if you're going to try and make sense of that with your logical mind, you're not going to be present to the moment. But if you surrender to wherever it is he's taking you, then by the time he says action, you realize that he has taken you somewhere. He's taken you exactly where he wants to take you and he starts the scene from that place. It's like a brushstroke that he's just painted across you."

There was a tradeoff to Lynch's idiosyncratic approach. "The downside is that he was so absolutely focused on the episode he was directing that he was not actually great at serialized television," says Peyton. "He was just not thinking about the next episode, because he's not directing it. His obsessions—chewing gum, giants, whatever—those were always in his episodes, even if they weren't in the episodes on either side of it." More often than not, it was up to Frost to figure out how to turn Lynch's impressionistic flourishes into something with actual, coherent relevance to the show's narrative.

David Lynch—an actor's director

It was, to say the least, an unconventional approach to network television. But owing, perhaps, to the show's out-of-the-box success, ABC executives largely stayed out of the way. The few objections they raised were typically related not to violence, or general weirdness, but to sexual content. When Standards and Practices objected to a scene in which Ben Horne refers to his penis as "little Elvis," the production simply gave him a little Elvis Presley doll to hold during the scene—sneaking by, with the thinnest of justifications, for what he was actually talking about. Other times, the references seemed to go over the network's head altogether. When Ben and his brother Jerry Horne (David Patrick Kelly) devour brie-and-butter sandwiches, Ben remarks, without further explanation, that the gooey, creamy sandwich reminds him of Ginny and Jenny down by the river. The erotic subtext of this comment is obvious, but the network's concerns were different. "David goes, 'You want to see the stupidest thing you've ever seen in your life?'" says Sherilyn Fenn. "I'm like, 'Sure.' And he says, 'Network notes.' It was the sandwich scene, and it was: 'How big is the sandwich? What's on the sandwich? What kind of sandwich? What comes out of it?' And he just threw them into the air."

And then there's *Twin Peaks'* most iconically racy scene: one involving a cherry stem. In her eagerness to help with Cooper's investigation, Audrey Horne has maneuvered and manipulated her way into a job at the casino/brothel One Eyed Jack's, where Jacques Renault deals cards (and which, unbeknownst to Audrey, is both owned and frequented by her own father). Despite the confidence Audrey projects, she's doing a pretty clumsy job of being an undercover agent; when asked for her name, she says "Hester Prynne," apparently unaware that someone might recognize her pseudonym as one of the most famous heroines in American literary history.

But when Blackie, the proprietor of One Eyed Jack's, calls Audrey out on the deception, Audrey improvises a backup plan. Taking the cherry from Blackie's cocktail, she puts the stem in her mouth and—after a slow, sensuous set of machinations with her tongue—drops it back on the desk, revealing that she's tied it into a perfect knot.

Twin Peaks had been built on happy accidents, and this one belonged to Harley Peyton. "It was just dumb luck," says Peyton. "I had a dear friend, and one night at dinner, she did that. She turned to me and said, 'You know, I can tie a cherry stem into a knot in my mouth,' and she did. Now, whether or not she fooled me or not . . . to this day, I do not know. But it was one of those things where I went, 'This is perfect for Audrey.' And one of the great things about working in television, when everything is immediate, is that you could write that cherry stem scene, and you're shooting it two weeks later, and then it's airing two months later, and then a month after that they're writing about it in *New York Magazine*."

"Look: It was, it was one of many scenes, one of the many pearls on the necklace," says Fenn. "To me, it wasn't bigger or smaller than anything else.

I don't know what it says about America, or the world, that all of a sudden I'm getting calls to go on so many talk shows. David Letterman, over and over. And I said, 'No. I am not getting approached with a cherry stem on a talk show.'" For starters, Fenn hadn't actually done the trick: during filming, an off-camera prop person had simply handed her a tied cherry stem to pop into her mouth. "I hate to burst your bubble, but that's how it works." It was only much later, when she accidentally locked herself out of her hotel room, that Fenn and a friend saddled up at a quiet bar and, just for the fun of it, actually attempted the cherry-stem trick themselves. "It can be done," she says. "It just takes a while."

This scene, Frost later revealed, drew extra scrutiny from the network. "I got an astonishing note from one of the censors," he said. "They thought the act of twisting the cherry stem was in some way a reference to oral sex. I called her up and said, 'What in the world would make you think that? You must have an absolutely filthy mind.' Censors, the whole idea is so childish. You feel like you're talking to hall monitors in school again."

If there was a sticking point with ABC, it was the same one that had made the series both bewitching and bedeviling to viewers: When the hell would we be told, once and for all, who had killed Laura Palmer? Seeking to quell doubters—and, perhaps, to quell the chance of a mass audience exodus, as *Twin Peaks* had shed more than fifteen million viewers between the pilot and the end of the season—an ABC spokesperson confidently assured reporters that the mystery would be solved by the season one finale.

This was news to Lynch and Frost. It wasn't just that they were firmly in lockstep in their refusal to solve the mystery so soon; it's that they hadn't even definitively agreed on the *identity* of the murderer, or where the show could go after the audience knew who had killed Laura Palmer. Their interest, as usual, went beyond a simple whodunnit, and they feared a network guillotine that would execute the series as soon as that baseline curiosity had been satisfied. "I never thought I'd be watching numbers like I am," said David Lynch. "But I love the cast, I love the place of Twin Peaks and the coffee and doughnuts. I don't want to say goodbye to them, so I'm sitting on the edge of my seat waiting to see what will happen."

So they devised the next best thing: a finale that not only left Laura's murder unresolved, but was packed with other mysteries, nearly all of which ended on tantalizing cliff-hangers. "We had no guarantee that ABC would ever renew us," says Frost. "I intentionally structured that last hour so that if ABC was really curious about who killed Laura, they'd have to pick up the show."

The season one finale, which was written and directed by Mark Frost, packs in so much incident that it feels, at times, like an arch parody of soap opera plotting. Nadine Hurley (Wendy Robie) attempts suicide. Lucy Moran reveals that she's pregnant. Leland Palmer, upon learning that Jacques Renault has been arrested as a person of interest in Laura's murder, sneaks into the hospital and strangles him to death. Leo Johnson burns down the Packard sawmill, leaving the fates of Shelly Johnson and Catherine Martell in question, before getting shot by Hank Jennings. Dr. Jacoby, attacked by an unseen assailant, has a heart attack. Still undercover at One Eyed Jack's, Audrey discovers, to her horror, that her first "client" at the brothel is her own father.

The episode saves its biggest jolt for last. After Cooper returns to his hotel room, exhausted after a long evening spent undercover, he opens the door and is shot in the stomach three times by an unseen assassin. The cheeky parallel to *Dallas's* infamous "Who shot J. R.?" cliff-hanger—which led to what was, at the time, the highest-rated episode in TV history—doesn't entirely obviate the very real stakes of the show's beloved hero bleeding out from a gut shot.

And yet: "Who shot Agent Cooper?" was no "Who killed Laura Palmer?" And the subset of viewers who expected a resolution to the latter question were not won over by the slew of new questions that had been presented instead. On May 24, 1990—just one day after the season one finale aired—ABC's *Primetime Live* aired a ten-minute segment asking *Twin Peaks* diehards about their reaction to the episode. They were, to say the least, less than pleased. "I'm angry. I feel used," complained one viewer. "Here we were, going through all these weeks, hanging on for this, you know? And they don't tell you anything," said another. One clip simply shows an entire room of people chanting, "We want to know!" over and over again.

The days of ABC being hands-off with *Twin Peaks* were coming to an end. The people wanted to know, and the network, like all networks, was in the business of giving the people what they wanted—even if they'd need to go twelve rounds with Lynch and Frost to do it.

ALBERT ROSENFIELD

"I reject absolutely revenge, aggression, and retaliation. The foundation of such a method . . . is love."

At the height of *Twin Peaks'* popularity, there were two characters who proved so popular with audiences, and so indelible to the show's writers, that they were considered prime candidates for a possible spin-off. One—as most David Lynch fans could recite as confidently as the alphabet—was Audrey Horne, who would have moved to Los Angeles and gotten involved in a mystery in a nascent version of what eventually became the film *Mulholland Drive*.

The other—less commonly known, though no less intriguing—is FBI Special Agent Albert Rosenfield (Miguel Ferrer). "We talked about that for a little bit," says Mark Frost. "I guess it probably would have been something like the precursor of the Blue Rose association. I was going to have him investigating paranormal cases. We would have brought the conspiracies back to Twin Peaks—they would have been related—but we would have stolen *The X-Files'* thunder."

What made Albert such a standout character in a standout ensemble? Much of it comes down to the actor who played him. Albert, says Frost, was written with Miguel Ferrer in mind, and offered to him without an audition, or even a meeting about the role. Though he'd happily subverted cliché with Cooper and Truman's relationship, Frost says, he felt *Twin Peaks* still needed an antagonist Fed, who could bluster into town and instantly establish himself as "the meanest guy in the FBI." Ferrer—who'd managed, impressively, to be the most punchable character in *RoboCop*, a movie full of punchable characters—was the actor for the job.

Much of what Albert says and does seems designed to alienate viewers who, like Cooper, have become infatuated with the small-town quirks of

Albert Rosenfield, making friends wherever he goes

Twin Peaks. He snorts at both the professional conduct and personal grief of kindly Doc Hayward, rolls his eyes at Big Ed's (Everett McGill) sad story about how Nadine lost her eye, and picks constant fights with Sheriff Truman, emerging as the one character who can reliably get under Harry's skin. When Truman finally throws a punch at him, Albert responds like a schoolyard snitch, informing Cooper that he plans to press charges.

Despite it all, Albert quickly emerged as a fan favorite, ensuring that *Twin Peaks* would have a skeptical outsider's perspective as Cooper became an insider. "I think Albert says the things the rest of us would like to say," said Ferrer. "The audience, at some point, wants to ask, 'Who are these crazy people?' and there's Albert to say it for them."

But even as he sits in judgment of the town's "morons and half-wits, dolts, dunces, dullards, and dumbbells"—his words, not mine—Albert, too, reveals hidden depths. In one of season two's more remarkable character swerves, Albert makes yet another crack at Truman's expense. When Truman threatens to punch him again, Albert retaliates instead with a rapid-fire monologue, written by Frost, that reveals the beating heart underneath his snarky veneer:

> While I will admit to a certain cynicism, the fact is that I am a naysayer and hatchet man in the fight against violence. I pride myself in taking a punch and I'll gladly take another because I choose to live my life in the company of Gandhi and King. My concerns are global. I reject absolutely revenge, aggression, and retaliation. The foundation of such a method . . . is love. I love you, Sheriff Truman.

As Albert leaves the room, leaving Harry in a state of silent wonder, Cooper offers an explanation: "Albert's path is a strange and difficult one." Who can relate?

Miguel Ferrer is one of the actors who appeared in *Twin Peaks: The Return* but died, sadly, before the show premiered. Due to his obligations to *NCIS: Los Angeles*, his *Twin Peaks: The Return* scenes needed to be filmed on weekends, and he died at age sixty-one, of throat cancer, less than a year after Lynch's production wrapped. "I would bet a bag of gold that not a single crew member or cast member that may have been disappointed to work a bunch of Saturdays regrets doing it," said singer and actress Chrystabell, who appeared as FBI Special Agent Tammy Preston in a number of scenes with Ferrer, in a tribute penned after he passed.

Ferrer's return to the world of *Twin Peaks* offers a wonderful swan song that adds a few more iconically caustic moments to Albert's already lengthy list. ("Fuck Gene Kelly, you motherfucker," he snarls as he stumbles through heavy rainfall.) It also meant he was frequently paired with

David Lynch, returning as FBI Deputy Director Gordon Cole. At times, their scenes seemed to channel their real-life friendship: "Albert, sometimes I really worry about you," says Gordon late in the season, squeezing his shoulder, in what feels, unmistakably, like one friend's concern for another. The scene was emotional to watch after Ferrer passed away; it's even harder to watch now that Lynch is gone, too.

But *The Return* also gives Albert a parting gift: a moment that seems to point to a happy future for *Twin Peaks*' most cynical character. During their investigative jaunt to Buckhorn, South Dakota, Tammy and Gordon spot Albert on a dinner date with Constance Talbot (Jane Adams)—a coroner who distinguished herself, in an earlier scene, by dropping a series of deadpan jokes about the headless corpse in her custody. ("Yeah, I'm still doing stand-up on the weekends," she sighs when no one laughs.) But Constance just hadn't found the right audience yet. If there's anyone who can appreciate how far gallows humor can take you in this line of work—and how good a person you can be underneath—it's Albert.

Chapter 4

FILLED WITH SECRETS

It's September 30, 1990, and after four long months, you're ready, at last, to see what the two-hour premiere of *Twin Peaks* season two has in store. You've speed-read Jennifer Lynch's tie-in novel *The Secret Diary of Laura Palmer*—released just two weeks earlier—to absorb any extra clues that might be hiding between its covers. You've invited some friends over, put on a pot of coffee, and even picked up a cherry pie for the occasion. You're a big enough fan that you've followed the industry chatter about the show between seasons, so you know that no less an authority than ABC's Bob Iger has vowed that viewers "will see the killer, and know it's the killer," by the end of the premiere. At the very least, you think, you'll finally find out who shot Agent Cooper.

And then—of course—the David Lynch–directed episode begins with eight unbroken minutes of Cooper bleeding out on the floor of his hotel room. His first visitor is a new character: an elderly Great Northern employee later described by Albert Rosenfield, accurately, as "the world's most decrepit room service waiter." His second visitor is the Giant (Carel Struycken)—a supernatural figure, like the Man from Another Place, who seems only to speak in riddles. It is mesmerizing television. It was also doomed to immediately alienate anyone who had grown frustrated with *Twin Peaks*' elliptical plotting—especially those who suspected the show might be using its strangeness to disguise a lack of coherency or substance at its core.

Twin Peaks entered its second season as the Schrödinger's cat of TV shows: both a critically adored, attention-grabbing phenomenon and a series that had tested the patience of ABC's parent company, Capital Cities—so much so, according to one source at the time, that they'd seriously contemplated canceling *Twin Peaks* until they got word that Fox might make a splashy bid for season two if ABC passed. In many ways, *Twin Peaks* had become the victim of its own success. "Because the show had debuted to almost Super Bowl numbers, they saw any decline in that as a sign of, *Oh, well, just like we thought, this was just a fad and no one's going to stay with this show*," says Frost.

For those who were actually working on the show, the show's success was undeniable, and the attention was overwhelming. "The question every writer hates is, 'What are you working on?'" says Harley Peyton. "But there are times when you love getting that question." Following its abbreviated first season, the show had taken an extended victory lap in the cultural zeitgeist. In the promotional sprint for the season two premiere, David Lynch was hailed the as "Czar of Bizarre" on the cover of *Time Magazine*. Sherilyn Fenn, Lara Flynn Boyle, and Mädchen Amick were on the cover of *Rolling Stone*. "It was a sign we'd arrived," said Lara Flynn Boyle. "I'll tell you when I realized the show was a really big deal," says Fenn. "I went to New York and people were screaming 'Audrey! Audrey!' in the street. And I just kept walking. It didn't even click. And my agent grabbed my hand and said, 'Sherilyn, they're calling for you. And I turned around and looked at this huge group of people, and I was like, 'Oh, my God. This is a thing.'" And Kyle MacLachlan hosted the season premiere of *Saturday Night Live*, complete with a joke about spoiling the killer's identity in the opening monologue and a lengthy, loving *Twin Peaks* parody sketch in which pretty much the entire *SNL* cast got into *Twin Peaks* cosplay.

"You had this very weird division," says Peyton. "The old pros . . . they understood how lucky they were, and they were really enjoying it. They knew what to do, and every day they were there to work. And the kids were completely losing their minds. And how could you not? They were in the middle of the most insane thing. They found themselves almost being fetishized, in a way. It was this weird dynamic. It's not like there was *trouble*, but there were complications. Lives were being completely upended."

▲▲

But the run-up to season two was also checked with disappointments. Two weeks before the premiere, *Twin Peaks* had been up for seven Emmy Awards, including Outstanding Drama. It won none. "We were in the lobby together, our little group—and then, huddled on the other side of the lobby, were all the people who go to the show every fucking year," said Harley Peyton. "They all knew each other, they all hung out with each other, they all loved to talk to each other. And I remember Mark and I looking at each other—probably with more pride than was necessary—and thinking, *We don't belong here*."

An additional complicating factor was ABC's decision to move *Twin Peaks* from Thursdays at nine PM, where it aired against NBC's ratings juggernaut *Cheers*, to Saturdays at ten PM. "ABC almost certainly has made a big mistake," wrote *Entertainment Weekly*'s Ken Tucker at the time. "Quite aside from the fact that a large portion of the show's audience probably will be out on Saturday nights, the move eliminates one of the prime pleasures of *Peaks*: the opportunity to discuss the latest episode's twists around the office water cooler the next day." (Writing this now, at a time when virtually all such discussions take place online, it's amusing to think that *Twin Peaks'* watercooler chatter suffered because its fans couldn't literally gather around a water cooler after it aired.) Bob Iger said *Twin Peaks* had been moved to Saturday, in part, to take pressure off its need to perform. But as far as both Lynch and Frost were concerned, it was a fatal mistake. "The people who like *Twin Peaks* are party people," said Lynch on an appearance on *Late Night with*

David Letterman. Even an ABC promo poked fun at the unconventional decision. "Diane, I've had a dream. In it are Laura and an ABC executive. They say they've hidden *Twin Peaks*, but what night? Finding the killer is child's play compared to the programming sleight of hand," narrates MacLachlan over clips of the show. "*Saturday!* Who'd think to look for it there?"

For at least some of the executives, Mark Frost suspects, literally making it harder to watch *Twin Peaks* was the plan all along. "What you have to get into when you talk about season two was the incredible antipathy to the show from the parent company of ABC, Capital Cities," says Frost. "They loved what they were getting from the ratings bonanza. That was like nothing that sorry-ass company had seen in many years. But this was a family-owned business. I remember meeting [Thomas Murphy], who was the chairman. And everything we did seemed to piss this guy off. I think it was an affront to his sense of what was good, and honest, and decent. And I'm sure that it was entirely his doing that we got moved to Saturday nights—which was basically a death sentence at that time. They felt they could just squeeze the last drops of blood out of us, and then just discard us to, you know, the elephant graveyard. And there was nothing straight about that. That was underhanded. That was something that contributed as much as anything to the momentum falling apart. There was just no way we were going to be able to sustain what we had started."

Iger, the show's original champion, found himself managing an increasingly tense situation between the executives who didn't believe in the show and the creators who felt they were being set up to fail. "Bob, to his credit, was always open and up-front with me," says Mark Frost. "I felt he never lied. Everything that he had to do to hurt the show, he did so reluctantly, and he basically told me that."

How best to reintroduce *Twin Peaks* to the world under these fraught conditions? To address ABC's concerns that viewers might have lost the show's thread in the intervening four months, the show's brain trust toyed with a number of ideas—including a special episode, set in-universe as a *Twin Peaks* public access bulletin, that would recap the events of the first season.

But there was another, splashier option that nearly came to pass: a season two premiere directed by Steven Spielberg. By the time the first season had concluded, Spielberg's admiration for *Twin Peaks* was no secret. In fact, Iger said, he fielded calls from both Spielberg and George Lucas, who expressed interest in the possibility of developing their own TV shows for ABC. "That notion, that directors of that caliber would be interested in making television shows, was unheard of until we started making *Twin Peaks*," he said.

But it was serendipity, says Harley Peyton, that almost led to Spielberg actually helming a *Twin Peaks* episode. Attending a get-together with his then girlfriend—a close friend of Kate Capshaw—Peyton says, "I was literally at Steven's house when he walked through the room and said, 'Okay, I've got to find out who these *Twin Peaks* writers are, because they're going to be the hottest writers in Hollywood.'"

In the conversations that followed, Spielberg's admiration for the show was clear, and he eventually met with Frost and Peyton about the possibility of directing the season premiere. "He said, 'Great. Just make it as weird as possible, and I'm all in,'" says Peyton.

It was at this moment—and *only* at this moment, says Peyton—that David Lynch became truly dedicated to *Twin Peaks*. During the show's first season, Lynch himself had downplayed his role, telling one reporter that—apart from the episodes he personally directed—he had little involvement with the day-to-day production of *Twin Peaks* and didn't intend to. "I think he just saw it as a TV thing he knocked off. He's a moviemaker, that's his passion, and that's what he does," says Peyton. "And then, I think, two things happened that changed it forever. One: He was on the cover of *Time Magazine*. And this was when being on the cover of *Time* meant a lot. And it's not for

The Elephant Man, or any of the amazing movies or art that he's made. It's because of *Twin Peaks*. And two: 'Oh, and by the way—*Steven Spielberg* is going to direct the first episode.'" We'll never know what Spielberg's *Twin Peaks* would have looked like; if Lynch wanted to direct an episode, everyone agreed, it was his to direct. "It was almost like David went, *Wait a minute. I cocreated this thing, and I need to focus on it now*. And on some level, because it's always like this with David, *I need to make it mine*."

Enter the Giant. By the beginning of season two, Mark Frost—who admitted to having some questions about the Man from Another Place—had learned to trust Lynch's flights of fancy. When Lynch called Frost and exclaimed that there was a giant in Cooper's hotel room, Frost simply replied, "I believe you."

Soon to be as iconic in *Twin Peaks*' supernatural pantheon as Michael J. Anderson's Man from Another Place or Frank Silva's BOB, the Giant was played by Carel Struycken, a seven-foot-tall Dutch actor. "I was already a hardcore *Twin Peaks* fan," says Struycken. "I remember being incredibly nervous about doing it, because I thought, *I can't screw this up*. And then when I came on the set, David Lynch got off his chair, shook my hand, and said, 'Everything is going to be peachy keen.'"

Struycken still had his doubts as he watched eighty-nine-year-old actor Hank Worden play out his scene as the elderly waiter delivering Cooper a glass of warm milk, apparently oblivious to the three gunshot holes. "Hank was kind of shuffling into the room, and everything was going extremely slow," says Struycken. "I remember being very worried. I thought, *Oh, people are going to switch to another channel if this takes too long*." After the take, Struycken recalls, Lynch had one note: Do it even slower.

In his first appearance, the Giant gives Cooper (and the audience) three more clues to chew on: "There's a man in a smiling bag," "The owls are not what they seem," and "Without chemicals, he points." The first pays off almost instantly, when Cooper notices Jacques Renault's corpse hanging limp in a sagging body bag. (This macabre image came directly from Lynch's fraught time as a young man in Philadelphia, when he became fascinated by the morgue across the street. "The bags had a big zipper, and they'd open the zipper and shoot water into the bags with big hoses. With the zipper open and the bags sagging on the pegs, it looked like these big smiles. I called them the smiling bags of death," he said.) But it's the second clue, "The owls are not what they seem," that captured the imaginations of *Twin Peaks* fans—even if the show's own writers weren't entirely sure what it meant. "There were things sometimes that were just like, *Oh, that's cool,*" says Peyton. "It wasn't like an owl figured deeply into the plot in some way. That was just adding, I think, to the general mystery."

Once Cooper has been rescued—you didn't really think *Twin Peaks* was going to kill off Dale Cooper, did you?—the episode gets back to the plot. There's a lot of it; when Lucy tells Cooper that Leo Johnson has been shot, Jacques Renault has been strangled, Josie Packard and Catherine Martell are missing, and the sawmill has burned down, he replies, with apparent sincerity, "How long have I been out?" But that's old business. In the episodes that follow, we spend time with Shelly and Bobby as they scheme, unsuccessfully, to cash in on Leo's vegetative state after the events of the season one finale; meet Jean Renault (Michael Parks), Jacques's sadistic elder brother, who seeks revenge on Cooper for Jacques's death while drugging Audrey and blackmailing Ben for her safe return; and try to suss out the identity of M. T. Wentz, a mysterious food critic rumored to be plotting a review of the Double R Diner. The latter subplot—a rare instance of Norma Jennings getting her own self-contained story—was "ridiculous stuff," allows Peyton. But it was also an opportunity to work with a Hollywood legend: Jane Greer, best remembered today for costarring with Robert Mitchum in the 1947 noir classic *Out of the Past*, was cast as Norma's semi-estranged mother, who turns out to be the mystery food critic who gives her own daughter's diner a withering pan. "Mark is a huge movie fan, and so any opportunity . . . I think a lot of it was just, like, 'Let's fucking work with Jane Greer, for God's sake,'" says Peyton.

To its ever-growing web of romantic entanglements, *Twin Peaks* added one more that would span the rest of the series: the question of whether the father of Lucy's unborn child was Deputy Andy or the slick, smarmy menswear salesman Dick Tremayne (Ian Buchanan). It wasn't exactly a fair fight: Andy, by then, was among the show's most beloved characters, while Dick spent a decent chunk of his early arc encouraging Lucy to get an abortion—no small thing on American television in 1990. "People were saying, 'It must be great to be off the soaps and be on this primetime show,'" says Buchanan. "And I said, 'Well, yeah, except that it's kind of like a soap. We're doing this love triangle, which is all you ever do on a soap." Tasked almost exclusively with serving as comic relief, Buchanan was completely unaware of the darker side of *Twin Peaks'* story. "I'd go into the makeup trailer skipping and whistling, and there would be buckets with fingernails and hair and blood and stuff," says Buchanan "I'd be like, oh my God, what's going on? I was as oblivious as Dick."

▲▲

Even in this generally strong run of episodes, you can feel *Twin Peaks* struggling, at times, to balance its always-idiosyncratic blend of plots, tones, and characters. "On most television shows—the ones that run for five, or six, or seven years—the writers get bored writing the same thing every week, and the actors get bored playing the same thing every week. You either try to make it fresh or you make the mistake of trying to change everything," says Harley Peyton. "And the funny thing about *Twin Peaks* is that it managed that seven-year arc in, like, eighteen months."

The result, at its best, was a kind of controlled insanity. In one memorable scene, Leland Palmer returns to the Great Northern, having decided he's ready to go back to work. His judgment is questionable; his hair has inexplicably turned white overnight, and he's spent the whole morning belting out the nonsense song "Mairzy Doats" on an enthusiastic but maddening loop. But when Leland barges into Ben Horne's office, Ben and Jerry don't roll their eyes and ask him what he's doing. They grin at each other and start dancing along to "Mairzy Doats," with Ben doing a tap dance on his own desk while Jerry does the worm on the carpet below. "We just joined in his madness," says David Patrick Kelly. "We said, 'Okay, we live here too.'"

Not every new idea was so potent. "You start seeing what people are really like with a second season. It was so popular that the next obvious thing for a lot of them is the movies. Getting out there and getting on with it," said Lynch. "When everyone came back for the second season, all of the young actors wanted to do different things," says Peyton. "Sherilyn Fenn did not want to be the fetishized bobby soxer anymore. In fact, she said, she wanted to be more like Katherine Hepburn. It was the same thing with Lara Flynn Boyle. She comes back, and she doesn't want to be the insanely sweet girl next door anymore. Suddenly, she wanted to smoke and wear sunglasses. They all came in with their own ideas. It certainly wasn't *our* idea."

One actor who was reluctant to voice his concerns about his character was James Marshall. "I was scared to say anything, because it was my first time, and all the other actors were like, 'Well, you just say something,'" says Marshall. "I felt like I kept playing the same scene over and over again, with either Donna or Maddy or a memory of Laura. It was always getting together, looking into each other's eyes, and then crying and kissing."

Marshall ended up at the center of one of season two's more infamous moments: the three-way performance of "Just You," an original song written by Angelo Badalamenti and performed, in character, by Marshall, Lara Flynn Boyle, and Sheryl Lee. By now, the love triangle between James, Donna, and Maddy Ferguson is threatening to boil over. When better for all three to cut a demo for a gooey, falsetto song about being in love forever? "Oh my gosh. I don't even like thinking back on that," said Lara Flynn Boyle. "I can't even listen to it," says James Marshall.

Making James Hurley into a secret doo-wop rock god was not Marshall's idea. "I used to go to the set with my guitar, and between takes, I'd just go back and quietly play the guitar during the day," says Marshall. "It got around that I play, and David said, at one point, 'Would you like to do something on the show?' But I was twenty-two years old, and when I got around David, I'd clam up because I got nervous. I didn't think it was my place to be saying anything. So I said, 'Why not?' I was picturing: James is plugging his guitar into the amp, and it's the end of the day. He starts playing a nice, slow lead, and the camera pulls back. Have the camera go out one of the windows, and then out of the house, then you just keep going. More of a montage, less showing off. But I didn't get the chance to finish my thought, because David said, 'What about a song?'

"And it just turned out awful. They put it in C, and I was having trouble with C. And when we did the actual singing, it was terrible. I mean, we had to take a few times to record it, because even David was going, 'James, I thought you could do that!' And I was like, 'Look, I thought I could too!' We did take after take, and it barely got better. But David loves it. He *listens* to it. I don't like it, but it's actually better for the show than if I had played well. It plays to the innocence of it. It's beyond cheesy. Beyond sweetness. It actually makes your teeth hurt."

Even this polarizing scene turns out to be integral to the show's larger tapestry. Immediately after the "Just You" recording—which ends with Donna catching Maddy making goo-goo eyes at James and storming off, with James trailing behind her—Lynch delivers what might be the single scariest moment in the entire series. As Maddy sits in the living room, she suddenly sees BOB stalk into the scene, walk directly into the center of the shot, and climb over the couch in front of her, staring directly into the camera until his face completely fills the frame. It's not just that BOB is menacing toward the screaming Maddy; it's that he's menacing toward *us*, the audience—almost openly taunting anyone who was naive enough to let the teen drama of "Just You" distract from the true dangers faced, every day, by a young woman like Maddy or Donna in *Twin Peaks*.

It's also a reminder that—whatever frustrations ABC and the audience had with the lack of resolution—"Who killed Laura Palmer?" remained, by far, the most potent plot device in the *Twin Peaks* toolbox. The best of the show's new arcs follows Donna as she takes over Laura's Meals on Wheels route—following, quite literally, in the footsteps of her friend, and getting

"Together, forever, in love."

a glimpse of a side of her life she kept entirely private by bonding, as Laura did, with the agoraphobic Harold Smith.

The Harold Smith drama is *Twin Peaks* at its best: Unexpected, suspenseful, and ultimately very sad. What it is *not*, to the frustration of some increasingly disgruntled viewers, was an answer to the question, "Who killed Laura Palmer?"

If this frustration was a problem baked into the show's very premise, it was one that had been supercharged by ABC's misleading marketing, which set false expectations over and over again. Bob Iger, remember, had vowed that viewers would "see the killer, and know it's the killer" all the way back in the season two premiere.

That was, to say the least, disingenuous. The answer the episode provided, while haunting, was hardly definitive. From the subjective perspective of Ronette Pulaski, *Twin Peaks* shows us for the first time—but not the last—what happened in the train car on the night Laura was murdered. As directed by Lynch, it's impressionistic and nightmarish: rapid cuts between Laura screaming in terror and BOB bellowing in what plays like a strange mix of ecstasy and agony, with his most animalistic howl coming only after Laura's screams finally fall silent.

Even as late as this episode, Frank Silva still believed that he was playing a real person, not a possessing spirit. "A lot of us didn't know who BOB really was. I don't think David did. I certainly, at first, thought he was real," said Silva in a 1993 interview with the magazine *Wrapped in Plastic*. "I just thought he was this really whacked-out crazy guy. An intense, crazy guy." At the time, he may even have been right. In that interview, Silva recalled feeling that his own tearful screams had a twinge of regret in them. "Maybe David clicked that together. Rather than BOB being just one person, maybe he was two, maybe he was three—or he was the entity that possessed people and there was this sense of remorse after it all happened. Because that's what I got from doing the scene."

Of course, BOB being the killer was too simple an answer for fans who had spent months swapping their own theories. "Everybody was saying, 'Is Frank really the killer? Is BOB really the killer?' Because why would David be so explicit as to show this scene with BOB as the killer?" said Silva. Indeed, speculation ran wild on alt.tv.twin-peaks. Maybe the choppy ambiguity of the train car flashback was a mask for what was *actually* happening: BOB, slamming his fists onto the dying Laura's chest in an attempt to revive her, then screaming in grief when she died despite his best efforts.

The answer, in short, wasn't good enough. *Twin Peaks* viewers may not have had enough context yet to understand precisely who BOB was, but they were right to distrust that the answer they'd been given was the whole story. TV audiences abhor a vacuum, and ABC's executives—even the ones who were bullish on *Twin Peaks*—were increasingly concerned that the show's steadfast refusal to provide a clear, definitive answer to its central mystery would alienate even its biggest fans. "The entire show hinged on the question of who killed Laura Palmer, and I felt David was losing sight of that, laying breadcrumbs in a way that felt random and unsatisfying," said Bob Iger. Once again, he pressured Lynch and Frost to reveal the killer earlier than they'd ever planned. This time, they relented. "Everybody wanted it revealed. There was so much pressure. People getting crazy to find out who did it," said Lynch. In the end, even the director who had sworn never to give up creative control again threw up his hands. "By the time Bob Iger came to us and said, 'You gotta solve this mystery,' I was sort of fed up anyway," he said. At long last—and for better or worse—audiences would find out who killed Laura Palmer.

BENJAMIN HORNE

"Sometimes the urge to do bad is nearly overpowering."

If you had let Richard Beymer choose, he wouldn't have played Ben Horne at all. After meeting David Lynch for the first time, Beymer recalled, "Johanna Ray called and said, 'He wants you to play a character called Dr. Jacoby,' then she called again and said, 'No, he wants you to play a businessman named Ben Horne.' I thought, *Shit, Jacoby sounded so much more fun*."

Beymer was wrong, though it's easy to see why he had his doubts. Ben seems, at first glance, like a generic villain straight out of the night-soap playbook. An insufferably self-satisfied businessman who fancies himself a community leader—but doesn't, you know, actually offer any leadership—Ben appears to be your textbook rich asshole, from the Gordon Gekko suits to the omnipresent cigar he's always puffing away on.

But Ben's public image as a "glad-handing dandy"—as Cooper pegs him in the show's pilot—isn't just a cover for the darker side of his accumulated business interests, or his own reflexive greed. It's also a smokescreen for the truth at the heart of his character: Ben Horne is a total freak, and the consequences of his power, and how he chooses to wield it, are very real. As one of Twin Peaks' nominal leaders, both his weirdness and his malice makes him a corrosive force for the entire community, spewing depravity from his lofty perch and letting it pour over the town like acid rain seeps into groundwater.

The first hint of Ben's true rapaciousness comes early. In "Episode 2," an awkward family dinner is interrupted by the arrival of Ben's brother Jerry, who has flown in from a trip to Paris with an armful of brie-and-butter sandwiches. At that point, "I still hadn't a real handle on the character yet," reflected Beymer. "He hadn't done enough." The script called for Ben to take a bite of the sandwich. "I think, *I'm supposed to be this wealthy guy, I've got my Armani suit on. I'm supposed to be dignified, right?"* said Beymer. But the small, polite bite Beymer took before continuing with his dialogue wasn't what Lynch had in mind. In the nine or ten takes that followed, Beymer kept dutifully taking bigger bites, only for Lynch to call cut and tell him he still needed to go even bigger. It was only when Beymer completely filled his mouth, after a bite so big that his subsequent dialogue could barely even be understood, that Lynch was satisfied.

It's a very funny scene. It's also Ben Horne in a nutshell: a man who wants nothing but the finest things in life, and in outsize, absurd proportions, as fast as he can possibly consume them. That's true in his baseline epicurean instincts—Ben seems to have much of Shakespeare's writing committed to memory, and according to his *Twin Peaks* trading card, the cigars he's always smoking are illegal Cubans—but also in his uglier business instincts. Not content with merely owning half of Twin Peaks, he masterminds the plot to burn down the Packard sawmill. And as the owner of One Eyed Jacks, he takes evident delight in being the first to have sex with every new girl brought into the brothel.

It's this latter sin that leads Ben to his most important role in the first half of *Twin Peaks*: presenting a red herring. Laura Palmer was employed at One Eyed Jacks before she died, and Ben later confesses—to his own daughter, who was the target of his unwitting lust during a different masked encounter—not just that he had sex with Laura, but that he loved her. The deeper you dig into this plot thread, the uglier it gets. Jennifer Lynch's novel *The Secret Diary of Laura Palmer* reveals that Ben Horne secretly purchased Laura a pony for her twelfth birthday, which means he started grooming her around the same time BOB started sexually abusing her. His obsession ran deep, and he seems to have felt remarkably little shame about it. Though their trysts were nominally secret, Ben, we learn, brazenly kept a picture of Laura on his desk, where anyone could see it—including Leland, who met with Ben regularly, or Audrey, who was comparatively ignored by her own father. Even Laura, from beyond the grave, seemed to be pointing the finger at Ben: "Someday, I'm gonna tell the world about Ben Horne," she wrote in her secret diary. We never actually see them interact; Beymer declined to return for the prequel movie *Twin Peaks: Fire Walk with Me* because he disliked the scene written for Ben, which would have seen him withholding cocaine from Laura until she gave him a kiss. But odious as that is, I've never fully understood his objection. That desperate behavior seems, to me, squarely in line with Ben's disturbing fixation on Laura.

Ben didn't kill Laura, of course. But the revelation of the actual killer presented *Twin Peaks* with an interesting challenge: If Ben Horne wasn't a red herring, what was he?

The answer, as anyone who has made it through the entirety of the series can attest, is some of the most fascinatingly off-kilter material in season two. "I have never seen a character change as much as my character through the course of a series," said Beymer. "Normally, when a character is established, the character usually stays that way." Exonerated for the murder, but floundering in business, Ben has a mental breakdown that leads him to believe he is actually Robert E. Lee at the Battle of Gettysburg. Dr. Jacoby, who never met a strange case he didn't enjoy, suggests letting the delusion play out, believing that Ben's sanity will be restored if he can come to terms with his own lost cause by reversing the outcome of the Civil War through the vast array of miniature models spread across his office. He only snaps back to normal after Jacoby, role-playing as Ulysses S. Grant, surrenders.

Twin Peaks never really reckons with the weirdness of making "What if the Confederacy won the Civil War?" into the catalyst for Ben's face turn, but it's worth sitting with this for a moment. Here is a rich, powerful white man turning the Lost Cause into his own personal odyssey—a pathetically ahistorical one in which it's hand-waved that Lee was fighting to preserve the enslavement of black Americans, and in which the real human cost of war is reimagined as literal toys for Ben to move around. It's so self-absorbed it would be comical—if it didn't feel like a barely exaggerated version of the Confederate whitewashing that still haunts the United States today.

Once he snaps out of his Robert E. Lee persona, the rest of the series finds Ben striving, vocally, to be a better man than the one we've known—albeit in the same fumbling, self-absorbed way he does everything else. He gives up his cigars for celery; spearheads a campaign to save the endangered pine weasel; and strives, with a surprising amount of success, to rebuild his badly damaged relationship with Audrey. Whether all this stems from an *actual* epiphany, or just his latest cynical business scheme, is one of season two's more intriguing open questions. It's impossible to ignore that Ben's sudden interest in protecting the pine weasel dovetails conveniently with his business incentives for preventing the Ghostwood development. Owing in large part to Beymer's committed performance, it's hard not to root for Ben to find his better angels—maybe pretending to be better can, over time, have the side effect of *making* a person better?

Like many of the characters in the season two finale, Ben's ultimate fate was left maddeningly unresolved. In one of the season's soapier subplots, Ben is revealed as Donna Hayward's true father. He tells her—in his typically myopic fashion—because he's newly committed to telling the truth but lunkheaded enough not to realize when the truth might cause more harm than good. Doc Hayward responds to this intrusion by punching Ben, which sends him careering into a fireplace and then to the ground, unconscious or worse. It was hard to believe *Twin Peaks* would ever have killed off Ben Horne—among other things, the town's doctor was literally right there—but his fate wasn't officially cleared up until Mark Frost's book

The Secret History of Twin Peaks, which reveals that Ben survived and sold off the Horne family's tract of the coveted Ghostwood land... to a private prison. One step forward, two steps back.

Twin Peaks: The Return brings Ben back into the story possessed by something unexpected: quiet, haunted regret. He's as verbose as ever. ("A prophet is without honor who eats his own profits," he lectures Jerry, who has stumbled into a fortune by being in the vanguard of Washington's legal weed push.) But he's also unmoored: acrimoniously divorced from his wife, Sylvia (Jan D'Arcy), disturbed by the abuses of his grandson Richard (Eamon Farren), and apparently disconnected entirely from his children. Johnny, his autistic older son, remains in Sylvia's care; neither Audrey, his apparent successor, nor Donna, the illegitimate daughter he longed to connect with, ever appears in a scene with Ben again. Instead, most of his scenes are with Beverly Paige (Ashley Judd), a married employee who he flirts with but ultimately declines to sleep with. Apart from Jerry, who pops in and out like a zany sitcom character, Ben seems to be totally alone.

How did his life go so wrong? There are moments, throughout *Twin Peaks*, when Ben seems self-aware enough to long for a younger, uncorrupted version of himself. After being arrested on suspicion of Laura's murder, he and Jerry share a childhood memory of sitting in their bunk bed, watching an older girl dance on a hook rug. When he fears losing everything, he pulls out an old home movie of his father breaking ground on the Great Northern. And in *Twin Peaks: The Return*, he waxes nostalgic about a green bicycle purchased for him by his father. "I loved that bike," he says with a smile. It's a pathetic, quixotic nostalgia that's painfully familiar in our modern cultural climate, which offers endless, desperate paeans to a bygone era that never actually existed. At least we were better *then*, this kind of thinking always seems to say—except we probably weren't.

Chapter 5

I PROMISE, I WILL KILL AGAIN

During the filming of the *Twin Peaks* pilot, Sheryl Lee gave Ray Wise a present: a photograph of her, taken when she was in the fourth grade. "She wanted me to have it," says Wise. "I put it in my wallet, and I carried that wallet with me throughout filming the rest of the episodes. Her picture, as a little girl, was always with me."

For Wise—who had his own two-year-old daughter at home—the role of a grieving father had always felt very personal, and he had invested much of himself to ensure that the magnitude of Leland Palmer's despair always felt real. For the scene in which Leland jumps onto the casket at Laura's funeral, he called upon his own memory of a grief-stricken family member pulling a body out of a casket. When Leland went to the morgue to identify Laura's body, Wise reflected on his own family, before every take, to conjure up the necessary emotion. "It was difficult," says Wise. "There were several pictures of me and David and Michael Ontkean taken at the time, and you could see my eyes were just constantly full of tears." During one take of a scene in which Sarah interrupts Leland as he dances with Laura's homecoming photo, the shattered glass cut Wise's hand open. The injury wasn't scripted, but he didn't break character. Instead, Wise began smearing his own blood across the photo, as helpless to undo the bloodshed as he was on the night Laura was killed.

After the broadcast of "Episode 14"—the one that reveals, at last, that Leland was Laura's rapist and murderer—fans scrutinized that scene, and others, for clues they might have missed that Leland was the killer all along. When Leland objects to Hawk taking Laura's diary, is he a grieving father trying to protect his daughter's privacy, or a cunning killer afraid of what it might reveal? When Sarah Palmer cries, "Don't ruin this too!" after Leland leaps onto Laura's casket at the funeral, what does she mean by *too*? What else has Leland ruined?

In the context of the killer reveal, those scenes have a richness and resonance that makes *Twin Peaks* rewarding to revisit. They were also, to borrow a term from David Lynch, happy accidents, because at the time they were filmed, none of the show's writers, directors, or actors had any idea that Leland was the killer. "Everyone always thought we knew, and we didn't," said Sheryl Lee. "We just really, really, really, really didn't know."

The exception—sort of—was David Lynch and Mark Frost. Though neither was interested in writing the mystery's solution in stone, they'd privately agreed early on that Leland was a strong contender. "We knew, but we didn't even hardly whisper it when we were working," said Lynch. "We were pretty sure it was him. Even before we started shooting season one," says Frost. "It was one of those moments—if you were writing it as a scene—you know: *They look at each other, their eyes meet. They both realize they've gotten the same idea at the same time.* And then we had to reckon with, *Well, Jesus, that's pretty heavy.* Because what you're writing is a tale of horrific and disastrous abuse, and that's taking us into a whole new area."

At the same time, Lynch and Frost didn't want to preclude the possibility of a better answer emerging as the story of *Twin Peaks* continued to develop. During the pilot, Duwayne Dunham recalls, Lynch invited everyone working on the show to write their best guess for the killer's identity and put it in a sealed envelope. As the show continued, a number of the actors passed the time by treating "Who killed Laura Palmer?" as a parlor game in which they happened to be major players. Everett McGill believed Big Ed was a plausible suspect. Often used as comic relief, David Patrick Kelly decided to play up Jerry's sadism in one scene—in which he taunts One Eyed Jacks Madam Blackie by withholding drugs—to plant the seed that Jerry Horne could be the killer. "I thought, for a while, that *I* was the one who killed Laura Palmer," says Russ Tamblyn. "I asked David [Lynch] one time. I said, 'So, Dr. Jacoby: Did he kill her? And he said, 'Well . . . I haven't decided yet.' He wanted me to just play it straight. To play it—if I *was* the killer—like I could be just a good liar."

Others concluded, reasonably, that there was no point in guessing at an answer that was probably still in flux. "Nobody knew," said Kyle MacLachlan. "I didn't really think about it, because I didn't think they knew. I thought they were trying to come up with it, so it was like, *I'm not going to guess at something* they're *guessing at*," says James Marshall. "I just wanted to make sure it wasn't me," says Sherilyn Fenn. "Knowing David, it could have been anybody. It could have been a tree," says Michael Horse.

As far as I can tell, none of the show's fans were galaxy-brained enough to guess a tree had killed Laura Palmer—but that's about the only possibility that *didn't* come up, at one point or another, in the months of feverish speculation over who killed Laura Palmer (or, in alt.tv.twin-peaks shorthand, WKLP). Just in the days leading up to the climactic episode airing, users exchanged lengthy, generally well-reasoned arguments for candidates as varied as Sheriff Truman, Deputy Andy, Doc Hayward, and Harold Smith. One widely circulated theory used Otto Preminger's 1944 noir *Laura* as a template to speculate that Laura Palmer wasn't dead at all—that the killer, whoever he or she was, had actually killed Maddy Ferguson, and that the real Laura was now wandering around *Twin Peaks* disguised as Maddy.

In a preview of what awaited future puzzle-box shows like ABC's *Lost*, HBO's *Westworld*, and Apple TV+'s *Severance*, these obsessively detailed theories were frequently juxtaposed with paranoia that the solution couldn't possibly live up to the extended buildup. "Am I the only one experiencing a crisis of faith?" wrote one alt.tv.twin-peaks poster. "I waken in the middle of the night in a cold sweat imagining a world in which no one knows who killed Laura Palmer. I imagine Lynch and Frost just making it up as they go along, snickering about attempts to identify the killer where none exists. I see them ultimately making an arbitrary choice of culprits, a totally unsatisfying conclusion to the mystery. Are we being treated to an excruciatingly slow fuck destined to end in a whimper of an orgasm?"

Despite all that hand-wringing, the answer, of course, wasn't entirely arbitrary. If it hadn't been written in ink—"the spotlight fell on different people at different times," Frost once allowed—it had certainly been written in pencil. "Nobody else really felt right," says Frost. "And in fact, anybody else, by the time we got there, would have felt like a cop-out."

Even as the late-breaking clues seemed to point to Leland—who struck some viewers as such an obvious suspect that they wrote him off as a red herring—Ray Wise invented his own theories that would let him off the hook. "I thought Ben Horne would be a good one, or his brother. Or even Sheriff Truman. I thought, *Wow, wouldn't that be a nice twist?*" says Wise. "I was just hoping it was anybody but me."

When it came time to formally break the news to Wise, the *Twin Peaks* brain trust threw an informal ceremony. "I came into this room in the studio. It was dark, and there was no furniture, except for a lava lamp in the corner," says Wise. "Mark Frost, David Lynch, Richard Beymer, and Sheryl Lee were sitting cross-legged on the floor. I went and sat down with them, and David leaned over and tapped me on the knee. And he said, 'Ray, it's you. It's always been you.' And I thought to myself, at that moment, *Oh, no, no, no, this can't be. This can't be. It wasn't always me. You just came up with that.*"

Wise's grief wasn't just the realization that the character he had so closely sympathized with was complicit in Laura's demise. He also guessed, correctly, that Leland's arc on *Twin Peaks* would be coming to an end. "I knew that *something* would have to happen to me—that I would be gone. I didn't want to leave town; I didn't want to go to jail; I didn't want to commit suicide," he says. And while Lynch confirmed that Wise would soon be written out of the series, he offered the consolation of a powerful climax to Leland's story. "David explained to me that it would be a beautiful ending," recalls Wise. "That I would die in the arms of Cooper and look down this tunnel. And at the end of that tunnel would be my daughter, Laura, holding her arms out to me and forgiving me. I could hardly complain about that."

For Leland to reach that final, cathartic vision of grace, *Twin Peaks* puts him, and the characters around him, through hell first. *Finally. Saturday, November 10th. Find out who killed Laura Palmer. Really.* That's the text of the advertisement ABC ran in the week leading up to the show's long-awaited reveal. If it has a whiff of desperation to it, it was also a self-inflicted wound. Why, someone might reasonably ask, did the network need to convince viewers that Laura's murderer would actually be revealed this time? Maybe misleading the audience a few times before that wasn't a great long-term strategy.

But any sense of relief at the mystery's resolution was doomed to be short-lived. It's as if Lynch and Frost—unhappy at having been strong-armed into revealing the murderer—deliberately crafted an episode so punishing that both the network and the show's fans would regret pressuring them into an answer. The *Twin Peaks* pilot had spared audiences the brutality of actually witnessing Laura's murder because the script kicked off hours after she had been killed. "Episode 14," by contrast, would give audiences every second of Maddy Ferguson's shock and terror as she realizes she's going to die at the hands of Laura's killer—the uncle who she came to Twin Peaks to support in the first place.

In an echo of the way "Just You" lowered the audience's defenses for BOB's sudden appearance earlier that season, "Episode 14" falsely sets up a much gentler way for Maddy Ferguson to leave Twin Peaks. As Louis Armstrong's "What a Wonderful World" spins on the record player, Maddy sits between her aunt and uncle. When she nervously confesses that she's decided to return home to Missoula, Leland tells her he understands completely, says he loves her, and kisses her hand. It's not hard to imagine what a more conventional TV show might do with this character—send her wistfully out of town, perhaps, to return late in the season as a wild card whenever James and Donna's relationship is getting a little stale.

That's not, of course, what happens. But the secrecy of that decision remained paramount to the few who knew, and they had reasons to be wary: According to Robert Engels, it was eventually discovered that someone in the costume department had been leaking scripts to the *National Enquirer.* Before "Episode 14" was filmed, the production sent a memo to the cast and crew insisting that all discarded script pages be shredded, fearing that *Twin Peaks* diehards would dig through the garbage for clues. "They didn't want the crew, or anyone else in the studio, to know," says Wise. And to ensure that absolute secrecy would be maintained, the few who *did* know agreed on what was then an almost unheard-of precaution at the time: filming the same scene, with multiple actors playing the murderer, to obscure which solution would actually air. Ray Wise, Richard Beymer, and Frank Silva were each tasked with stepping into the role of the killer—which meant, in practice, that Sheryl Lee needed to act out Maddy's murder, in full, three times.

Footage from two of those murders would make it to air. (The scene of Ben Horne murdering Maddy has never been released in any form.) BOB, this episode formally confirms, is an occupying spirit who has possessed Leland. Sarah Palmer has been drugged, having a brief vision of a pale horse before passing out in the living room. Just above her—in one of the recurring mirror images that defines *Twin Peaks*—we learn Leland and BOB are one and the same when Leland grins at his reflection in the mirror and sees BOB grinning back.

BOB is clearly responsible for the murder, but exactly when and how frequently BOB takes control of Leland—or whether Maddy ever sees BOB as a distinct physical presence, as we do—is an open question. Lynch freely cuts between Wise and Silva during the murder. BOB/Leland repeatedly punches her in the face, then caresses her. He kisses her and calls her Laura as she chokes on sobs while bleeding from her eyes, nose, and mouth. He slams her into a picture frame while gleefully taunting her about her plan to return home. It's obvious by then that she can't possibly escape, let alone survive—but her eyelids are still twitching when he uses a penknife to insert a small letter *o* under her fingernail. We don't actually witness the moment of Maddy's death, and it's unclear how much longer she holds on, or what he does to her in the meantime.

How is possible that this nightmarish sequence aired on ABC in 1990? Even the people who made it aren't sure. "I didn't know how shocking it would be for TV. I knew how shocking it was for me to do. I don't think *ABC* can believe ABC showed that," said Sheryl Lee. "Violence will get through nine out of ten times," said Lynch. "There were some pretty strange and violent things in *Twin Peaks*, and they got by. If it's not quite standard it sneaks through, but it could be that the 'not quite standard' things make it even more terrifying and disturbing: the kind of thing they don't have names for. They're not in the book so they go right through."

What *is* clear is the effect it had on the actors who filmed it. "That day was the hardest. Absolutely," says Wise. "It was a twelve- or fourteen-hour day, as I recall. It had to be very well-timed, and done just right, to smash Maddy's face into that picture on the wall, and then to throw her onto the couch. It was extremely physical, and the adrenaline was really pumping all day. We were all exhausted at the end of it, and certainly no one more than Sheryl."

"It was a brutal day," recalled Sheryl Lee. "I had a brilliant doctor tell me that the only part of an actor that knows that they're acting is their mind. So, if you're crying real tears, your body still goes through the chemical response of real tears. If you're acting afraid, if you're feeling fear—which most actors are in that moment—then whatever chemicals are released when your body is afraid, the adrenaline, all that stuff that goes on, it really does take a toll on your system."

The tragedy of Maddy's murder is compounded by the dramatic irony that Cooper, for all his preternatural investigative talent, has missed that the killer has been right in front of him all along. "It is happening again," warns the Giant in a brief vision—a rare moment of desperate clarity from a supernatural being who normally speaks in riddles. But it's too late; Cooper's deductive powers have already failed. He has already arrested Ben Horne on suspicion of Laura's murder, and even as the killer claims another victim, Cooper is sitting in the Roadhouse having a beer with Sheriff Truman and the Log Lady.

Just as it was in the pilot—when everyone seemed to understand, without even being told, that Laura had been murdered—the characters in the Roadhouse suddenly grasp, on an intuitive level, that something awful has happened. Donna begins sobbing hysterically. Bobby, smoking at the bar, suddenly looks almost painfully childlike, lost and forlorn. Even Cooper, normally so unflappable, gets a little glassy-eyed.

Behind the scenes at the Roadhouse

In one of his interviews with François Truffaut, Alfred Hitchcock laid out a scenario that remains an unmatched practical definition for the importance of suspense. If a bomb suddenly goes off in the middle of a scene, he says, the audience is merely surprised. But if the director *cuts* to the as-yet-unexploded bomb under the table—and then back to the characters, sitting and chatting, totally unaware that their lives are in mortal danger—the scene suddenly becomes a nailbiter that a director can milk for minutes of screen time.

As "Episode 14" ends, *Twin Peaks* is at a fascinating crossroads. *We* know Leland is the killer, but none of the characters do. There are unexploded bombs for the plot to deal with—at some point, Maddy's parents are going to start wondering why she hasn't returned to Missoula yet—but in narrative time, only two weeks have passed since the morning Laura's body was found. One can imagine a version of the second season that spends the rest of its run following BOB as he takes Leland on a secret serial-killing spree while Cooper tries, with mounting horror, to solve a new rash of murders.

Instead, the show lets the audience simmer in suspense for a single, tense episode before BOB-as-Leland's crimes are revealed. Having apparently gotten away with murder once again, he's positively giddy—almost recklessly so—as he drives around town with Maddy's corpse stuffed into a golf bag. It's fascinating to watch Wise play BOB pretending to be Leland; when Cooper and Truman tell him they suspect Ben Horne murdered Laura, he excuses himself to cry, then bursts into barely stifled giggles when he's alone. Later, he seems to be on the verge of beating Cooper to death with a golf club just for the fun of it. Most alarmingly, he awkwardly goads Donna into dancing with him—drawing, cruelly, on the paternal relationship Leland has forged with her since childhood—and seems prepared to murder her when Sheriff Truman interrupts. The mask is obviously slipping, but BOB, in his triumph, just isn't that worried about covering his tracks anymore; he can, after all, abandon Leland and find another vessel.

That's exactly what happens in the subsequent episode, which returns to the Roadhouse with a grab bag of characters—Cooper, Truman, Leland, Ben Horne, Albert Rosenfield, Ed Hurley, Major Briggs (Don S. Davis), and the elderly room service waiter—for an Hercule Poirot–style deduction scene in which writers Mark Frost, Harley Peyton, and Robert Engels labor, heroically, to make coherent sense out of the oddball dreamworld clues that have led to this point. The Man from Another Place danced, like Leland dances; the "gum that's going to come back in style," Leland happily exclaims, is the same kind of gum he enjoyed as a child. (If this sounds, to you, like the product of hasty reverse engineering, you're right: "That was just kind of, you know, cleverly looking back and making it all work," says Engels.)

In the Red Room

But the result is Cooper remembering the key detail that eluded him all the way back in the show's second episode: "My father killed me," whispered Laura in the Red Room dream just before she kissed him. Back at the sheriff's station, they make BOB sit down for an interrogation, in which he happily confesses to Laura's murder. It's a dead end for Leland, but what does he need Leland for, anyway?

Given that he had no idea he'd be asked to play a killer, Wise is shockingly credible as BOB—but it's when BOB departs Leland that Wise, as promised, gets to do his best work, as Leland is flooded with the shock and grief of what was done to his own daughter, with his body and in his name. Cooper's natural sympathy to the esoteric makes him an ideal guide for Leland's final moments, which are sublime. As Cooper recites from *The Tibetan Book of the Dead*, Leland cries out: "I see here. She's there. She's beautiful. Laura." And then he dies.

More complicated is what Leland leaves behind. Is Leland responsible for these crimes? If he is, *how* responsible is he? It's a question *Twin Peaks* would go on to revisit in ways that do more to muddle than clarify it.

Lynch, when asked, was blunt: "He's a victim." But asked decades after the episode aired, the writers don't even agree. "I'd say Leland *sort of* knew," says Engels. "I don't think Leland had any idea," says Peyton. "I always thought that the more helpless nature of the people who were possessed by him made more sense than Leland being conscious of the evil he was perpetrating on others." For Mark Frost, the truth was somewhere in the middle: "We thought, 'How can you reckon or deal with or depict something this evil unless, you know, the man is clearly either mentally ill or possessed?'" he says. In 1990, he called BOB "a creature from somewhere else, and maybe he's only from within Leland. We don't exactly say where he's belched up from. He is somebody who kind of went along for the ride."

Ray Wise, for his part, believes Leland knew all along. "I don't know if what I have to say about it explains it fully, but I was always Leland, even when I was BOB," says Wise. "BOB was more like a character that Leland was playing. He wasn't any kind of an evil entity taking over my body and mind. He was, for want of a better word, another personality that took over at times. But in my mind, I was always Leland."

This debate plays out, fascinatingly, among the show's major characters, who can't even agree on what literally just happened in front of them. When Truman says Leland was crazy, Albert counters that other witnesses have, independently, reported seeing a man who looks exactly like BOB. "This is *way* off the map. I'm having a hard time believing," confesses Truman. "Harry, is it easier to believe a man would rape and murder his own daughter? Any more comforting?" replies Cooper.

It's here, I believe, that any thinking viewer must depart from Cooper. It may be less comforting, but it is, unfortunately, easier to believe. "The devil made me do it" is a fiction spun by those who refuse to take responsibility for their actions. A recent study says that 20 percent of women self-report an incident of childhood sexual assault. *Twin Peaks*, to its credit, allows for both: Ben Horne may not have murdered Laura Palmer, but that doesn't make his relationship with her any more defensible. You could say the same thing about Leo Johnson, Jacques Renault, Dr. Jacoby, or any of the other men innocent of Laura's actual murder, but unquestionably guilty of harming her.

Maybe that's why, in the end, it feels like Albert delivers the most clarifying answer about what happened to Laura. "Maybe that's all BOB is: the evil that men do. Maybe it doesn't matter what we call it."

DENISE BRYSON

"My recent experiences taught me never to judge too quickly."

Denise Bryson's reputation precedes her. When Cooper learns that Bryson, his former partner in an Oakland drug bust, has been brought in as the DEA's point person on the missing cocaine he's accused of stealing, he's delighted. Denise is "one of the finest minds in the DEA," says Cooper. "Harry, we're in very good hands."

But when Denise walks into the room, Cooper hardly recognizes her. When they'd worked together in Oakland, Denise—a trans woman—had not yet transitioned. Cooper, caught off-guard, calls her by her deadname. "It's a long story, but actually, I prefer Denise, if you don't mind," says Denise, smiling. And to *Twin Peaks*' eternal credit, Cooper's response is, "Okay."

It would be inaccurate to say that *Twin Peaks* nailed trans representation when Denise was introduced in 1990, though its small-town characters are believably awkward in what you must assume is their first encounter with a trans person. In the scene that follows, Hawk declines to shake Denise's outstretched hand, and Truman makes a crack under his breath about how the Great Northern, where Denise is staying, is in for a real surprise. But Cooper—recognized by then, by the audience, as the show's paragon of moral rightness—is unquestioningly accepting of Denise's identity. She hasn't been in the room for thirty seconds before they've moved on to more important business: the particulars of Cooper's drug case and the high quality of breakfast at the Great Northern.

Though she appears in just three episodes of the original series, Denise Bryson stands out as one of the most memorable guest characters in *Twin Peaks*' second season. Some of that, admittedly, is due to the actor who plays her: David Duchovny. Though Duchovny had barely acted when he was cast in *Twin Peaks*, it was just a few years later that he landed a lead role in Fox's

The X-Files—a show that, at the height of its popularity, probably made him more famous than anyone else in the *Twin Peaks* cast.

To hear Duchovny tell it, he only landed the role because another, more famous actor turned it down. "I believe that my part was inspired by James Spader and written for him," said Duchovny. "He wasn't able to do it, and I was looking for any job I could get. It wasn't like, 'Gee, I'm a fan of *Twin Peaks*.'"

Casting director Johanna Ray recalls multiple men arriving in drag for their audition to play Denise. Duchovny didn't go that far, but he acknowledges his first attempt to play Denise was more over-the-top. "I must have auditioned much more stereotypically effeminate, and then when I put on the makeup and everything, it became clear to me that less was more," he said.

After that initial introduction at the Sheriff's Department, *Twin Peaks* largely does right by Denise. She explains that she realized she was a woman during an undercover investigation, when she discovered she felt more at home in women's clothing. There's a quick, heartfelt moment when Cooper—in the midst of a heated conversation about the investigation—accidentally deadnames her. Denise quickly corrects him; he apologizes, she says it's okay, and they both move on. But even as the show acknowledges her transness, Denise is equally defined, as Cooper told Harry and Hawk, by her intelligence as a law enforcement agent. She sees through the unconvincing attempt to frame Cooper immediately, and masterminds the sting that leads to the downfall of Jean Renault.

This leads to a sequence in which Denise appears in drag as a man. "You can call me Dennis," she says, walking into the room dressed as a stereotypical businessman—not because of any social pressure, but because it's a role she thinks might be useful in infiltrating Renault's camp. Still, it's Denise being a woman that saves the day; wearing the uniform of a Double R Diner waitress, Denise holds Renault's attention just long enough to pass a gun to Cooper.

Denise appears for just one scene in *Twin Peaks: The Return*, but it's one of the show's most memorable—so much so that it's routinely quoted by people who haven't seen a frame of *Twin Peaks*. When Gordon Cole announces his intention to launch an investigation in Buckhorn, South Dakota, he needs to clear it with his superior officer: Denise Bryson, who has climbed the ladder to become the FBI's chief of staff. It's in this scene that Gordon Cole, played by Lynch himself, gets the last word on Denise—one that was almost instantly adopted as a rallying cry by the LGBTQ+ community and its supporters. "When you became Denise, I told all your colleagues, those clown comics, to fix their hearts or die," says Gordon.

"I said, 'We've got to bring [Denise] back. And I think she's the head of the FBI,'" says Mark Frost. "But I'll give David the credit. He came up with 'Fix your hearts or die.' I've seen people carrying that poster at protests over the last few months. There are probably hundreds of tattoos."

Fix your hearts or die. If that sentiment, in the end, turns out to be *Twin Peaks*' greatest legacy, it's a worthy one.

Chapter 6

WHEN YOU SEE ME AGAIN, IT WON'T BE ME

From the day it premiered, *Twin Peaks* had a problem. Audiences wanted to know who killed Laura Palmer; David Lynch and Mark Frost weren't interested in telling them who killed Laura Palmer. When they agreed to reveal the killer, the network was apparently vindicated. Some seventeen million viewers tuned in—the highest ratings the show had achieved since the season two premiere.

But now that the murder mystery had been resolved, the show had a new, even more vexing problem: If it wasn't about solving the murder of Laura Palmer, what *was Twin Peaks* about? Even Bob Iger concedes he may have been too hasty. "Looking back on it now, I'm not convinced I was right," he said. "Deep down, I felt David was frustrating the audience, but it may well be that my demands for an answer to the question of who killed Laura Palmer threw the show into another kind of narrative disarray." Mark Frost agrees. "We paid a big price for it. You know, that was something that contributed as much as anything to the momentum falling apart." David Lynch was even blunter. "That killed *Twin Peaks*," he said. "Totally dead. Over. Finished."

The problem, of course, was that *Twin Peaks wasn't* finished. It was in the middle of its second season, and the story would continue, one way or another, for at least thirteen more episodes. "Especially network television—when you're dealing with twenty-two episodes, and the production monster's chasing you, you don't really have any other choice," says Mark Frost. "I don't think it had been fully figured out," says Scott Frost. "Production is like jumping out of a plane. And you *have* a parachute, but it's actually not attached to you yet."

The resolution of Laura Palmer's murder isn't so much a period at the end of a sentence as it is an ellipsis: Leland may be dead, but BOB is still out there, hunting for another host.

Or, to put it another way: With the central mystery resolved, the show's writers had unprecedented freedom to redefine what *Twin Peaks* could be. "I don't know if there was a master plan there at all. We got so good at resolving things we thought up that we were kind of fearless about what we put in," says Robert Engels. "That was one of the things that was fun about the show—that we had the sense that we could pretty much do or try anything," says Harley Peyton. "There were times when that took us down weird avenues, but there were times when it took us in absolutely the right direction. I think we took some wrong turns along the way, but that, to me, is part of the process, and part of making something under sort of insane circumstances."

There's a palpable sense of desperation as *Twin Peaks*—just one episode removed from Leland's death—manufactures another, flimsier reason for Cooper to stick around town. Targeted (correctly) by the FBI's internal affairs division for his extralegal undercover mission at One Eyed Jack's and (incorrectly) for stealing a large amount of cocaine, Cooper is suspended from the FBI and forced to hand over his badge and gun. *Twin Peaks* had already flirted with turning Cooper, a consummate outsider, into a Twin Peaks insider. (At the very least, it was hard to imagine him saying goodbye, forever, to the Double R's coffee and cherry pie.) But Cooper's dismissal from the FBI, even temporarily, altered the show's fundamental building blocks in a way that proved challenging to reverse. So much care had been put into crafting the show's look and feel: What happened when you upended it? "We were doomed the day that Agent Cooper turned in his black suit for lumberjack flannel," says Duwayne Dunham.

Perhaps the most charitable reading is that *Twin Peaks*—having faced such a seismic rupture when Laura's grieving father was revealed as her rapist and killer—had no choice but to reconstitute itself. Emerging from a coma, Nadine Hurley was reinvented as a teenager; facing public shame and financial ruin, Ben Horne simply lost his mind.

But no character faced a more radical reinvention than Catherine Martell. You can see the seeds of where *Twin Peaks*' second season was going in a plotline that unfolds alongside the revelation of Laura's murderer: The sudden arrival of a Japanese businessman known only as Mr. Tojamura, who Ben Horne courts as a major investor in the Ghostwood Estates project. But "Mr. Tojamura" isn't a Japanese businessman at all; it's Catherine, wearing yellowface as part of her long con to manipulate Ben into giving up the Ghostwood land.

Where does an idea like this come from? In her 2011 autobiography, Piper Laurie revealed that after Catherine disappeared in the sawmill fire, David Lynch reassured her she would eventually return, in disguise, as some kind of businessman. He left the businessman's ethnicity up to her; after reflection, Laurie decided Catherine would pretend to be Japanese. "David wished me to keep it a secret from the entire cast and crew. Not even my agent or my family was to know. That was important to him. I wasn't to tell a soul," she said. A press release was dutifully issued revealing that "Fumio Yamaguchi," a Japanese actor who was said to have trained under Akira Kurosawa, had flown over from Japan specifically to work with David Lynch despite speaking no English whatsoever. His lines, the network claimed, would all be learned phonetically. "Piper loved it," says Peyton. "That was the whole idea: That she just showed up in costume one day and we would see how long it took for people to go, *Wait a minute . . .*"

It probably goes without saying that this subplot has not aged especially well. It's not just that Laurie's performance in these episodes falls under the long, lamentable tradition of white actors attempting to pass themselves off as Asian through stereotypical accents and cakey makeup. It's that—especially in the era of high-definition remasters—Catherine's disguise is laughably unconvincing in execution.

And yet: Those who were on set with Laurie insist that the gambit actually worked. Her commitment to the bit included picking small fights with the directors through her "interpreter," and those who shared scenes with "Yamaguchi"—including Laurie's most frequent scene partner, Jack Nance—failed to recognize her under the wig and makeup. "I did not know. Really, I didn't," says Michael Horse. "And I was standing right next to 'him.'" Even the few who suspected something was off about "Fumio Yamaguchi" didn't recognize their costar; skeptical about the sudden arrival of this previously unknown Japanese screen legend, Peggy Lipton guessed the actor was Isabella Rossellini in disguise.

Twin Peaks had always managed to juggle its darkest moments with its silliest. (Most people remember the sprinklers going off right before Leland died, but how many remember foppish Dick Tremayne is the one who set them off when he lit a cigarette in the Sheriff's Department?) But the show's unique tone was becoming harder and harder to balance. "If we made mistakes along the way, one of them was maybe falling in love with comedy a little too much," says Peyton. "This is the thing you always have to be careful of as a writer: Are you entertaining yourself, or are you entertaining the audience? We were certainly entertaining ourselves, and the hope was that we would entertain the audience as well." After Leland died, "I don't think [*Twin Peaks*] ever fully got back to quite that sense of darkness that existed at times, and that mystery," says Scott Frost. "But that's a hard thing to sustain. I have no answers as to how one would have done that."

No sustained analysis of season two would be complete without a brief survey of some of the show's wackier storylines. Nadine Hurley waking from a coma with the strength of a superhero and the mind of a teenager? "I was a big comic book fan, so I brought in Nadine's superpowers, which I thought was hilarious. That's on me," says Harley Peyton. The emergence of Lana Milford (Robyn Lively), a black widow who seduces both of the elderly Milford brothers while turning every other man in Twin Peaks—even, uncharacteristically, Cooper—into a drooling idiot? "That was meant to have a supernatural aspect, but that supernatural aspect never actually comes in, so it's just unresolved," says Peyton. Ben Horne, trying to reverse the Civil War while delusionally believing himself to be Robert E. Lee? "That idea came about at the same time Ken Burns' [*The*] *Civil War* miniseries happened. Had that miniseries not come out, I doubt that story ever would have gone into the series," says Scott Frost. That one, at least, came with a bonus: "I remember getting called down to the set when Richard Beymer and Russ Tamblyn were singing together because they were laughing so hard. The first time they sang together since *West Side Story*," says Robert Engels.

And then, of course, there's what Harley Peyton acknowledges as "the most grievous thing I ever did in the *Twin Peaks* universe": James Hurley's brief, stand-alone detour into a film noir after he crosses paths with a femme fatale named Evelyn Marsh (Annette McCarthy). "James is just such a wonderful actor, and he had this wonderful vibe that sort of made him a perfect fit for that kind of story, which is why we wanted to do it in the first place," says Peyton.

At this point in the story, James's love life has gone full *Peyton Place*. "The only thing I really, really wish they would have done is kept James with Donna," says Marshall. "I thought those two represented the audience, a little bit. Like they were the innocent ones amongst this craziness. With Laura, he was repeating his abuse cycle, if you want to break it all down. Her dysfunction matched what he was comfortable with. But he was kind of falling in love with Donna without knowing it. When Laura died, the reality of their attraction came around. And when they got together, they should've stayed together. They could help each other through their grief, and you actually see two people heal while everything else is going crazy. Instead: Evelyn Marsh."

In a rare subplot that takes place entirely outside Twin Peaks, James—on a sullen solo motorcycle trip after Maddy is murdered—suddenly wanders into a James M. Cain novel. *Twin Peaks* had nodded at classic noir tropes before; Neff (Mark Lowenthal), the insurance agent who alerted Catherine Martell to a shady policy in the show's first season, was named in tribute to the protagonist of Cain's 1943 crime classic *Double Indemnity*. This particular subplot owes Cain an obvious debt and stretches across five episodes, as the married Marsh picks up James at a bar, hires him as a mechanic, sleeps with him, and frames him for killing her husband before having a change of heart and letting him go.

It is as paint-by-numbers as a noir story can get, and those responsible for translating it to the small screen were just as dubious of the storyline as the audience. "You hadn't seen a character like Evelyn in *Twin Peaks*. She felt like she came from, I don't know, *Dynasty* or something," says Duwayne Dunham, who directed one of the episodes in which the Evelyn Marsh subplot unfolds. "I regret that I didn't do a better job with it. But it just didn't fit. It was completely wrong, and it was wrong for James. James—that character—would not be attracted to that. James was one of the Bookhouse Boys." Marshall agrees. "I think there were a lot of actors on the show who were reputable, seasoned actors—who've been around a long time—doing exactly what I was scared to do: going to production and fighting for their parts," he says. "It was a learning experience. I *could* have done that. Maybe it would have changed something."

It didn't help that, in the scramble to complete the season, the production had brought some unexpectedly ill-equipped people into the *Twin Peaks* fold. With a résumé that included scripts for *Moonlighting* and *thirtysomething*, Jerry Stahl looked, on paper, like the kind of forward-thinking writer who might slot neatly into the show's inner circle. But Stahl was also, he later revealed, a habitual cocaine and heroin user who was so deep in the throes of addiction that he shot up twice on his way to meet with Frost for the first time. The meeting went poorly, and Stahl promptly went on a bender so wild that he completely lost track of his deadline. "So enfeebled were my perceptions, I thought that only a day or two had passed when the *Twin Peaks* messenger showed up at my Lookout Mountain hideaway and asked for the draft. To say I was unprepared is like saying the A-bomb broke a lot of windows," Stahl wrote in his 1995 memoir *Permanent Midnight*. "How to explain that I'd mistaken seven days for one and a half?" The script he turned in—half-baked and streaked with his own blood—ultimately resulted in an episode credited to Stahl, Frost, Harley Peyton, and Robert Engels, after the latter three writers pitched in to fix it.

A similarly expanded pool of directors brought similar problems. As Diane Keaton—yes, *that* Diane Keaton—recalled, the one episode she directed came with a single, simple instruction from David Lynch: "Do whatever you want." But the problem, more often than not, wasn't when a director brought their own ideas to the table; it was when they tried, and failed, to do a cover band version of David Lynch. "So much happened on the show where I didn't know if my character was coming or going," said Lara Flynn Boyle. "I called [David Lynch] every day, like, 'Oh my God, they're ruining the show.' He got sick of hearing from me," says Sherilyn Fenn. "This costumer, in the second season, said, 'Oh, I've got 20 hula skirts.' And I was like... 'Do you think *Twin Peaks* is just this random, let's-be-weird-to-be-weird? Because it isn't. It never was.'" "It just was getting weird for weird's sake," agrees Duwayne Dunham. "My thing is: That's not an accurate understanding of David's work. It's *not* just weird for weird sake. There's a purpose and a reason. That's why, in David's hands, he can make that stuff work."

The problem reached its nadir in "Episode 21," the first (and only) episode directed by Uli Edel. As the director of the acclaimed, noir-ish drama *Last Exit to Brooklyn,* Edel had earned a reputation as a talent to watch. But his abrasive style clashed with the cast of *Twin Peaks,* who were justifiably confident, by then, that they knew what they were doing. During the filming of one scene, "Uli said, 'You're just furniture to me, man. Just go where I tell you,'" says Michael Horse. "So I go to the crew and said, 'This guy, Uli, is he good?' And they said, 'Yeah, he's really good.' And I went to Uli and said, 'Hey, man, you can say that to me. But if this isn't Emmy-quality shit, I'll come to your house and kick your ass.'"

Horse's conflict with Edel was a representative example of the cast's larger sense that *Twin Peaks* had been handed to some unfit caretakers while Frost and Lynch were busy elsewhere. "I hope I'm not making anybody mad, but they claimed David and Mark were totally on top of the *Twin Peaks* stuff—that they were giving yeses and noes and overseeing everything in every detail. But I know that, working with David, it was a way different show. So I just don't believe that," says James Marshall. "I *do* think that it had an effect on the show. How could it not? You could be the most talented person on earth. You're not going to be able to imitate David Lynch."

It's true that the Leland reveal in "Episode 14" was Lynch's last writing credit, and that he didn't direct another *Twin Peaks* episode until the season two finale. But while there are *Twin Peaks* fans who believe season two's missteps were due to Lynch's absence, it was Mark Frost who spent some time away from the show during its perceived dip in quality. Just as Lynch spent a chunk of *Twin Peaks*' first season directing *Wild at Heart*, Frost took a leave of absence from season two to direct *Storyville*, a moody, James Spader–starring political thriller. "His absence made things complicated. Certainly for my relationship with David," says Peyton.

By this point, Harley Peyton and Robert Engels—long established as two of *Twin Peaks*' most reliable writers—had been given producer credits and taken on some duties that, today, would fall under the umbrella of "showrunning." When Frost went to New Orleans to shoot *Storyville*, he left Peyton in charge. "It's not like I had to somehow convene a writer's room and figure out what we're going to do next. We *know* what every episode is going to be, and Mark was talking to me every day," says Peyton. "But one night—at, like, almost midnight—my phone rings, and it's Todd Holland. And Todd is freaking out because he just got off the phone with David Lynch, who gave him a raft of script notes that were going to impact his shooting the following morning. Now, I'm already a little irritated, so I say, 'Look. Ignore David's notes. He has no business calling you up at eleven o'clock at night with script notes. Just shoot your day and let it be.' He's very thankful, and I feel I've done my job.

"My phone rings the next day. And David yelled at me for ten minutes. And I'm telling you: Ten minutes is a long time to have someone yell at you. His temper . . . you didn't see it very often, but I saw it, and he was fucking furious, yelling at the top of his lungs: *How dare I? What the fuck am I doing? Who the fuck do I think I am?* The phone call, obviously, did not end well. And my relationship with David—whatever relationship I had—that was the end of our relationship."

The disagreements among creatives at the top of the show were further complicated by the actors, who continued to use their own power to try to shape the stories written for their characters. "There were some political things that were starting to happen, and I just got out of the way for the whole thing," says James Marshall. "There were several other actors on the show who were vying for different things, and it was like . . . I didn't want to be involved in that."

Most significant was the scrapping of a plotline that had been simmering since the beginning of season one: The flirtation between Cooper and Audrey Horne. "As far as I remember, we all believed that they were a couple or going to be a couple," said Tina Rathborne, who directed one of season one's many sexually charged scenes between Audrey and Cooper. "Audrey's seduction of Coop seems part of the dual lesson that Coop is learning. He's learning about his more innocent side, and he's learning about his darker side, that he's willing to be seduced by this young girl. This young, somewhat raunchy girl. But he's also willing to defend his higher side."

In season one, Cooper's so-called "higher side" seemed to win out. When he found Audrey waiting for him, naked, in his bed at the Great Northern, he let her down by gently explaining that what she really needed was a friend. But owing to MacLachlan and Fenn's undeniable on-screen chemistry, the writers kept looping Cooper and Audrey back together. Audrey goes undercover at One Eyed Jack's to help the man she calls "my special agent"; Cooper risks his career to rescue her. When Audrey meets Denise Bryson and feels threatened by the presence of Cooper's female FBI peer, she marks her territory by planting a kiss on his lips. If the writers *didn't* want the audience to be invested in a romance between Cooper and Audrey, they

Audrey in saddle shoes

were doing a very, very bad job backing away from the story. That's because they had every intention of doubling down on what had obviously emerged as the show's most potent will they/won't they. "David took me to dinner and basically asked me if I was in love with Kyle," says Sherilyn Fenn. "And I burst out laughing. Not even slightly! He's a great guy, he's a nice person, but that's it. I didn't have any feelings that way. At all. The truth is that as human beings, he and I didn't have that kind of chemistry. But those characters, for some really weird reason, did." Peyton adds, "We were going to do a—'romance' may be the wrong word, but certainly an *exploration* of the relationship between Audrey and Cooper. That didn't happen, and it didn't happen because Kyle refused."

For years, the official story has been that MacLachlan rejected the plotline because he didn't believe Cooper would get involved with a high schooler. There's a solid plot justification for that argument; Cooper did, after all, gently reject Audrey for the same reason back in season one. But whatever the merits of that argument, there's no question that off-screen dynamics were also in play. At the time, MacLachlan was dating Lara Flynn Boyle, whose push for Donna's unconvincing bad-girl makeover in season two was judged, by some, to have been a response to Sherilyn Fenn getting more attention for her coquettish performance.

"I still remember talking with Mark [Frost]," says Peyton. "Mark was saying, 'No, we're going to draw a line in the sand. We can't do this. We planned this pretty carefully, and it's going to upend our second season.' Then Kyle went into Mark's office with David. I remember waiting and waiting and waiting. And then he came out and said, 'No, we're not doing it.' And that was because David was the one who was basically saying, 'We're going to go with what the actors prefer.' I think when Kyle made it very clear he didn't want to do it, and he gave the reasons, David said, 'Fine. That's what we'll do.' The thing about David that I learned over time is that he will sort of do anything for the actors. And because he'll do anything for them, they will do anything for him."

Whatever the underlying reasons for it, even those who were frustrated by MacLachlan's justification now concede it was better that the Cooper-Audrey plotline didn't move forward. "It's hard to say, because nowadays, *I* would say, 'No, we can't do that, because he's in a position of power and she's much younger.' All the things Kyle was saying. It's easy to say he did it because of Lara Flynn Boyle. But who knows why?" says Peyton. "I mean . . . he did end up with a love interest who was the same age [as Audrey]. And she was from a *convent*, for crying out loud."

Cooper's formerly cloistered paramour was Annie Blackburn (Heather Graham), a half sister of Norma Jennings whose sudden arrival in Twin Peaks was written to fill in the gap where the Cooper/Audrey romance would have been, and actor Heather Graham knew what she was walking into. "I think a lot of people were bummed out that he wasn't with Sherilyn

Fenn. That romance had been so juicy to people," she says. And Graham counted herself among those who had followed every beat of that will they/won't they love story. "I watched *Twin Peaks* religiously. I was obsessed," she says. "I mean, I was such a nerd. I was just so excited to meet every single actor. And I had a huge crush on Kyle MacLachlan. It wasn't so hard for me, because I honestly had this massive crush on him."

Prior to being cast in *Twin Peaks*, Graham had already made her way into the outskirts of Lynchland by costarring, opposite Benicio del Toro, in a Calvin Klein commercial Lynch directed. But playing a woman capable of instantly bewitching Dale Cooper would be an entirely different challenge, and Graham met Lynch at his home to discuss the character—after he showed off another ongoing project. "He was doing some kind of experiment where he was putting meat into this kind of art piece and letting ants crawl on it," says Graham. "It was so interesting and bizarre."

Graham recalls Lynch describing Annie as "a finely tuned machine. Like a Ferrari or a sports car that's very amazing—but that it can be easily thrown off-balance, if something goes wrong." Harley Peyton had a blunter appraisal: "Sad to say, Annie was—at least when the character was initially conceived—a damsel in distress. And not a great deal more than that," he said.

Audrey, for her part, got a new love interest of her own—though not before the show teased a flirtation between Audrey and Bobby, who was briefly positioned as Ben Horne's new right-hand man. "I don't know if they were definitely going to go with it. I *thought* they were definitely going to go with it, and we had those moments," said Dana Ashbrook. "I think it was either a MacGuffin, or a change of someone's mind, or I don't know. It was so on the fly, always, the story." In the end, Bobby stayed true to Shelly—though not before Gordon Cole planted a kiss on her—and Audrey got her own new love interest in John Justice Wheeler, a dashing young businessman/pilot played by Billy Zane. "It was Harley who came up with [John

Justice Wheeler]," says Mark Frost. "When we said, 'Okay, well, who's going to sweep Audrey off her feet?' he said, 'Well, it should be a singing cowboy.'"

Wheeler does, in fact, throw on a cowboy hat, take Audrey on a picnic, and serenade her with a rendition of the cowboy folk standard "Bury Me Not on the Lone Prairie." Fenn herself was unconvinced. "He's a really nice guy. But the first time I met him was at six in the morning. And he goes, 'What would you do if I leaned over the table and kissed you?' And I go, 'I'd have a problem with that.'" Still, Wheeler's routine is enough, apparently, to knock Audrey's crush on Cooper out of her brain entirely; the episode's script describes her as "warm and certain" as she reassures Wheeler that she doesn't have feelings for anyone else.

With Cooper and Audrey splintering off into their own separate love stories—and much of the other main cast engaged in their own semi-standalone arcs—*Twin Peaks* needed both a villain and an event to justify weaving everything back together. If there was anything that bound *Twin Peaks'* many threads in the back half of the second season, it was the simmering threat of Cooper's insane former partner Windom Earle (Kenneth Welsh), revealed early in season two as having escaped custody and hell-bent on revenge. Though it wasn't clear at the time, Earle's clash with Cooper would become *Twin Peaks'* most significant arc following the resolution of Laura's murder. "That was supposed to be short-lived," says Robert Engels. "I talked those guys into hiring [Kenneth Welsh]. He was a friend of mine, and they just loved him, so that character became bigger."

Earle's introduction had the benefit of giving *Twin Peaks* an excuse to delve into Cooper's past—something that was clearly on the minds of the show's writers, as Scott Frost's tie-in book *The Autobiography of F.B.I. Special Agent Dale Cooper: My Life, My Tapes* was published shortly before the climax of the second season. As a young agent, we learn, Cooper fell in love with Caroline Earle (Brenda E. Mathers), the wife of his FBI mentor and ex-partner Windom. The story gets a little muddy from here—decades later, Mark Frost's book *Twin Peaks: The Final Dossier* would hand-wave any discrepancies by stating that the records had been doctored by a bad actor—but the important part is that Windom Earle killed Caroline and wounded Cooper, resulting in scars both mental and physical.

After escaping a mental institution and stalking Cooper to Twin Peaks, Earle engages Cooper in a grotesque version of the daily chess game they played when they were partners. Whenever Earle takes a piece, he commits an equivalent murder; the loss of a pawn, for example, leads to the murder of a drifter with no direct connection to the larger narrative.

Once Cooper realizes the game Earle is playing, he's savvy enough to build a strategy not aimed at winning the game, but at protecting the pieces remaining on his side of the board. Still: You'd think he'd be smart

Windom Earle in his lair

enough to realize that protecting his queen is paramount—especially since he's simultaneously falling in love with Annie Blackburn, whose innocence and lack of worldliness makes her an especially ripe target. And you'd *definitely* think he'd be smart enough to recognize the danger when the Giant literally appears in front of him, waving his arms and mouthing the word *no*, after Annie suggests she'll enter the Miss Twin Peaks pageant. But when Cooper falls in love, it seems, his deductive powers vanish; just a few episodes earlier, he flirts with Annie at the Double R, then walks right by the not-especially-well-disguised Windom Earle.

All these plotlines converge in the penultimate episode of *Twin Peaks*, which also turns out to be the last gasp of the comedy-focused storytelling that had come to the forefront of the first season. The Miss Twin Peaks pageant was designed, among other things, to bring the increasingly scattered group of characters back together: Donna Hayward, Shelly Johnson, Lucy Moran, Nadine Hurley, Lana Milford, and Annie Blackburn all compete, and Norma Jennings, Doc Hayward, Pete Martell, and Dick Tremayne all play a role in judging the pageant. Though she had been targeted by Windom Earle alongside Donna and Shelly just a few episodes earlier, Audrey is noticeably absent for much of the competition. "I called David right away and said, 'I'm not doing it,'" says Fenn. "No fucking way. Audrey was there, but I didn't, like, parade up and down a fucking catwalk in a bathing suit."

Goofy as it is, the levity feels welcome before *Twin Peaks* takes its final plunge into the darkness. Lana Milford does something called "contortionistic jazz exotica," and Lucy Moran does a dance that ends in the splits, which led to actress Kimmy Robertson needing to reassure people that there was no damage to the baby. (Robertson, for the record, was not actually pregnant.)

But when Annie Blackburn is crowned Miss Twin Peaks—after a speech that leans heavily on the words of Chief Seattle, a leader of Washington's Suquamish and Duwamish tribes—Earle, who has infiltrated the Miss Twin

Peaks pageant disguised as the Log Lady, makes his move. A queen has been crowned; he's ready to claim her.

It's a strong cliff-hanger for the season finale, but that's not how it originally aired. By this point, ABC's scheduling of *Twin Peaks* had become erratic, with lengthy hiatuses in December and January—a problem further exacerbated by coverage of the Gulf War. "The thing that really hurt us was we were preempted for six out of eight weeks when the Gulf War started," said Mark Frost. "Every night everybody was watching reporters standing in front of bombs falling in Baghdad, and this was not a show that benefited from people not seeing it for six weeks." After the memorably bizarre cliff-hanger of "Episode 23"—which concluded with Josie Packard, revealed as the mysterious shooter who shot Cooper in the season one finale, somehow trapped in a drawer pull in a Great Northern Hotel room—ABC put the show on hiatus. That troubling sign prompted a fan campaign called COOP, or Citizens Opposed to the Offing of Peaks, to place hundreds of phone calls and send thousands of letters and packages, some containing logs or donuts, to ABC. David Lynch goosed the campaign further in a February appearance on *Late Night with David Letterman*, where the host gamely posted Bob Iger's mailing address. ("I love annoying these network weasels," said Letterman.)

ABC relented, and *Twin Peaks* returned on Thursday, March 28—an escape, at last, from the wasteland of Saturday night. But the reprieve was short-lived. Less than a month later, on April 18, 1991, "Episode 27" aired—a return to form that ended, promisingly, with BOB reemerging from the Black Lodge. But anyone intrigued by that cliff-hanger was forced to wait nearly two months, to June 10, when the network unceremoniously dumped the final two episodes as a double feature. Though *Twin Peaks* hadn't been formally canceled, everyone involved knew the writing was on the wall. "As a phenomenon," Mark Frost conceded a month before the season two finale aired, "the show is over."

JOSIE PACKARD

"Do you hear me now—as a rustling in the curtains, a murmur in a crowd, an echo without an origin?"

"WHAT HAPPENED TO JOSIE?" bellows BOB, gleefully, after Josie Packard dies. It's not often that *Twin Peaks* viewers find themselves on the same page as BOB—but by the end of her story, what else is there to say?

What happened to Josie? Let's start at the beginning. Josie Packard's face is the first we see in *Twin Peaks*. Just before Peter Martell walks down to the lakefront and discovers Laura Palmer's body wrapped in plastic, we see Josie Packard, applying makeup. It's an image so unexpected—and so irrelevant, apparently, to everything that comes after it—that some viewers took it as a clue Josie might be Laura's killer. Why else would David Lynch open *Twin Peaks* with a character who turns out, in the end, to be only peripherally connected to the show's big mystery?

There are overarching explanations worth considering. *Twin Peaks* is a show obsessed with thematic doubles, actual doppelgängers, and mirror images. That opening image of Josie, stoically applying red lipstick in a mirror, finds its own dark mirror image in the series finale: Cooper's doppelgänger cackling into the mirror, his face red with blood. By then, Josie has already exited the story—swallowed up by the Black Lodge in a way that even *Twin Peaks* struggles to explain.

Even by *Twin Peaks* standards, Josie is carrying some dark secrets. *The Secret History of Twin Peaks* reveals that she was born Li Chun Fung in Guangzhou, China, to a high-ranking member of the Triads and a heroin-addicted sex worker. (There's a hint, perhaps, that Josie's tragic fate was sealed from the start: The book translates Li Chun Fung as *upright autumn bird*, which certainly sounds like an owl that's not what it seems.) She ended up at a boarding school in Shanghai, where she started her own drug and prostitution rings. Even after she launched a successful fashion label, she maintained her ties to the criminal underworld, finally going into hiding—under the alias Josette Wong—after she was suspected of orchestrating her father's murder. Escape came in the form of Andrew Packard (Dan O'Herlihy), a successful international businessman who fell in love with her and swept her away to Twin Peaks. In a soapy turn, we eventually learn that Josie was secretly involved with Andrew's business partner, Thomas Eckhardt (David Warner), and orchestrated the boat explosion that led to Andrew's death. In a *very* soapy turn, we then learn that Andrew anticipated the hit and faked his own death, leaving Josie unwittingly caught in a game between two rich assholes.

But the overheated specifics of Josie's life are almost beside the point. What matters, to paraphrase Dr. Jacoby, is that Josie had secrets, and that most of her life seems to have been an elaborate performance. Josie is one of the two non-white regulars in *Twin Peaks*' sprawling cast, and unlike Hawk, who has deep roots in the region, she's an outsider whose closest family tie is the sister-in-law who openly hates her. "Josie Packard" seems to have been yet another performance, and as she did for most of her life, she seems to have survived in Twin Peaks by finding and targeting those who could be useful to her.

For starters, *The Secret History of Twin Peaks* heavily implies Josie didn't need those weekly English lessons with Laura Palmer; according to the book, she fluently spoke six languages, so all of her malapropisms were deliberate. In *The Secret Diary of Laura Palmer*, Laura describes those language sessions as being more like "poorly executed seductions" on Josie's part. "The more she comes on to me the less I respect her," she writes. Was Josie just another person who couldn't resist Laura? Or did she see a strategic advantage in cozying up to the daughter of Leland Palmer, a powerful lawyer who served as the personal counsel to the even-more-powerful businessman who wanted her land?

Maybe, like many who build their lives on deceptions, Josie's motives were opaque even to herself. Her relationship with Sheriff Truman certainly feels calculated, and she spends much of it feeding him misinformation in an attempt to frame Catherine Martell for the sawmill fire. It's a well-executed plan, but even then, her lies are catching up to her, and she commits an increasingly brazen series of crimes to try to stay ahead of them. We learn, eventually, that Josie shot Cooper because she feared he had learned the truth about her. She shoots and kills two more people before the show ends, apparently willing to do almost anything that might give her enough time to find another escape hatch.

Josie's character arc, which can feel scattered and strangely paced—the less said about her time as a live-in maid for Catherine, the better—was shaped in part by the needs of actress Joan Chen, whose unpredictable schedule regularly caused headaches for the show's production. "Joan Chen had this whole life and career out of the country," says Harley Peyton. "She would go back and forth, and she was frequently not available when we wanted her to be available." In the end, it was Chen who asked to leave *Twin Peaks*, and Lynch who crafted an exit so bizarre that the actress later wondered if it might have been his way of getting revenge against her for quitting.

Mark Frost swears that wasn't the case. "It was a creative way to park the character in some way. In case she ever changed her mind, to be honest," he says. But even now, it's hard to make sense of what happens to Josie. In "Episode 23," Cooper finally catches her in the act of committing a crime. Josie draws a gun, willing to shoot the FBI agent if it means she might be able to slip the noose yet again. Harry's arrival, gun drawn, seals her fate, but Josie's story doesn't end in a pair of handcuffs. She suddenly collapses, dead—replaced, from Cooper's heightened perspective, by a gleeful BOB and a brief dance by the Man from Another Place. For all his intuition, not even Cooper gets the final answer the audience does: Josie's face, trapped in agony, in the drawer pull of the hotel room's bedside table.

There were just six episodes of *Twin Peaks* after Chen left the show, but she haunts the rest of the series—though only a few of those moments actually made it to air. Doc Hayward's autopsy reveals, inexplicably, that Josie weighed sixty-five pounds at the time of her death. The original script for "Episode 27" included a quick cut to Josie, still trapped in the knob and screaming, as BOB emerges from Glastonbury Grove. In the same episode, Pete Martell mutters "Josie, I see your face," while staring at a Great Northern fireplace, and Ben Horne seems startled by something he sees (but we don't) in the wooden wall. Most intriguingly, photos taken by Richard Beymer reveal that Joan Chen's stunt double was on set for the *Twin Peaks* finale. According to actor Frank Silva, her body would have been seen trapped in the curtains of the Red Room, implying that Josie had also been ensnared by the dark forces of the Black Lodge.

When *Twin Peaks* ended, fans had understandable questions about Josie's ultimate fate. Even by Lynch's esoteric standards, the Log Lady introduction he later wrote was no help: "A hotel. A nightstand. A drawer pull on the drawer. A drawer pull, on the drawer of a nightstand, in the room of a hotel. What could possibly be happening on or in this drawer pull? How many drawer pulls exist in this world? Thousands. Maybe millions. What is a drawer pull?" Some speculated that Judy, the mysterious figure namechecked by both David Bowie and a monkey in *Twin Peaks: Fire Walk with Me*, was intended to be Josie's sister in a nascent version of the script—a claim screenwriter Robert Engels answered, vaguely, by saying, "Yes. Yes, I think that is true."

All of this straw grasping points to a larger truth: With the exception of Cooper's replacement by the doppelgänger in the season two finale, Josie's fate was the question that most haunted *Twin Peaks* fans. It haunted Joan

Chen as well. In a 2014 post on her personal blog, she blamed herself for Josie's abrupt exit from *Twin Peaks*. "I have made countless stupid mistakes in life and wanting to be written out of *Twin Peaks* was among the stupidest," she wrote, saying that she had "naively rebelled" against playing a character written as an exotic flower. When *Twin Peaks: The Return* was announced, she expressed a "glimmer of hope" that Josie might return, and when she wasn't approached to join the cast, she even wrote a letter to Lynch, in Josie's voice, hoping he might reconsider.

"I write to you from the wooden drawer knob in which I have been trapped for the past two decades, yearning restlessly for an escape," the letter begins. Channeling Josie, Chen describes longing for her own physical body while watching an endless parade of hotel guests coming and going, and dreaming of her twin sister, Judy, rescuing her, allowing them to inhabit one body as they'd once inhabited one womb. "My time in purgatory has been served, don't you think?" she pleads "Isn't it time I at least got to meet my maker one last time?"

It is, in its way, probably the best answer *Twin Peaks* fans will ever get about what happened to Josie. It was largely ignored; Josie goes all but unmentioned in *Twin Peaks: The Return*. "I think we might have had room to do something with Joan Chen if Michael Ontkean had come back," says Mark Frost. "I remember bringing it up a couple of times: 'I mean, she *is* trapped in a doorknob. I suppose we could bring her back, you know?'"

What happened to Josie? I guess we'll never truly know. Sometimes the Black Lodge wins; sometimes, when you're gone, you can't come back.

Chapter 7

AND NOW, AN ENDING

Imagine what it's like to hit your final deadline on the biggest project of your career. Everything you've done has built up to this moment. But this project isn't merely the long-awaited culmination of months of work; it is, potentially, a make-or-break moment that will determine whether you'll either keep the job you have or put out your shingle and find something else to do for a living.

Now: Imagine that your boss—widely lauded as a genius—has been a little asleep at the wheel lately. Imagine you've been toiling, in relative obscurity, in his absence. Imagine that he suddenly comes into the office, at the eleventh hour, and says, 'Oh, this is what you've been working on? This doesn't work for me. I'm going to do my own thing.' Imagine that he doesn't even bother to tell you what he's doing.

Are you getting angry yet? Then you have some idea of the outrage Harley Peyton felt when he learned that David Lynch had shown up to work one day and thrown out pretty much everything but the basic structure of the script that he, Mark Frost, and Robert Engels had written for the *Twin Peaks* finale. "I remember hearing from some production people, 'You know, David's not even doing the script. He's just tossing it.' And I can't tell you the umbrage I felt," says Peyton. "I was outraged. I thought, *How fucking dare you?* I was really furious. Usually, when that stuff happens, it's a shit show—for someone to just come in at the last minute and change a bunch of things. And then I saw the episode and went, 'Oh my God. It's perfect. This may be one of the best television episodes ever.'"

To understand what makes *Twin Peaks*' season two finale one of the strangest, most mesmerizing hours in network television history, you need to start with the bones of that largely unused script. Just as he had in season one, Mark Frost had responded to the uncertainty of *Twin Peaks*' renewal with a game of chicken: *Look how many cliff-hangers I can squeeze into this thing.* Even if you ignore Cooper's surreal trip into the Red Room, which takes up the bulk of the episode, the finale script leaves a staggering number of characters in limbo. Nadine's memory has returned, leaving Ed and Norma's future once again in question. Leo Johnson is booby-trapped with a cage of deadly spiders. Ben Horne might be comatose, or even dead, after a head injury caused by Doc Hayward. Andrew Packard, Audrey Horne, and either Catherine or Pete Martell—the script says Catherine, but Lynch swaps in Pete—might be dead after an explosion in a bank vault.

It's not that *Twin Peaks* was actually going to write off all those characters if it had been picked up for a third season. Sherilyn Fenn says Audrey Horne was always intended to survive everything. "I said to David, 'What the hell?' And he said, 'It's the fucking stupid-ass network notes and they wanted a stupid-ass cliffhanger, so you're it. I'm not going to kill Audrey,'" says Fenn. "There was absolutely no way Pete Martell wouldn't come back," says Harley Peyton. But while those after-the-fact reassurances might give fans some closure, the reality was that *Twin Peaks* was willing to let its story end with a sizable chunk of its characters in mortal peril, risking the possibility that viewers would never learn whether they lived or died.

Both the original finale script and Lynch's filmed version take us into the Black Lodge. Where they diverge, most sharply, is the nature of the Black Lodge. "Whenever David directed, things changed," says Robert Engels. But the changes had never been as dramatic as this. In the original script, Truman sees a woman in chainmail guarding the entrance to Glastonbury Grove. When Cooper enters the Black Lodge through a hole that opens in space, he briefly finds himself transformed into a ten-year-old boy and encounters his own father as the clerk of a shabby motel. Soon after, he enters a bizarre, chessboard-themed version of the Great Northern. Windom Earle shows up and does a song and dance routine; Cooper ends up menaced by BOB, who's dressed as a syringe-wielding dentist, until Laura Palmer appears, bathed in beatific light, to save him.

By all accounts, David Lynch was particularly incensed by what he saw as a complete misrepresentation of the Black Lodge. "That's the only time David ever really got mad at me on that second season," said Sabrina S. Sutherland, a production coordinator who would go on to be an executive producer on *Twin Peaks: The Return*. "He did not like the script that had been written. He came to me, and he was screaming at me: 'Did this script go out to everybody?' Because my job was distributing the scripts. And I said: 'Yes.' And he was so upset. So he rewrote it and took out stuff that he didn't like, and made new scenes to make it more like his and Mark's original vision of *Twin Peaks*." When location liaison Barry Gremillion, still working from the original finale script, asked Lynch a logistical question, Lynch replied: "I wouldn't pay too much attention to that script if I were you."

It's not quite fair to say Lynch tossed the original script entirely, but much of what he kept shifted dramatically in tone. "David did something that he didn't with any other script: He got in there, and he edited, and maybe wrote things himself. If that had happened on anything close to a weekly basis, it probably would have been a disaster. But it worked really well here," says Peyton. In the script, Nadine's realization that she's not actually a high schooler rings with shticky comedy; in Lynch's version, it's full of despair, as a troubled, sobbing woman realizes, once again, she's become completely unmoored from reality. In the script, Doc Hayward rushes to Ben Horne after causing his head wound; in Lynch's version, he merely falls to his knees and screams. In the script, Hawk and Major Briggs have arrived to try to rescue Leo from the spider trap; in Lynch's version, we get only a brief glimpse of Leo, trapped and alone, with no indication whatsoever that anyone even knows where he is.

What Lynch introduces, instead, is a series of callbacks and inspired, surreal touches. Some are blatant: When Heidi the waitress shows up late for work at the Double R, Bobby and Shelly repeat their banter from the pilot almost word for word. Some are subtler: establishing shots that give us one more look at iconic locations, such as the bridge Ronette Pulaski crossed in the pilot. And some are simply examples of Lynch pulling his favorite tricks one last time. Just as he did in the season two premiere with the room service waiter, Lynch stretches the bank-vault drama to nearly unbearable length by casting eighty-five-year-old actor Ed Wright as bank manager Dell Mibbler, then following him for every moment as he slowly dodders around the vault. The scene is full of uncanny, Lynchian details. A guard we've never met picks up a ringing phone and shouts, "It's a boy! It's a boy!" Meanwhile, a woman sits slumped in a chair in the far background, her mouth wide open, totally uncommented on, sleeping or maybe, quietly, dying. There are flashes of love and warmth; in the Double R Diner, which doesn't appear at all in the original script, Lynch shows us Major Briggs and Betty, sitting on the same side of a booth, sharing coffee while gazing lovingly into each other's eyes. But even this moment of harmony is quickly disrupted. Dr. Jacoby brings Sarah Palmer into the diner, apparently possessed, with a cryptic message for Briggs: "I am in the Black Lodge with Dale Cooper . . . I am waiting for you."

These flourishes—so unlikely to be appreciated at the time, as ABC buried the finale in the back half of a two-hour block—feel much more significant now, when first-time *Twin Peaks* viewers are almost certainly binge-watching the show instead of trying to follow it across ABC's erratic scheduling. It was as if Lynch had glimpsed a future in which audiences might view this finale with eyes fresh enough to appreciate everything he was doing, and crafted an episode that would keep the fandom engaged, and desperate for resolution, even decades later.

The episode's centerpiece is Cooper's entrance to the Black Lodge—seen here, at last, not filtered through Cooper's dreams, but as an actual, tangible place a person can enter with the proper knowledge and preparation. Windom Earle, whose real goal was entering the Black Lodge, drags Annie along with him. Somehow, both men have intuited the dream logic by which the Black Lodge operates. When Earle drags Annie across the threshold, she becomes catatonic and pliable; when Cooper arrives with Truman, he insists, without further explanation, that he needs to go on alone. In another small full-circle moment just before we're plunged into the Black Lodge, Lynch reveals that Cooper is a man changed by his time in Twin Peaks. Where Cooper eagerly quizzed Truman about the Douglas Fir trees that so entranced him in the pilot, he instantly recognizes the twelve trees of Glastonbury Grove as sycamores.

Where the Black Lodge in the scripted version of the finale had an almost Tim Burton-esque flair, Lynch's version hews closely to the template he established with the Red Room: red curtains, zig-zag floor, plush black leather chairs, and a replica of the Venus de' Medici. His grandest addition is a solo performance of "Sycamore Trees"—an original song written by Angelo Badalamenti, with lyrics by Lynch—by the jazz legend Jimmy Scott, which Cooper watches blankly. A genetic disorder called Kallman syndrome had left Scott with an unusually high contralto and a unique timbre, and Scott "does things to a song that nobody else does. So he's an original, an original voice," said Lynch. "It's haunting. And it's so pure soulful."

There's no need for anything else; what's terrifying, in the end, is that the Black Lodge doesn't need to be anything more than an endless liminal space of identical hallways, in which every path seems to loop back to what the Man from Another Place calls "the waiting room." Given the urgency of finding Earle and saving Annie, why does Cooper stop in this room and sit? Perhaps it's the supernatural version of what he says about whittling in the *Twin Peaks* pilot: "It's what you do in a town where a yellow light still means 'slow down,' not 'speed up.'" Maybe, when you're in the waiting room, what you do is wait.

If the Black Lodge seems to abide by its own dream logic, it might be because Lynch—even more so than usual—was operating on instinct, letting his muse guide him from scene to scene. "It was such a strange atmosphere because nobody had the slightest idea of what was going to happen," says Carel Struycken, who delivers several cryptic lines of dialogue (including the revelation, apparently, that the Giant and the room service waiter are one and the same, just as BOB and Leland were). "I had much more of a sense that David was improvising. After every scene, people would kind of walk up to him and say, 'Okay, what's next?' And he would just come up with something. Most of the dialogue got handed to me on little scripts of paper, torn out of a notebook, and then I had to quickly try to figure out how to say it backwards."

The challenge was multiplied for Sheryl Lee, who appears as both Maddy Ferguson and Laura Palmer—rendered here not as an angelic figure saving Cooper from BOB, as she was in the original script, but as both an enigmatic, riddle-spouting Laura and her terrifying doppelgänger, who climbs over a couch and breaks the fourth wall as BOB once did. Once again, Lynch is complicating the question of who Laura really was. "Watch out for my cousin," says Maddy Ferguson—apparently trapped, like Laura, in this liminal space. But her phrasing is ambiguous. Is she asking Cooper to protect Laura or warning him that Laura is dangerous? It's a question

Twin Peaks has been asking, in its own oblique way, from the very beginning; it's a question *Twin Peaks* will be haunted by for the rest of its run.

Sheryl Lee reveled in the unique difficulty of such scenes. "I love the creative challenge of working in the Red Room," said Lee. "It's completely different from any other set. It's almost like I have to leave the logical part of my brain at the door when I walk on that set behind those curtains. It is, in a way, like working in a dream world where time and logic are stretched. It's like working in a different dimension, honestly, doing everything we do in there. If I overthink it, I get in my own way."

Eventually, Cooper pushes past enough doppelgängers to find a disturbing pastiche of the night Caroline Earle was murdered: a bloodied Annie Blackburn, lying on the ground next to a Cooper doppelgänger. Or is it Caroline? The Black Lodge is a place where personal identity becomes porous, and the damsel in distress here cycles, both physically and mentally, between Caroline and Annie. "It was really fun to be doing the talking-backwards stuff," says Heather Graham. "It's exciting when you're working with someone who's so creative. Where it's not just like, *Oh, the studio's controlling what they're doing and they have to just follow this formula.* It's like: *Oh, you're really going with this really artistic person who's just making up all this totally crazy stuff about people talking backwards.*"

Are there any rules in a place where reality itself seems to be in flux? It's only when Windom Earle appears, offering to let Annie live in return for Cooper's soul, that the cosmic, unknowable logic of the Black Lodge asserts itself. Though Cooper agrees, BOB instantly appears and calls the whole thing off; Earle isn't allowed to take Cooper's soul, and as punishment BOB will take his instead. In a matter of seconds, Cooper's greatest enemy is reduced to a husk, replaced by an enemy that's infinitely more terrifying: a cackling, blank-eyed doppelgänger of Cooper himself.

Cooper runs. (Wouldn't you?) But Lynch has established, by now, that the Black Lodge isn't a place that's so easily escaped. It's only when the doppelgänger grabs Cooper that we return to Glastonbury Grove, where Truman is shocked to see Cooper and Annie materialize on the ground.

Cut to the Great Northern—and the cliff-hanger that would haunt *Twin Peaks* fans for twenty-five years. Cooper wakes up in bed, attended by Truman and Doc Hayward. He seems foggy and strange after his experience in the Black Lodge—asking about Annie in the same emotionless monotone with which he insists he needs to brush his teeth.

Once alone in the bathroom, he squeezes the toothpaste tube like a particularly destructive toddler still figuring out how the world works. He smashes his face into the mirror, cracking open his forehead—and, of course, sees BOB grinning back at him. "How's Annie?" he cackles repeatedly, openly mocking human empathy or connection. The doppelgänger has escaped the Black Lodge; Cooper, we have to assume, is still waiting there. And that's the idea, and the image, that *Twin Peaks* goes out on.

It is one of the cruelest twists in television history, and Lynch—having otherwise departed so dramatically from the script's version of the Red Room—shot it more or less identically to how it was originally written. "My memory is that I came into the room and said, 'Okay, the ending has to be Cooper looking in the mirror and seeing BOB,'" says Peyton. "And Mark said, 'Yeah, I wrote that yesterday.'"

In its own quiet way, *Twin Peaks* had been building up to this moment all along. There is a moment in Scott Frost's *The Autobiography of F.B.I. Special Agent Dale Cooper*—published a month before the finale aired—in which the fourteen-year-old Cooper, while suffering from an asthma attack, receives an unsettlingly familiar nocturnal visitor. "A man who I have never seen was trying to break into my room," writes the young Dale. "He kept calling my name and said that he wanted me. He then screamed, and after a

"How's Annie?"

moment it turned into a kind of roar as if he were some kind of animal. I told Mom about it and she said that she knew about 'him,' and that she has the same dream, and that I must never let the man into my room."

Decades later, it is still hard to watch this episode without wanting to reach back in time and shake a bunch of ABC executives by the shoulders. How do you see an episode this unique and compelling—with a cliff-hanger so potent—and not roll the dice on another season of *Twin Peaks*? "I think there was probably a real shot. But not fifty-fifty. Let's put it that way," says Robert Engels. "David tried to get the show back on the right track, but it was just too late. It had to end. It just got too strange," says Duwayne Dunham. "In a way, I can't fault [Bob Iger] for canceling us for season three," says Mark Frost. "Given what I know about executives, I might have done the same thing. You know, it's self-preservation. That's what the business is about."

But before the network formally canceled *Twin Peaks*, there were, at least, preliminary conversations within the show's creative team about what might happen in the third season. "It would have looked at least in part like [*Twin Peaks: The Return*], because I had already come up with the battle between the good and the evil Cooper and how that was going to play," says Mark Frost. "I think I even mentioned that to ABC as the place that we would go, which I thought would have really revitalized their audience engagement. But it was clear that they already sort of moved on. They were looking for another dopamine hit."

Harley Peyton is still intrigued by the possibilities. "As a writer, you go, 'Okay, Cooper has BOB inside of him. We have to get BOB out sometime during the season,'" says Peyton. "I think it would have had to do with the various characters on the show—but Harry, first and foremost—figuring out that something was horrifically wrong. And, I think, Cooper doing what Leland did . . . which is leaving a trail of bodies behind him. I don't see how you avoid that. It would have been really fun and crazy and insane to do. And while Leland ended up dying at the end of his discovery, Cooper would not. That does get very interesting. There was some rich text to work with, which, of course, sadly, I never got to work with."

Another Peyton concept for season three—unfortunately unrealized—would have been formally inventive in a way that was basically unheard of on network television at the time. "I had convinced Mark to let me write an episode where we just did a stationary camera on a booth at the Double R Diner," says Peyton. "It would be stationary for the entire episode, and the entire episode would just be different characters sitting in that same booth, having conversations. The conversations would advance the plot, but what I *really* wanted to do—although they probably wouldn't have let us do it—was just have the booth be empty for, like, sixty arduous seconds."

The Autobiography of F.B.I. Special Agent Dale Cooper leaves another intriguing clue for where the third season might have gone. The book features occasional references to Cooper's long-estranged elder brother Emmet, who avoided the Vietnam draft by fleeing across the border to Canada and working as a lumberjack. According to author Scott Frost, Emmet wasn't his idea. It was a request from Mark—who had concluded that Tony-winning actor Roger Rees would make a great elder brother for Cooper if the show were picked up for a third season—and asked him to insert a few tantalizing references to Cooper's brother into the already-completed manuscript in case they ever needed him. "I think that was part of Mark's understanding—which I didn't really have yet—of the desperate nature of the writer's room. You know, *Oh, God what do we do* this *week?*," says Scott Frost.

For years, some of the best information about *Twin Peaks'* scrapped third season came thirdhand, via illustrator Matt Haley. When CBS/Paramount was preparing the *Twin Peaks* Definitive Gold Box Edition—a luxe set collecting the entire series across ten DVDs released in 2007—Haley, a longtime *Twin Peaks* fan and comic book artist, pitched a graphic novel that would be included with the box set and finally tie up the season two cliff-hanger. When he reached CBS's Paula Block, who was then in charge of managing the *Twin Peaks* license, she was frank: "That's a really great idea. Mark will probably say yes; David will probably say no." Still, the possibility was intriguing enough that—at the price of one dollar—she gave him the exclusive rights to a *Twin Peaks* graphic novel for eighteen months on the condition that both creators signed off on the idea.

"I spent six solid months watching the show and taking copious notes," says Haley. As Block predicted, Frost quickly gave his approval. He also connected Haley with Robert Engels, who agreed to write the comic, which would have run either sixty or eighty pages. "I was keen to use whatever notes they had for the proposed third season," said Haley in 2007. "Bob told me they really wanted to get away from the high school setting, so after the resolution of the Cooper BOB possession plot point, they would have cut to something like 'Ten Years Later,' and then shown us a Twin Peaks where Cooper had quit the FBI and had become the town pharmacist, Sheriff Truman had become a recluse, etc. He also mentioned they were going to have Sheryl Lee come back yet again, this time as a redhead, and probably have her character killed by BOB again. There were also some vague ideas about BOB and Mike being from a planet made of creamed corn, something about Truman driving Mike backward through the portal into the Black Lodge." ("I have no idea what Bob was talking about," says Frost when asked about these ideas. "That was something that was not on my radar.") Audrey and Ben Horne, Haley adds, would have been side by side in the hospital, recovering from the injuries they sustained in the season two finale. The comic might even have answered one of the still-unresolved mysteries that bedevils *Twin Peaks* fans today: "I feel like Josie Packard came back in some way, but I could be wrong about that," Haley recalls. (In the end, it didn't matter; Lynch spent a weekend contemplating the pitch, but turned it down.)

Of course, no one knew any of this back in 1991. But the *Twin Peaks* fans who had stuck with the show all along, and were now grieving its demise, received an unexpected consolation prize just a few weeks after the season two finale aired. In an interview for a June 28 newspaper column by the Pulitzer-nominated pop-culture journalist Noel Holston, Mark Frost revealed that a *Twin Peaks* film, cowritten by Lynch and Robert Engels, would go into production by the end of the summer. "If the movie works, I suppose there's an opportunity to do, like, a *Star Trek* movie every couple of years, if that's what we want to do," said Frost at the time.

But the movie also represented the first irreconcilable break between the two creators' visions for *Twin Peaks*. Where Frost saw an opportunity to push *Twin Peaks*' story forward, Lynch, with the help of Engels, was already looking backward. "I was in love with the character of Laura Palmer and her contradictions: radiant on the surface but dying inside. I wanted to see her live, move, and talk," Lynch later said. His movie would do what *Twin Peaks* itself never could: bring Laura Palmer back to life.

WINDOM EARLE

"Think of all the hapless sinners wondering where their soul's destination lies."

Twin Peaks is so frequently dinged for losing its way after the murder of Laura Palmer is resolved that it's startling to realize how early, and how carefully, Windom Earle is seeded into narrative. We hear about Earle no fewer than three times before Leland is unveiled as the killer. Early in season two, Albert Rosenfield comes to town and warns Cooper that his former partner has escaped a mental institution. Four episodes later, Gordon Cole—a friend even higher up the FBI ladder—makes his own trip to Twin Peaks to give Cooper an envelope, which contains Earle's opening move in the chess game that dominates the back half of season two. Even BOB gets in on the fun; shortly before abandoning Leland as his vessel, he snarls a taunt: "I have this thing for knives. Just like what happened to you in Pittsburgh that time, huh, Cooper?"

What happened to Cooper in Pittsburgh that time? It's another five episodes before we get the whole story. Earle was Cooper's mentor and friend—a man who, per *The Autobiography of F.B.I. Special Agent Dale Cooper,* had helped to shape Cooper's life and career since they first met at an FBI job fair. They played chess every day for three years; Cooper never won a game. "I suspect there is much I can learn from this man," said the young Dale at the time. Even in the TV series, Cooper seems cowed by Earle's intellect. "Windom Earle's mind is like a diamond. It's cold and hard and brilliant," he says.

At the very least, you have to give him credit for planning ahead. What Earle was *actually* up to, Cooper eventually learned, was a scheme so elaborate it borders on the surreal. He committed at least one murder (and probably more), covering his tracks but ensuring his wife, Caroline, would witness the aftermath of the crime. He simultaneously encouraged a flirtation between Cooper and Caroline by engineering a series of apparently random encounters between them. Once Caroline was a federal witness and Cooper was assigned to protect her, Earle pretended to leave town, leaving *just* enough clues to make both Cooper and Caroline suspect he had gone insane while secretly monitoring their safe house. Then—once they'd consummated the affair he'd worked so hard to nudge them into—Earle snuck in and stabbed them both, killing Caroline and giving Cooper a lifelong case of survivor's guilt.

But wait! Literally all of that was a cover story for his real goal: Gaining entrance to the Black Lodge. While cleaning up some inconsistencies between that book and the TV series, *The Secret History of Twin Peaks* also deepens Earle's connection to the show's lore by revealing that he was a key member of Gordon Cole's Blue Rose task force. He was also, Major Briggs reveals, a major player in Project Blue Book, becoming dangerously obsessed with the woods surrounding Twin Peaks.

Did you get all that? Windom Earle feels a little bit like what you'd get if you took a few of pop culture's most iconic villains and threw them in a blender. He is, like Hannibal Lecter, a tactical mastermind, thinking a half-dozen moves ahead of his adversary. He is, like James Bond's nemesis Ernst Stavro Blofeld, a master of disguise—using three distinct costumes and characters to insinuate himself with Audrey, Donna, and Shelly as he slinks around Twin Peaks. He conjures up the gleeful, ghoulish malice of the Joker, pretending to be an old friend of Doc Hayward's and leaving, as his address, the cemetery where the actual, long-dead man is buried. He soliloquizes like a Shakespeare villain—usually at Leo Johnson, whose stupor makes him an easy audience—while demonstrating abilities that seem, at times, to border on the supernatural: In one surreal, unexplained moment, he suddenly has chalk-white skin and a black tongue.

Or, to put it another way: Windom Earle is a lot. Actor Kenneth Welsh was a close friend of *Twin Peaks* writer Robert Engels, who recommended him for the role, and Welsh really makes a meal out of it. To be clear, that's not a complaint. As *Twin Peaks*' second season drifts toward a series of fruitless detours, Earle's lurking presence provides some much-needed ballast, drawing many of the show's characters back together and giving Cooper a compelling reason to keep kicking around Twin Peaks.

But if Earle was initially conceived as a more verbose, intellectual alternative to the feral evil of BOB, the character always threatened to descend into pure camp. That indulgence would almost certainly have been completed in the season two finale as originally scripted, which included—and this is not a joke—a Black Lodge–set sequence in which Earle, in top hat and tails, performs the Cole Porter standard "Anything Goes." Credit belongs to David Lynch for reworking the excesses of the season two finale, including dumping most of the florid dialogue written for Earle. Sometimes less really is more: He's never scarier than when he suddenly rants "Take a look at that! Twelve rainbow trout!" at Annie Blackburn. But in every version of this story, Earle's arc was destined to conclude the same way: in defeat.

In the end, what I like best about Windom Earle is how easily he's snuffed out. Having traveled across the country and wormed his way into the Black Lodge, he's ready for his crowning triumph: Taking Dale Cooper's soul. But the moment he tries—stabbing Cooper just as he'd stabbed him years once before—BOB appears and literally reverses time to prevent the attack. "HE IS WRONG. HE CAN'T ASK FOR YOUR SOUL. I'LL TAKE HIS," BOB snarls. Earle screams, but even his death rattle is stripped away from him. "BE QUIET," BOB orders, and he immediately falls silent, completely at the mercy of the Black Lodge's rules, inscrutable to any mortal dumb enough to enter it.

The message is clear. When compared to pure, carnal evil of BOB, Earle is a joke—someone to be dispatched without a second thought so the finale's true horrors can be unleashed. Maybe it's best to return to a chess metaphor: Windom, in the end, is a pawn who thought he could promote himself into something much, much stronger. But let's be honest: He was never going to make it all the way across the board.

Chapter 8

THE LAST SEVEN DAYS OF LAURA PALMER

It does not take a PhD-level degree in semiotics to decode the opening scene of *Twin Peaks: Fire Walk with Me*. After the opening credits, which play out over fuzzy blue static and a bluesy Angelo Badalamenti number, the camera pulls out to reveal that everything we've seen so far has been unfolding on a TV screen. That doesn't last long. Just seconds after the image becomes clear, the TV explodes in a shower of sparks—violently destroyed by a pipe.

TV is dead; long live *Twin Peaks*. The series—the movie seems to be saying—has finally broken out of the medium that had both spawned and restrained it. In *Fire Walk with Me*, there would be no breaks for commercials or scheduling snafus that made the story impossible to follow; no concessions on sex or violence to please a TV network's Standards and Practices department; and no hand-wringing executives, or even other creatives voices, urging Lynch to do anything besides tell his story exactly as he wanted to tell it.

It had not been an easy path to get here. Noting, correctly, that the series had maintained cultural cachet abroad even as audiences in the United States bailed, mega-producer Aaron Spelling had considered reviving *Twin Peaks* as a TV series that could be syndicated for both the remaining fans domestically and a hungry audience internationally. But Spelling balked at the $500,000-per-episode cost, and the *Twin Peaks* continuation project ultimately emerged as the first film in a three-picture deal Lynch signed with French producer and distributor CIBY 2000.

But if this *Twin Peaks* continuation was going to be a film, it was heading into largely uncharted territory. With the exception of *Star Trek*, there were few precedents for TV shows successfully making the leap to the big screen, and the established narrative was that *Twin Peaks* had lost its way long before cancellation, alienating even its most loyal fans by the time ABC finally put the show out of its misery. If audiences hadn't bothered to keep up with the show when it was beamed into their living rooms—or so the logic went—why would they drive to a movie theater and pay a premium for more *Twin Peaks*?

That's part of the reason Frost preferred the idea of a sequel movie, which would, at least, give those who had stuck with *Twin Peaks* some closure on the many cliff-hangers of season two. Frost says the sequel movie he'd had in mind would have been a similar story—albeit much more compressed—to the story that unfolded decades later in *Twin Peaks: The Return*. He was much less enamored of a prequel. Though he signed off on *Fire Walk with Me*, and is credited as an executive producer, he played no creative role in its screenplay, which was cowritten by David Lynch and Robert Engels.

When asked today, Frost is not merely polite about *Fire Walk with Me*. He seems sincerely appreciative of what the movie accomplished, and he seamlessly integrated many of its ideas—and added coherence to the ones that felt fascinating but half formed—into *Twin Peaks: The Return*. But there's no way around the fact that *Fire Walk with Me* was also Lynch asserting complete creative control over *Twin Peaks* for the first time, and doing so with the assistance of another writer who Frost had personally brought into the *Twin Peaks* fold. "That was not great for Mark and [Engels], who'd been friends for years," says Harley Peyton.

For Engels, the collaboration was a natural progression of a rapport that had developed during *Twin Peaks*' second season. "David and I started to write more together and became friends during production of the show," said Engels. "After the show stopped, David and I began to work on a couple of different scripts." One such script, *The Dream of the Bovine*, concerned men who used to be cows, and included a character, to be performed entirely in drag, that they'd written for Marlon Brando. (He declined.) When Lynch told Engels that Francis Bouyges, the head of CIBY 2000, was intrigued by the idea of a *Twin Peaks* movie, they didn't waste any time. They began writing the script that became *Twin Peaks: Fire Walk with Me* that afternoon.

Engels, for his part, is happy to give most of the credit for *Fire Walk with Me* to Lynch's creative energy. "I was the typist," he says. "I don't mean that as a complaint, but I would type it out. And the great thing about David is: It's bottomless. We just kept going. We obviously knew it had to be cut back, but then you'd think, *Well, maybe they'll do two movies.*" As Engels recalls, the goal, from the start, was that *Fire Walk with Me* could serve as both prequel and sequel to *Twin Peaks*. "We wanted to show how Laura got there and what happened after. That was our concept, to do both ends," he says.

The net they cast was unusually (and, based on what Lynch eventually shot, needlessly) broad. They toyed with everything from a prologue set during the 1953 presidential inauguration of Dwight Eisenhower to an elaborate origin story for the evil denizens of the Black Lodge, who had come from a planet made of creamed corn and were desperate to return to it. "We would hit on something, and then we would do ten pages of that," said Engels.

None of that was actually filmed, but it does give some sense of the rambling creative process that led to *Twin Peaks: Fire Walk with Me*. The final cut of the movie, which spans two hours and fourteen minutes, also has a full ninety-two minutes of deleted scenes—essentially a second feature film, left entirely on the cutting-room floor. "We shot over a million feet of film in forty-two days," recalls director of photography Ron García. As the subtitle on Lynch and Engels' screenplay indicates, the excesses of *Fire Walk with Me* would eventually be pared down so the film could tell a more focused, harrowing story: "Teresa Banks and the Last Seven Days of Laura Palmer."

There was, theoretically, a template for the Teresa Banks investigation to follow: Scott Frost's *The Autobiography of F.B.I. Special Agent Dale Cooper*. The book includes exhaustive notes from Cooper's time as the lead agent on the Teresa Banks case, including the discovery of the letter *T* under her fingernail and an encounter with the obstructionist Sheriff Cable (Gary Bullock)—a belated justification for Cooper's initial tetchiness with Truman in the *Twin Peaks* pilot. Teresa Banks was BOB's first known victim, but the circumstances of her murder and the subsequent FBI investigation had been described only briefly and hazily in the original series. Including it would also ensure that Cooper, *Twin Peaks*' most popular character, would play a key role in a Laura Palmer-centric prequel that otherwise had no obvious place for him.

There was just one problem: Kyle MacLachlan wasn't interested in playing Cooper anymore. "I think these characters on *Twin Peaks* are kind of cartoony, which is fun but it's not really what I'm hungry to do," he told the *Los Angeles Times* in 1990—and that was *before* the show's second season premiere, when *Twin Peaks* was still the hottest thing on TV. During the second season, he became increasingly concerned that he would be typecast as Cooper. "I was pretty naive about it. At the time I felt like I was trapped in this stale role," he later reflected. If the show's cancellation gave him the excuse to take on new challenges, returning for *Fire Walk with Me* could send the opposite message: That he wasn't capable of much more than *Twin Peaks*.

Laura and Cooper, together at last

He also acknowledged feeling "fairly resentful" about Lynch and Frost's absences during the production of *Twin Peaks*, and frustrated that Lynch wasn't willing to seriously engage with his doubts about the *Fire Walk with Me* script. "I remember it being very violent and disturbing in a way that the show hadn't been," said MacLachlan. "The show *had* been disturbing, but not quite as in-your-face, you know? I think I was sort of, 'Oh, can't we go back to the way it was in the show?' And obviously David wasn't interested in doing that. He was interested in taking it further, you know? And I was resisting that."

So MacLachlan declined to return as Cooper—a loss so significant that it briefly killed *Fire Walk with Me* outright. "The story as conceived relied heavily on the Cooper character," said Lynch/Frost Productions chief executive Ken Scherer in July of 1991. "Kyle no longer wants to do the role. That's unfortunate for *Twin Peaks* . . . We're all very sad." Just a month later, the *Los*

Angeles Times reported an about-face: MacLachlan had "dropped his reservations," and *Fire Walk with Me* was on track to start production in September after all. "We might even have gone on without Kyle, rewriting the script, but his decision to do this makes a great deal of difference," said Lynch/ Frost Productions publicist Gaye Pope at the time.

In reality, MacLachlan had offered a compromise: five days of shooting. It was far less time than Lynch needed to shoot the entirety of the Teresa Banks investigation as scripted, and it resulted in what MacLachlan later acknowledged as "the crack" in their relationship. "I really abused the relationship," he said in a 2000 profile. "I don't know if David and I will work together again. I hope so."

On paper, MacLachlan's polished FBI loafers might have seemed impossible to fill. But MacLachlan's skepticism also led to another one of Lynch's "happy accidents" (albeit under unhappier circumstances than usual): the creation of a brand-new FBI agent named Chester "Chet" Desmond (Chris Isaak), who handled the Teresa Banks investigation in Cooper's absence. As Johanna Ray recalls it, finding the right actor to play Desmond wasn't especially challenging. "Chris Isaak was easy. I was a huge fan of his and David liked him," says Ray. And Lynch and Isaak already had a history; Lynch had scored a pivotal scene in *Blue Velvet* with an instrumental version of Isaak's "Gone Ridin'," and played a major role in saving Isaak's music career when he used "Wicked Game" in *Wild at Heart*, prompting a belated spike in radio play that turned Isaak's 1989 album *Heart Shaped World* from a flop into a multiplatinum hit. "It was like having the laundry call and say, 'We found a lottery ticket in your jacket, and oh, by the way, it's a winning number,'" said Isaak.

Though Isaak had virtually no acting experience when Lynch cast him in *Fire Walk with Me*, his stiffness turns out to be an asset. It's hard to imagine Cooper—or at least, the boyish, cheerfully quirky version of Cooper that had become the character's default mode for much of *Twin Peaks*—at the center of this very strange investigation. Chet Desmond's unfamiliarity to the audience makes him the ideal point of view for this deliberately jarring reentry into the *Twin Peaks* universe, which accrues much of its power by veering away from everything fans might have expected from a *Twin Peaks* movie.

Desmond is joined in the investigation by fellow FBI agent Sam Stanley (Kiefer Sutherland), who was briefly name-checked by Cooper in the *Twin Peaks* pilot: "Don't go to Sam. Albert seems a little more on the ball." Sam, a dweeb in a bowtie who follows Desmond around like an eager puppy, is played against type by Sutherland, who recalled *Fire Walk with Me* coming at "an odd time for me, working-wise and professionally." Stanley's grab bag of eccentric traits includes the ability to appraise, with apparent accuracy, the total cost of every object in a room, but Sutherland—who was largely

"You stick with Chet. He's got his own M.O."

unfamiliar with *Twin Peaks*—feels, in retrospect, that he played Stanley too *straight*. "I think had I known the show a little better and known how quirky it was—even though I think my character *was* quite quirky—I might've gone a little farther with it," he said.

It's Gordon Cole—played, of course, by Lynch himself—who sets the story into motion. Instead of a traditional briefing on the Teresa Banks murder, Cole introduces Desmond and Stanley to Lil (Kimberly Ann Cole), a red-haired woman in a red dress who does an odd little dance. Stanley is puzzled, and so are we, but Desmond is kind enough to decipher it. Lil was grimacing and making a fist to warn them about a sour, possibly violent reception from the local authorities; she was walking in place to indicate that legwork will be required; and she was wearing a tailored dress, which Desmond says is Gordon's code for drugs. Most notable is the blue rose pinned to Lil's dress. "But I can't tell you about that," says Desmond. It's a scene that almost seems to be poking fun at viewers and critics who approach Lynch's images as codes that can be cracked (even if the blue rose itself proved tantalizing enough that Lynch and Mark Frost formally explained its meaning, twenty-five years later, in *Twin Peaks: The Return*).

Gordon's code was designed to prepare Desmond and Stanley for some unpleasantness when they arrived in Deer Meadow, Washington, but it's hard to overstate the ugliness of their reception. The Deer Meadow sheriff's department is as hostile as advertised, and in ways that seem specifically engineered to make it feel like the evil doppelgänger of Twin Peaks' dependable law enforcement branch. Desmond and Stanley are met with days-old coffee by a smirking deputy sheriff and a cackling receptionist—two obvious stand-ins for fan-favorites Andy Brennan and Lucy Moran, but drained of charm and filled back up with menace. When Sheriff Truman flipped over the corpse in the *Twin Peaks* pilot, he remarked, with shock and dismay, it was Laura Palmer; Sheriff Cable has already shrugged off Teresa

Banks as an anonymous drifter and is openly disinterested in attempting to solve her murder. This is what passes for law enforcement in the darker vision of *Fire Walk with Me*; Truman, Andy, and Lucy don't appear in the final cut of the movie at all.

The doppelgänger effects are doubled when Desmond and Stanley follow a lead to Hap's Diner, the grim twenty-four-hour eatery where Teresa Banks worked part-time. If Twin Peaks' Double R Diner is, as Cooper once remarked, "where pies go when they die," Hap's seems to be where bad coffee and stale cigarette breath goes to die. They're greeted, if you can call it that, by a sour waitress named Irene, who asks if Desmond and Stanley would like to hear the diner's specials before snorting that the diner doesn't have any specials. She eventually tells them she thinks Teresa's death was "a freak accident," as if someone being beaten to death and floated down a river is just one of those things that happens sometimes. Across the counter, an old man repeatedly, uselessly asks, "Are you talking about that little girl that got murdered?" Every lead is a dead end; whether they knew Teresa or not, no one really seems to care that she's dead.

Maybe not even Chet Desmond, who is obviously capable but bored enough to trick Stanley into dumping his coffee onto his own lap for the fun of it. It's only when the investigation takes them to the Fat Trout Trailer Park, where Teresa lived before her murder, that Chet seems to recognize that something bigger and stranger must be happening. The catalyst appears to be a conversation with Carl Rodd, the cantankerous trailer park manager played by Harry Dean Stanton, who slips into a strange reverie in the middle of their questioning. "I've already gone places," he says haltingly. "I just want to stay where I am."

This line, which does not appear in the *Fire Walk with Me* shooting script, was reportedly conceived by Lynch on the day of filming. "Harry Dean Stanton sent chills down my spine," recalls Ron García. "He went deep down, and it scared the crap out of me. That's where he was, at that time." But unplanned as it was, it's the moment at which the petty cruelties of Deer Meadow and its residents give way to something more unfathomable. We know *something* needs to happen to Chet Desmond; there's a reason, after all, that it's Cooper who ends up as the lead agent on the Laura Palmer case. But the manner of his disappearance is a harbinger for just how powerful the Black Lodge can be. Finding Teresa's missing ring on a mound of dirt at the trailer park, Desmond touches it and promptly disappears. When Cooper himself arrives, now tasked with tracking down the missing FBI agent, he finds a car with "Let's rock" scrawled in cursive across its windshield.

Given that MacLachlan was only willing to give five days to the *Fire Walk with Me* shoot, David Lynch found a way to make the most of them. In the drab corridors of the FBI's Philadelphia field office, Cooper, Gordon Cole, and Albert Rosenfield are startled by the sudden arrival of Phillip Jeffries (David Bowie), a fellow agent who's been missing for two years. Jeffries raves like a lunatic about a meeting between the forces of evil that he witnessed above a convenience store; refuses to talk about someone named Judy; and disappears just as suddenly and inexplicably as he came.

It's a barnstormer of a scene, and it needed a performer who could equal its mesmerizing strangeness. It needed David Bowie, and David Lynch used his own considerable mystique to draw the iconoclastic performer into the world of *Twin Peaks*. "He was very hard to get through to," says Johanna Ray. "You had to get to his very personal assistant, who really arranged everything for him. And David ended up getting on the phone with her." As Ray recalls it, Bowie might even have been pitched a bigger role: "He was a choice to—oh gosh, I can't remember whether it was *him*, precisely—but, I think, to take over Kyle's role if he ended up not doing it."

Instead, it's MacLachlan's familiar diction to Diane that takes us out of the Deer Meadow prologue. "The clues that were found by Special Agent

Desmond and Agent Stanley have led to dead ends," he says. "The letter that was extracted from beneath the fingernail of Teresa Banks gives me the feeling that the killer will strike again. But like the song goes, 'who knows where, or when?'"

After all this strangeness, it's a relief when *Fire Walk with Me* finally cuts, at the thirty-three-minute mark, to the familiar Twin Peaks sign, with the warm, nostalgic theme song blasting over the soundtrack. The relief does not last long. This Twin Peaks is, admittedly, more inviting than Deer Meadow—but it's not the Twin Peaks we know from the TV show, because that's not the Twin Peaks that was occupied by Laura Palmer. By zooming in on Laura in the last week of her life, Lynch dials down the quirkiness while ratcheting up the horror. If the TV show, at times, seemed to lose track of the unspeakably awful violation at the heart of its story, *Fire Walk with Me* ensures that viewers will never forget it.

The sense of not-quite-rightness is heightened by the absence of many of the TV show's most familiar actors. Many—including Michael Ontkean, Joan Chen, Russ Tamblyn, Warren Frost, Michael Horse, Wendy Robie, and Don S. Davis—filmed scenes that Lynch ultimately cut from the movie. But a few other *Twin Peaks* regulars, including Sherilyn Fenn and Richard Beymer, opted out. Their absences may have been disappointing for fans, but neither was especially essential for the story *Fire Walk with Me* was telling. Audrey herself makes it clear several times that she and Laura weren't especially close, and Ben was just one of several older men who preyed on Laura.

But there was one major character *Fire Walk with Me* couldn't do without: Donna Hayward. When Lara Flynn Boyle declined an offer to return, the role of Laura's best friend needed to be recast.

Long before she was invited into the *Fire Walk with Me* ensemble, Moira Kelly had been a *Twin Peaks* fan. "It was such an event for me and my friends," she says. "We were pretty hooked. We had pie parties. To us, it was just like, *This is not like anything that anyone else is doing*. We felt like we were on the cusp of something amazing."

Kelly's first meeting with Lynch was appropriately Lynchian. "I was surprised to even get a call," she says. "I drove over to his house and walked into the sitting room, and there was a couch and a standing lamp—and nothing else. I said, 'Did you just move in?' And he said, 'Oh, no, Moira. I've lived here for years.' He was like a kid. He said, 'I've got to show you something. I've been working on gifts for friends. I want to know what you think of them.' And he opened up his refrigerator, and he had five or six wooden plaques—and on each was a beautifully labeled, beautifully dissected animal, like a frog or a little bird. My first thought was, *Wow, I'd love to get something like that*. And then the second thing I thought was, *You know, if this wasn't David Lynch, I don't think I'd be coming out of this house alive*."

Lynch and Kelly chatted amiably for forty minutes, but it wasn't until she walked to the door to leave that Lynch popped the question: "How would you like to be Donna?" Kelly replied that she'd love it, even as she recognized the unique challenge ahead of her. "I remember feeling absolute pressure," she says. "I knew people loved the show, loved the characters, loved the actors. And here I am, stepping into the role of a prominent character."

Kelly never spoke with Lara Flynn Boyle. "It wasn't that I didn't want to. I looked up to her, in a way," she says. But she was unsure, at that time, if Boyle had passed on *Fire Walk with Me* or if Lynch had simply decided to recast Donna, and she was hesitant to ask. Instead, she rationalized the differences between herself and Boyle in acting terms: Because Donna's life was so radically altered by Laura's murder, it made a strange kind of sense that she would look different, too. "There really *were* two Donnas," she says. "You know, we're embodying the same character, but they really are coming from very different places. I tried to convey the more naive, starry-eyed side of Donna, before the loss of innocence—the loss of idealism—that I think all young people kind of go through at some point in their lives."

The idea of revisiting a *Twin Peaks* character *before* Laura's murder also appealed to James Marshall. "I liked that *Fire Walk with Me* was before [the show]," he says. "Laura wasn't dead yet, and the lines were written . . . not *cocky*, but James has got a smile when he's saying them. And then he'd get pissed off, a little. He's got dynamics. He's not just very, very sad. There was almost this levity—even though it was heavy."

But if Laura's secret boyfriend was getting the chance to lighten up a little, her official boyfriend was reentering *Twin Peaks* at one of the darkest valleys of his own story. We know, through the stories Bobby Briggs tells in the original series, that Laura had him wrapped around her finger. But it's another thing entirely to watch Laura manipulate him into becoming a drug dealer, and eventually a murderer, with little more than a smile. Dana Ashbrook calls his dark scene in the woods with Laura—which culminates with Bobby shooting Deer Meadow's drug-dealing deputy while Laura, drunk and high, cackles maniacally—"one of my favorite scenes in the entire thing, including the series," owing largely to the intensity of Lee's performance. At one screening, said Ashbrook, "I was sitting next to my girlfriend and she said: '*Wow, Sheryl is so annoying in this scene.*' And she *was*. I remember her being annoying while filming. It was late at night; it was cold. It was an amazing kind of scene, and she really did go for being one of those people that are so out-of-control drunk that you cannot get them to sober up." Even her improvisations were provocations. "Sheryl was doing things like putting her finger in my ear, and I said "*Stop it*," said Ashbrook. "She just did that stuff. It was all her and not scripted."

That anecdote is one of many windows into the terrifying intensity with which Sheryl Lee threw herself into the last week of Laura Palmer's life.

Method acting is typically associated with a specific kind of very acclaimed, very difficult actor—one who is so committed to the integrity of his performance that he must stay in character at all times. The process often encompasses, and is used to excuse, bizarre behaviors and general peevishness toward a cast and crew for the duration of a shoot. This imposition should be tolerated, proponents argue, because the end result is a performance that simply couldn't be achieved any other way.

Sheryl Lee did not employ the Method technique in this fashion. She was, by all accounts, an incredibly personable and generous actress during the filming of *Fire Walk with Me*. On the last day of filming, she took the megaphone, thanked everyone who had worked on *Fire Walk With Me*, and gifted them custom-made lighters with the film's title stamped on them. By then, Ron García says, he was just relieved Lee had made it through the shoot intact. "The *danger* we thought Sheryl Lee was in. She almost had a complete breakdown," he says. "And that's what made that film so powerful. I think she's not the same person, after all of that. After I finished shooting, I could not watch it for ten years. Because I saw [what it did to] Sheryl Lee," he says.

If Lee was practicing her own version of Method acting, it was an unusually selfless one, in which all the pain and suffering Laura experienced was held inside herself, not inflicted on the other people working on the movie. "My process is different for every character I play, but I never played a character that required so much of my body, mind, heart, and soul that there was very little space left for me during that time—for me, Sheryl, during that time," said Lee in 2017. It wasn't until more than a week after filming had wrapped, when Lee had returned to Los Angeles, that she was standing in a grocery store line and realized, to her relief, that she was finally having her own thoughts, not Laura's.

Fire Walk with Me required Lee to be stripped naked, both literally and emotionally, and she agreed to everything Lynch asked—with one exception. "There was only one thing that David ever asked me to do that I said 'No way,'" said Lee. It was during a scene in which Laura is sexually assaulted in her childhood bedroom. By then, Lee had grown accustomed to playing the same scene several times to account for the ever-shifting identities in *Twin Peaks*—in this case, opposite both Ray Wise and Frank Silva, so the scene could be cut together to show both Leland and BOB raping Laura. But Lynch felt inspired to shoot the scene a third time with an even less conventional scene partner. When Lee asked who, Lynch said it was coming in right now—"And I just felt my blood turn cold. I knew that there was something I was not going to want to be doing," said Lee.

Lynch's idea? Shooting the scene again, with Lee staring into the eyes of a dead pig. A pig's head had duly been procured by the crew. When Lee said she wouldn't do it, she recalled, Lynch was incredulous: "Really? Why?" (It was Ron García who ultimately backed Lee, telling Lynch that the scene would pose possible dangers to Lee, if the pig's head fell, that the production simply wasn't prepared to address.)

This was the kind of thing Lynch simply hadn't had the time or license to do in his *Twin Peaks* episodes, and he was making the most of total creative control by following inspiration wherever it led him. During one memorably bizarre scene—as Lynch used a special camera designed for medical purposes to shoot extreme close-ups on the mouths of BOB, the Man from Another Place, and other assorted Black Lodge denizens—Ken Scherer confessed he couldn't figure out what was happening in the scene, but was confident it would result in a great cinematic moment. "This is the common feeling," wrote Charlotte Fraisse, who kept the official production diary.

Lee was fortunate enough to have her own sourcebook: Jennifer Lynch's *The Secret Diary of Laura Palmer*, which was released almost exactly one year before *Fire Walk with Me* began shooting. When Jennifer Lynch was twelve, she recalled, she told her father that she fantasized about stealing another girl's diary and seeing what it contained. "I wanted to know if she was scared of the same things I was, if she yearning for the same things I was," she said. Years later, David Lynch recalled the conversation and invited Jennifer to write the tie-in novel from Laura's perspective. "I had to basically become her," said Jennifer Lynch. Out of necessity, she was the first person, other than David Lynch and Mark Frost, to know who killed Laura Palmer.

Written when Lynch was in her early twenties, *The Secret Diary of Laura Palmer* is an accomplished and remarkably dark novel. Beginning in Laura's early adolescence, it spends nearly two hundred pages chronicling the five years in which Laura's natural entrance into young womanhood is poisoned by abuse—most notably by BOB, whose violations include inserting himself into the book's pages, but also by other men and women Laura encounters. The result, as Bobby screamed at Laura's funeral, is a portrait of how an entire community can fail a girl in trouble. "The girl who received this diary on her twelfth birthday has been dead for years, and I who took her place have done nothing but make a mockery of the dreams she once had. I'm sixteen years old, I'm a cocaine addict, a prostitute who fucks her father's employers, not to mention half the fucking town," writes Lynch in a characteristically wrenching passage.

Described by *The New York Times* as "a twisted variation on *The Diary of Anne Frank*," and by the *Associated Press* as "*Rebecca of Sunnybrook Farm* on a four-year bender," *The Secret Diary of Laura Palmer* became an unlikely bestseller. It was undeniably boosted by viewers desperately seeking clues to the "Who killed Laura Palmer?" mystery, but it was also an uncompromising and well-reviewed novel in its own right, and its influence on the arc of *Twin Peaks* was ultimately an indirect one. "Truth be told, I don't think my

All of Twin Peaks turns out for Laura's funeral

father ever read the diary—which is both totally expected and a little sad," said Jennifer Lynch in 2013. But the book had a major impact on Sheryl Lee, shaping her performance as she labored to bring Laura's traumas and tragedies to the big screen. "It helped tremendously," she said. "I felt like Jennifer was in my head, meaning Laura's head. And I always feel this intimate connection with Jennifer because of that. There's something there that connects us, having experienced that character that way."

Lee's other key resource was David Lynch himself. It was Lynch, after all, who felt he had spotted something remarkable about Lee in the brief video of Laura and Donna at a picnic that appears in the *Twin Peaks* pilot. That moment led him to create the character of Maddy Ferguson just to give Lee something bigger to do; now he had crafted an entire film around her—full of challenging scenes, but also a rare opportunity for a young, relatively untested actress to do career-defining work. "I would look at scenes and go, *I have absolutely no idea how I'm going to do this, but I know* [David Lynch] *will help me and guide me, and I can lean into that and trust him,"* said Lee.

Sound design had always been a key part of Lynch's creative process, and he used it liberally on set, playing music as a way of indirectly shaping the mood of a scene and the actors' performances. "I'd never been in a scene before where there were loudspeakers. They were playing kind of punky, underground rock," says Moira Kelly. "It was coming out of the high school, and he told everyone who was coming out the doors, 'Just move to the music. Come across and walk down the path.'" That instruction, vague as it was, was more than Lynch usually offered. "He gives very little direction," says Kelly. "It's almost like he knew, by casting you, that he had what he wanted in you. You brought that, and he would just let you explore that. If you were on the money, he would give you the thumbs-up and say, 'Hot dog! We can move on!'"

Music is also central to one of *Fire Walk with Me*'s most iconic and punishing scenes, as Laura and Donna take a trip to a grim, grimy bar on the other side of the Canadian border. As the thudding bass line of Angelo Badalamenti's "The Pink Room" drones on and on—played loudly enough that the scene's dialogue is subtitled—we spend nearly ten unbroken minutes watching grown men, including Jacques Renault, prey on teenage girls. Donna has followed Laura to this nightmarish place out of stubborn loyalty, but she's in over her head; in the end, it's Laura who saves *her* from hell, literally dragging Donna away from a man who has spiked her drink and seems prepared to rape her on a bar table.

"We were in there for fourteen or fifteen hours, with no air," says Ron García. "I finally told David, 'Everyone's gotta take a break here.' I didn't ask for anything until I thought we really needed it, but my job is to protect the crew, and also the actors." By then, the music had been so omnipresent that it was "in the cells of our being," said Sheryl Lee. "That was a tough shoot. You feel very exposed and very vulnerable," says Moira Kelly. "But what I really did appreciate is that everyone who was in that scene had already been there for hours, in a very vulnerable position. You know, there were a lot of topless people. Sheryl and I had been in that environment for a while, so it kind of allowed us to feel safer [when we were topless]. There was a camaraderie. You didn't feel, all of a sudden, like you were terribly exposed. I think that was on purpose, to make us feel comfortable. And I loved [David Lynch] for that."

The "Pink Room" sequence represents one nightmare for Laura: the possibility that Donna will be corrupted by her loyalty and proximity to her best friend. But as disturbing as it is to watch the bar's patrons descend on the girls like wolves seeking prey, *Twin Peaks* fans already know that Laura's greatest threat is under her own roof.

For Ray Wise, *Fire Walk with Me* was a chance to flesh out a side of Leland he hadn't even known about for much of *Twin Peaks*, and he eagerly took it. "Oddly enough, by that time—emotionally—I was able to handle it much easier than I had in the original series," says Wise. "It gave me a completeness of the character of Leland. Even though it was very dark, and the whole idea of doing that to his own daughter was just too terrible to even think about for long periods of time. But to do it fully . . . it gave me a kind of satisfaction that I hadn't really felt when I did the series. I was able to turn that little click in my brain that went from Leland to BOB, and it became easier and easier to do."

In the immediate aftermath of Leland's death in the original series, *Twin Peaks* worked overtime to make it clear that BOB, and not Leland, was responsible for Laura's rape and murder. "There are things dark and heinous in this world. Things too horrible to tell our children. Your husband fell victim to one of these long ago when he was innocent and trusting.

Leland did not do these things, not the Leland that you knew," says Cooper to Sarah Palmer on the day of Leland's funeral. He goes as far as speaking for Laura, saying that she welcomed Leland and forgave him.

It's a kindness that Sarah is grateful to receive in her time of unfathomable grief. But *Fire Walk with Me* at least raises the possibility that Cooper was too quick to absolve Leland entirely. As the movie fills out the details of Teresa Banks' murder, we see Leland pay her for sex, ask her to arrange an orgy with some of her friends, and hastily "chicken out" when he sees that one of the girls Teresa has invited is Laura. At no point, in any of these scenes, does Lynch depict Leland turning into BOB, or even seeing his reflection in a mirror. It's not that BOB doesn't exist in *Fire Walk with Me*; by the end, the movie has added extensively to the show's supernatural lore, revealing that the Man from Another Place is actually the arm Mike cut off and that BOB is harvesting something called "garmonbozia," which the subtitles translate as "pain and sorrow," from all the evil he inflicts on the world.

Still, the lines between Leland and BOB feel blurrier in *Fire Walk with Me*, and purposefully so. It's admittedly difficult to imagine Leland Palmer, respected lawyer and family man, bothering with Jack the Ripper–style flourishes like the letter under the fingernail that will later link Teresa's murder to Laura's. But it's troublingly easy to imagine Leland Palmer, respected lawyer and family man, murdering a sex worker who could utterly destroy his life if he missed even a single blackmail payment.

It's the thin line between BOB and Leland that makes *Fire Walk with Me*'s domestic scenes so hard to watch. Anyone who watched these scenes out of context, without any knowledge of BOB or the Black Lodge, would essentially be watching a straightforward depiction of abuse by a tyrannical patriarch. In one memorably horrifying dining room sequence, Leland taunts Laura about her lovers and insists she wash her hands. When Sarah

A family photo

gingerly tells Leland Laura doesn't like what he's doing, he snarls back, "How do you know what she likes?" That scene, says Ray Wise, "was chilling to *me*, when I did it. It was like I was outside of myself, watching myself do that. And scaring the hell out of myself."

Like any prequel, the greatest flaw of *Fire Walk with Me* is the difficulty it has generating suspense. Sheryl Lee is brilliant at conveying Laura's slow-dawning horror that her abuser is her father, but this isn't likely to be new information for anyone who bothered to go to a *Twin Peaks* movie. In fact, we've already heard about most of what happens in the movie secondhand, from recurring *Twin Peaks* characters like Bobby Briggs and Harold Smith. Most of all, we know, by the end, that Laura will be dead and wrapped in plastic, and that's exactly what happens, with Lynch directing a longer and more violent version of the railroad car murder than the impressionistic version he delivered in the season two premiere.

At the same time, one of the more unexpected things about *Fire Walk with Me* is that it is also, in a sense, the sequel movie Mark Frost had in mind. Owing to the nonlinear nature of time in the Black Lodge, Laura receives two nocturnal visitors in *Fire Walk with Me* who she never would have crossed paths with in life: Agent Cooper, who warns her not to take the gold ring that will later become important in *Twin Peaks: The Return*, and Annie Blackburn—bloodied after her time in Black Lodge during the series finale—who asks Laura to write a diary entry explaining that the good Dale is in the Lodge and can't leave. This latter thread, in particular, seems to be setting the stage for a sequel in which Cooper's allies discover Laura's note and save him from the Black Lodge. "I wouldn't mind if they turned this thing into a series of movies. We could just keep spinning the tale," said Michael Ontkean, who was ultimately cut from *Fire Walk with Me*, shortly before its release.

But any possibility of a *Twin Peaks* sequel movie was essentially obliterated by the dismal reception to *Fire Walk with Me*. On May 16, 1992, *Fire Walk with Me* premiered at the Cannes Film Festival, where Lynch had won the Palme d'or for *Wild at Heart* just two years earlier. Even as Lynch accepted that award from the jury, *Wild at Heart* was recognized as a polarizing choice to receive the festival's prestigious top award—but where that movie had, at least, divided critics and viewers, *Fire Walk with Me* was met with nearly uniform hostility.

Robert Engels strongly disputes the oft-repeated story that *Fire Walk with Me* was booed at Cannes. "There were no boos. I was there. There were no boos. There might have been a lukewarm reaction, but people weren't pissed off," he said.

But the reviews that emerged upon the movie's domestic release in August are uncontestable. *Fire Walk with Me* "proceeds from no artistic conviction, just from a cynical desire to squeeze a few more bucks from the already overworked corpse of Laura Palmer," wrote *The Boston Globe*'s Jay Carr. "David Lynch probably should have let Laura Palmer stay dead," wrote *The Hollywood Reporter*'s Robert Osborne. "It's not the worst movie ever made; it just seems to be," wrote *The New York Times*'s Vincent Canby. Harley Peyton recalls walking out of a *Fire Walk with Me* screening feeling rattled by how much he despised *Twin Peaks* without Mark Frost balancing out David Lynch. "I haven't seen it since, so in fairness, it could be tremendous," he says. "But I was so furious that Mark was not involved. I just hated it. I hated it from start to finish. That's probably unfair, but it just felt like such a betrayal to me. And how could it not feel like a betrayal to Mark?"

Fire Walk with Me opened in just 691 theaters in the United States, and was handily outgrossed in its opening weekend by the Nicolas Cage rom-com *Honeymoon in Vegas*, the horror sequel *Pet Sematary Two*, and the ninth weekend of Sony's hit *A League of Their Own*. *Fire Walk with Me* ultimately grossed $4.2 million—which was, even by the most conservative accounting, less than half of the movie's production budget. The movie's critical and commercial failure seemed to vindicate ABC's belief that *Twin Peaks* had lost its way, and lost any hope of a loyal audience in the process.

None of this surprised David Lynch, who had been preparing for a fall. "They warned me if you're on the cover of *Time*, you've got two years' bad luck coming," Lynch reflected a decade later. "And a black cloud did come over me, and when the black cloud comes over, there's nothing you can do about it. Nothing. And you look out and you wonder, 'How come these things are happening and people are saying these things?' It's just the way it is. It's just part of the deal. And then you wonder, 'How long will the cloud be there?'"

There was one major consolation: *Fire Walk with Me* had not been another *Dune*. "With *Dune*, I sold out on that early on, because I didn't have final cut, and it was a commercial failure, so I died two times with that," said Lynch.

"With *Fire Walk with Me*, it didn't go over well at the time, but I loved it so I only died once." Love it or hate it, Lynch had made the movie he wanted to make.

At the very least, the actors who starred in *Fire Walk with Me* were quick to realize they had made something special. The late Al Strobel, who reprised his role of Phillip Gerard/Mike, said:

> The critics—who I would think for the most part are educated, intelligent people—couldn't see that this was more a piece of art than it was a movie. The juxtaposition of horror and beauty, which is something I think David strived for there, has an elevating sense that brings out things in your mind and in your heart and in your soul, like a very fine piece of art. Like a painting does. And the critics didn't see that, and that made me angry, because I thought they would be intelligent enough to do so.

"The whole business about being booed at the Cannes film festival... I look at that as a red badge of courage, you know? Over the years, more people have gravitated toward it and seen it for what it really was, and is. I think it's David's masterpiece," says Ray Wise. For James Marshall, the film's complexity made it uniquely difficult to evaluate on a single viewing. "With poetry, you read it over and over again, and you get different stuff. When you first read a poem, it may seem stupid to you and you don't get it—but you keep reading, and it keeps opening up to you, if it's good. That's what David did. It's real poetry," he says.

In the end, *Fire Walk with Me* turned out to be a slow burn. In the years following its release—and especially as the next generations of *Twin Peaks'* fans discovered it—the movie's reputation shifted from messy to misunderstood to masterpiece. "I'm not at all surprised that it's now a classic to people," says Moira Kelly. "I *am* surprised at who actually approaches me with the DVD and asks me to sign it. It's all ages. All walks of life." At an event for *Twin Peaks: The Return*, Lynch acknowledged that *Fire Walk with Me* may simply have been too far ahead of its time. "People have revisited that film, and they feel differently about it," he said. "When a thing comes out, the feeling in the world—you could call it the collective consciousness is a certain way, and so it dictates how the thing's going to go. Then the collective consciousness changes and people come around. Look at Van Gogh: the guy could not sell one painting and now nobody can afford them."

A final victory lap came on July 16, 2014, when an invitation-only crowd packed into the historic Vista Theatre in Los Angeles for the premiere of *Twin Peaks: The Missing Pieces*—the never-before-released *Fire Walk with Me* deleted scenes, spanning a total of ninety-two minutes, that had long been described as a Holy Grail for the show's fans. Though the scenes don't tell a linear story, they add up to a kind of *Twin Peaks* tone poem, offering glimpses of the town and its residents in the days before Laura's murder brought all the darkness to the surface. Seeing them on the big screen, so many years later, was an intensely moving experience, recalls Ray Wise—including one scene depicting a happy dinner at the Palmer household. "Boy, there was some stuff in those pieces that should have been in the final cut," he says.

In the years following *Fire Walk with Me*'s release, Lee spent years processing what making the movie did to her. "I was still very, very young, and very inexperienced. So I didn't understand, necessarily—psychologically and emotionally and mentally—how to let it go enough. Now, films like this would have a therapist on set," said Sheryl Lee. "As I've gotten older and worked more and studied more, I think I've realized places that it affected me that I wasn't aware had affected me, when I was young." She makes it clear that she doesn't blame David Lynch, or anyone else who worked on the movie, for the toll playing Laura took on her. "Even though the role was challenging, there are films that I've worked on that were not supportive. That's really hard to deal with. This was not that. This was a wonderfully supportive, collaborative, safe environment," said Sheryl Lee. She has, however, seen *Fire Walk with Me* just three times, and told her son not to watch it until she's dead. "I felt like I got the opportunity to come full circle with her. It's very strange to play a dead person, and to never really get to experience her life force. I creatively longed for that," said Lee. "Laura had sort of haunted me."

As difficult as the production had been, that spirit, at last, had been exorcised: as Lee likes to remind audiences, after all of the darkness, Laura finally gets her angel as the movie ends. Shortly after *Fire Walk with Me* wrapped, Sheryl Lee wrote her own personal diary entry—addressed to Laura—which she only shared publicly a full decade later:

> Where do I begin? It has been a little over a month since we stopped filming. In a way, it seems like years and in another, only yesterday. As I sit down now to write this, so many emotions arise. The gift and the experience that you gave me are beyond expression of words. I am aware that your death also allowed an old part of myself to finally die . . . a very self-destructive part. Through you, I came face-to-face with my own dark side. I feel as if I have lived a whole lifetime in those two short months of filming. I will never forget how, the week after we finished, I suddenly became aware that my thoughts were my own again. My mind and my life had been completely occupied by you. You came to me morning, noon, and night—especially night. That was your time, the darkness of midnight. You continually wove your spirit into my

dream world, revealing bits and pieces of yourself, myself, and our fears and struggles. The thing I remember most about you, though, Laura, is your loneliness. That loneliness haunted me. Walking back into my empty hotel room by myself each day, left to deal with the fragmented pieces of my own life, your loneliness would still fill my room. My prayer is that you are now someplace where you are truly loved and at peaceful rest.

JUDY

We're not going to talk about Judy at all. We're going to keep her out of it.

Chapter 9

IS IT HAPPENING AGAIN?

The line could slip right by you: "I'll see you again in 25 years." Spoken by Laura Palmer in the middle of Cooper's nightmarish experience in the Black Lodge in the season two finale, it was originally written to close the loop on Cooper's first Red Room dream, which was captioned "25 years later" in the European version of the pilot.

But it had an entirely different resonance in 2012—twenty years after the release of *Fire Walk with Me*—when Lynch and Frost met at Lynch's private screening room to watch the season two finale for the first time since it had originally aired. "We honestly did not remember that that precise exchange was in the last episode until we sat down to screen the last hour," says Frost. "That moment happened, and we looked at each other, and I think, at that moment, we realized, *Okay, we're doing this.*"

On May 21, 2017—or, if you prefer, twenty-five years, eleven months, three weeks, and one day since *Twin Peaks*' original series finale—*Twin Peaks: The Return*, an eighteen-episode continuation of the original series, premiered on Showtime. It was promoted by the network as "A Limited Event Series," and it was unquestionably an event: the king of cult TV shows returning, after a quarter-century hiatus, to cement its singular place in television history.

Twin Peaks: The Return was only possible because *Twin Peaks*, despite its relatively brief run, never actually died. From the very beginning, the show had attracted an unusually devoted legion of diehard fans, and even when its popularity waned, that core group never fully moved on. *Wrapped in Plastic*, a *Twin Peaks* magazine coedited and published by Craig Miller and John Thorne, ran for seventy-five issues between 1993 and 2005, helping to keep the fandom alive by publishing interviews providing new behind-the-scenes information and in-depth essays that explored *Twin Peaks* from every conceivable angle. Also beginning in 1993, a *Twin Peaks* festival—still held annually in Snoqualmie and North Bend, Washington, where much of the pilot was shot—welcomed fans and *Twin Peaks* alums alike for location tours and trivia contests.

How was *Twin Peaks gaining* fans a decade after its abrupt cancellation? If the show had been ahead of its time when it aired on ABC, it was exactly on time to benefit from the DVD era. Previous home-video releases on VHS and LaserDisc had been specialty products that catered to those who already loved *Twin Peaks*. But with the advent of DVDs, binge-watching became the norm, and suddenly, the hyper-serialized quality that made *Twin Peaks* such a tricky sell when it was erratically scheduled on network television made it an irresistible prospect on DVD. There were hurdles for new viewers to overcome. When Artisan Entertainment released season one on DVD in 2001, they couldn't secure the rights to include the pilot and were forced into the unhappy compromise of including a lengthy plot summary in an accompanying booklet. Season two didn't receive a stand-alone release on DVD until April of 2007 and was quickly supplanted by the *Twin Peaks* Definitive Gold Box Edition that arrived later that year, which collected both seasons and—finally—the original pilot.

The show's influence could also be felt, more indirectly, in the TV shows that came after it. To paraphrase an oft-quoted piece of wisdom about the Velvet Underground: Not everyone watched *Twin Peaks*, but everyone who went out and created a TV show did. David Chase, the creator of HBO's

The Sopranos, cited *Twin Peaks* as the primary influence on the mob drama's trippy dream sequences. AMC openly cribbed from *Twin Peaks* for its murder mystery *The Killing*, which launched with a ubiquitous ad campaign asking, "Who killed Rosie Larsen?" In the run-up to its premiere, Donald Glover described his genre-bending FX dramedy *Atlanta* as "*Twin Peaks* with rappers." And the show's DNA can be found in half-remembered TV knockoffs such as FX's *Push, Nevada*, Fox's *Wayward Pines*, and ABC's *Big Sky*—and, more unexpectedly, in video games, where *Twin Peaks* has been cited as a key influence in everything from the *Alan Wake* series to Nintendo's *The Legend of Zelda: Link's Awakening*, whose creators actively sought Mark Frost's input.

By then, *Twin Peaks* had long stopped being described as a cautionary tale. When J. J. Abrams and Damon Lindelof pitched *Lost* to ABC in 2004, Lindelof recalled, copresident Lloyd Braun balked at supernatural elements like the smoke monster. "I don't want to do a *Twin Peaks*," Lindelof remembered him saying—meaning, basically, that he didn't want to do anything that might be deemed too weird by the network's audience. But by then, J. J. Abrams argued back, audiences were finally ready for what *Twin Peaks* had tried to do. "J. J. jumped in and said some version of this," said Lindelof:

> It's 2004. *Twin Peaks* has been off the air for thirteen years and you're still using it as a cautionary tale. But even if it is a cautionary tale, we should be so lucky if this show gets to be like *Twin Peaks*, because how many television shows get remembered the way *Twin Peaks* is remembered? *Twin Peaks* was amazing and maybe it didn't end well, but we can learn from its mistakes. We should be so lucky to be compared to *Twin Peaks*! We should aspire to *Twin Peaks*!

Braun conceded the point, and *Lost* premiered with its smoke monster intact.

The final factor in *Twin Peaks'* extended shelf life was the one that had never been intended: the sheer power of the shocking, unresolved cliffhanger that ended season two. If the goal had been goading ABC into picking up a third season of *Twin Peaks*, it failed. But it had the unexpected secondary effect of keeping the fandom in limbo—hopeful, somehow, that they would someday learn the fate of Dale Cooper. It was that audience that lined up to attend a massive 2013 *Twin Peaks* retrospective held at the University of Southern California, where Mark Frost couldn't resist teasing an audience hungry for more. "*Twin Peaks* is a continuing story," he said. "That comes from both David and myself."

Unbeknownst to the audience at the time, Lynch and Frost had already been discussing reviving *Twin Peaks* for a year. Their first conversation came in 2012, when Frost asked Lynch to meet him at the legendary Hollywood steakhouse Musso & Frank Grill. "My words to David at the beginning were, 'I don't necessarily think this is a TV show or a movie,'" says Frost. "'We're going to be filming every page of a novel, and novels have the luxury of beginning more slowly.' It is not, 'You have to grab the audience by the throat in the first thirty-five seconds or you've lost them'; it's, 'Let's take our time.' It's a value that has been almost lost in our culture. Good stories take time."

Lynch—who, in years of interviews, had repeatedly and firmly stated that *Twin Peaks* would never return—was willing to hear him out. "I never really thought about going back," said Lynch. "But I did think about the characters and the world, and I loved those characters and I loved that world." But Frost recognized that the sheer breadth of high-quality prestige TV shows on the air—many of which could trace their DNA back to *Twin Peaks*—opened a lane for *Twin Peaks* itself to return. "What I saw was that the TV landscape had shifted dramatically and people were obviously hungry for storytelling that has broken out of the box over the last ten years," says Frost. "I felt it was time to take a kind of evolutionary leap forward and that we should be a part of that."

Frost's ideas, while partially unformed, were remarkably similar to what ultimately ended up in *Twin Peaks: The Return*. "I had come up with a fair amount of it," says Frost. "Not *all* of it, by any means, but enough to hook him and to get us started talking. I had Vegas, at that point. We were in the middle of this big housing crisis, and I was seeing pieces about these urban neighborhoods, built outside of Vegas, that broke down before anybody bought into them. We were looking, obviously, to expand the show beyond just a town, and to talk a little bit more about what was happening culturally and politically in the country. That was kind of the keyhole through which I was seeing what the show might turn into."

You might notice that there's nothing in that concept that mentions Dale Cooper, Laura Palmer, or even Twin Peaks. That was by design. While the idea of a *Twin Peaks* reboot—like all reboots—was rooted in nostalgia, Lynch and Frost quickly agreed, says Frost, that a typical reboot was "the last thing either of us wanted to do." The show would employ the basic structure of a nostalgia-fueled reboot, and trade on the almost mythical reputation *Twin Peaks* had attained during its years off the air, to deliver the kind of storytelling that had very little chance of making it onto television in any other way.

"All we were doing for the first year was taking notes and creating stories. We didn't start writing, literally, for a year," says Frost. Just as it had been with the original pilot, Lynch and Frost's discussions were free-flowing and free-form. Any character from the original series, major or obscure, might warrant revisiting twenty-five years later; any idea, even one that seemed totally disconnected from what someone might expect from *Twin Peaks*, might be fair game. Sometimes their ideas aligned, and sometimes they diverged, but many of them ended up in the final script, which was written more like a film than a TV show, without any act breaks. After his writing sessions with Frost, Lynch would sit outside alone for hours, smoking and writing more new ideas onto legal pads. "I think the analogy I would use is, 'This is like the Beatles' *White Album*,'" says Frost. "There are Paul songs; there are John songs; there are Beatles songs. But they're all ultimately on the album. That's how people should think about it."

The story they were crafting also drew extensively on *Fire Walk with Me*, which Frost—despite his lack of creative input on the movie—had come to see as core to both *Twin Peaks* and its fans. "There were a few things he had done in *Fire Walk with Me* that I felt needed to be pulled into the larger universe of the show and the history, so we spent a couple days talking about those things after we looked at the movie," says Frost. "Some of them were my suggestions, some of them were his, about how best to make it all fit together—to make it cohesive." Long-standing mysteries—the disappearance of Phillip Jeffries, the identity of "Judy," the strange woodsman who joins BOB and the Man from Another Place in their meeting above the convenience store—would, at last, be explained.

And, of course, there was the cliff-hanger that had been unresolved for decades: the fates of both Dale Cooper, trapped in the Black Lodge, and the doppelgänger who took his place, who they nicknamed Mr. C. "We left off with the birth of Mr. C, when he cracked his head in the mirror," says Frost. "It felt right to pick up the thread with him." Cooper's journey, they knew, would be a complicated one, with mythological overtones. "I went back and started thinking about sources like the *Odyssey*," says Frost. "This is about a guy trying to get back to who and what he thought he was."

During this lengthy creative process, Lynch and Frost initially maintained strict secrecy, even keeping their families out of the loop. But it

Mr. C makes a terrifying first impression

soon became clear that there would be no point in moving forward if Kyle MacLachlan wasn't fully committed to playing both the hero and the villain. The project was clandestine enough that even MacLachlan couldn't be told about it over the phone. Instead, Lynch asked him to meet and told him in person. Despite MacLachlan's frustrations with the original run of *Twin Peaks*, he had, over the years, grown intrigued by the possibility of reviving the show—so much so that he would occasionally suggest that idea to Lynch when they met for coffee. Now Lynch was pitching the idea to him. "We've talked about this, David," MacLachlan said. "But if you need to hear it from me: Yes, I'm in." He was, in the end, the only actor permitted to read the entire script.

Which network would air the *Twin Peaks* revival? Though a bogus 2013 rumor about a *Twin Peaks* revival on NBC inspired network executive Jennifer Salke to investigate the possibility of a *real Twin Peaks* revival, Lynch and Frost already had their eyes on Showtime. As a premium cable network, it would enable them to craft a *Twin Peaks* without commercial breaks and include—and, based on Showtime's other hit dramas, probably *encourage*—as much sex and violence as they wanted. Best of all, the right-hand man to Showtime president David Nevins was Gary Levine, the ABC senior drama executive who had been a champion of *Twin Peaks* during its original run. "We've known Gary a long time. We trust Gary. We like Gary," said Frost.

This time around, the dynamic was reversed. Where much of *Twin Peaks*' original run had been assailed by skeptical executives, Lynch and Frost found themselves describing their *Twin Peaks* revival to an executive who was already presold on what they were selling. As a self-described "actual, genuine lover" of *Twin Peaks*, said Nevins, "I was begging them and hoping to pass muster with David Lynch." As Nevins recalls it, Lynch spent much of the meeting staring at a painting in his office of a little girl next to a bookshelf that looks like it may fall on her. "I have some very violent, weird imagery. I think he liked that," he said.

If it was a typically offbeat David Lynch encounter, it was also a reminder that Lynch benefitted from being paired with a partner who could focus on the practical side of a production so he could tilt all his energies toward the creative. For years, that role had been filled by Sabrina S. Sutherland. Their history dated back to her time as a production coordinator on the original run of *Twin Peaks*, when Sutherland had earned Lynch's ire by distributing the original draft of the season two finale he already intended to throw out. But in the years that followed, she became one of Lynch's most trusted confidants, working as an associate producer on his 2006 film *Inland Empire* and helping to manage his other artistic projects. She is the only person other than Lynch or Frost credited as an executive producer on *Twin Peaks: The Return*.

At the outset of the project, Sutherland was given the quixotic task of attempting to come up with an entire budget for the series based on early scripts for what eventually became the first two episodes of *Twin Peaks: The Return*, along with Lynch's descriptions of what the rest of the series would entail. "Mark is television, and he structured it like television," says Sutherland. "What was actually written, versus what David told me... I mean, that was already one hundred and eighty degrees. The first couple of scripts were—I won't say *mundane*—but there was just a lot that David envisioned that hadn't been written down."

Meanwhile, Lynch's and Frost's years of steady work had resulted in a behemoth of a script. "David Nevins knew we were working on it," says Frost. "I don't know that he was expecting us to drop the whole script on his desk." The completed draft, which spanned 334 pages, was enough to earn a thumbs up from Showtime.

After years of work, it was time to tell the world that *Twin Peaks* was going to return. On October 3, 2014, at eleven thirty AM—the time Agent Cooper arrives in *Twin Peaks* in the original pilot—Lynch and Frost simultaneously tweeted, "Dear Twitter Friends: That gum you like is going to come back in style!" The reaction was hopeful, if skeptical. The *Observer* speculated it might be a new DVD extra or package of deleted scenes; *Vox* guessed, cheekily, that Lynch and Frost were just feeling nostalgic after meeting Kyle MacLachlan for some pie. "It was fun to watch people realize what we were up to," says Frost. "You want to drop a rock in a pond and see how far the ripples go, and they went pretty far." It was three days later that Showtime formally confirmed that *Twin Peaks* would return, with Lynch directing every installment, as a nine-episode limited series.

Despite Showtime's enthusiastic press release, that last bit would prove to be a sticking point—one that nearly derailed *Twin Peaks: The Return* from happening at all. "There is a formula that people use to figure how long a page of script will take on-screen," says Sabrina S. Sutherland. "This formula is not necessarily accurate when it comes to how David envisions a scene." Duwayne Dunham—the editor of the original *Twin Peaks* pilot, who agreed to return for *The Return*—recalls his first conversation with Lynch about the series. "I said, 'How many hours?'" says Dunham. "And David said, 'Nine.' And I kind of giggled and said, 'David. Your nine is probably more like ten or eleven.' And he chimed in, laughing, and said, 'Or thirteen, or fourteen . . .'"

Lynch was enamored of the way a TV series could grow, bursting, kudzu-like, out of the confines of a three-act structure. "Any time limit is arbitrary and absurd," said Lynch in 1990, just a few months before the *Twin Peaks* pilot premiered. "There's no law that says you have to end a show at a certain time." He felt the same way a decade later. "I've never liked having to bend my movie scripts to an end halfway through. On a series you can keep having beginnings and middles, and develop story forever," he said in 1999. Of course, he expressed that sentiment while making *Mulholland Drive*, a TV pilot that ABC ultimately rejected despite Lynch's game efforts to accommodate the network's extensive notes by cutting his two-hour version down to eighty-eight minutes. "I feel it's possibly true that there are aliens on earth, and they work in television," he lamented. In the end, *Mulholland Drive* only emerged when Lynch revisited the pilot, filmed extensive new footage, and released it as a movie—one made, pointedly, with his complete creative control.

As Gary Levine recalls it, David Lynch personally turned up at the Showtime offices in January 2015. The script had ballooned to four hundred pages—"But this time, there are no dividers in the binder." Lynch explained that the show would be more than nine episodes, but that he had no idea how many more—and that he *wouldn't* know until the entire season had been shot. "It was a difficult level of flexibility for a big network to absorb," said Levine, who had risen from his role at ABC during *Twin Peaks'* original run to become president of programming at Showtime.

For the third time in his career—and to his great frustration—Lynch found himself arguing with a network that seemed openly skeptical of his vision for what a TV show should be. The problem came down to the nature of how the television business is financed. For *Twin Peaks*, Showtime intended to employ the same model it applied to its other shows: budgeting on a per-episode basis. If Lynch had no idea how many episodes of *Twin Peaks* he would make, how would Showtime know what to budget?

Negotiations continued for months, but neither Lynch nor Showtime were willing to give the other side everything they wanted. "I knew that he was not happy with where we were. We felt we needed more money, and, you know, they were being contentious about some issues," says Mark Frost. But he wasn't prepared for what Lynch decided to do next. It was Easter morning, April 5, when Lynch suddenly tweeted to his millions of followers that—after one year and four months of negotiations—he was walking away from directing the *Twin Peaks* revival because he felt the money Showtime was offering was insufficient for what the script required. "*Twin Peaks* may still be very much alive at Showtime. I love the world of *Twin Peaks* and wish things could have worked out differently," he concluded.

Showtime quickly issued a statement. "We were saddened to read David Lynch's statement today since we believed we were working towards solutions with David and his reps on the few remaining deal points," they said. "Showtime also loves the world of *Twin Peaks* and we continue to hold out hope that we can bring it back in all its glory with both of its extraordinary creators, David Lynch and Mark Frost, at its helm."

Frost, who had already started writing his tie-in novel *The Secret History of Twin Peaks*, was flabbergasted. While it wasn't *impossible*, with Lynch's blessing, that the *Twin Peaks* revival could go into production with a rotating group of directors—that was, after all, how the original series had been made—it was also counter to the plan he and Lynch had agreed on from the very beginning, before a single word had been typed onto a page. Now, without warning, Lynch was out. "The only problem for me was that he didn't tell me he was going to do it," Frost says. "David was, you know, very hard-headed. He did it while he was in Australia, and there were some communication issues, so I found out the same day as everyone else. Suddenly, three years of work go up in smoke. I didn't know what to think. I hoped it would work out, and I believed it would. But honestly—when you're talking about that much money, and that much effort—I was upset he didn't let me know he was going to do it. And I don't know why. I still don't know why. He never offered an explanation. If he'd *told* me, frankly, 'I'm doing this, and it's basically a negotiating strategy' . . . All he had to do was tell me. I would have supported him. I understand the dynamics of the business as well as anybody, and I would have said, 'It's a smart strategy. That's where the leverage is.' But I don't think he liked to think of it that way. I think he wanted to think of it as pure principle."

"I think, in some way, I was Mark's therapist during all of that," says his brother, Scott. "It was fraught with frustration at times for Mark. Particularly when it seemed as if the whole thing was about to collapse, Mark's head was, you know, sent into orbit. Like, 'Wait a minute. You're going to blow it, David.' He was not a happy camper. It was just, like, dealing with a madman."

Lynch had always maintained strong relationships with the show's actors, and they responded in kind. In the wake of his abrupt departure, more than a dozen *Twin Peaks* cast members took to social media to post short videos expressing their displeasure and encouraging Showtime to woo him back. "*Twin Peaks* without David Lynch is like a girl without a secret," said Sheryl Lee. "*Twin Peaks* without David Lynch is like a pie without cherries," said Peggy Lipton. "Twin Peaks without David Lynch is like drape runners without cotton balls," said Wendy Robie.

The campaign went viral, ensuring that each development in the standoff between Lynch and Showtime made a splash in the *Twin Peaks* fandom (and in the Hollywood trades). "I don't think they realized they were at war with an artist who was not going to back down. You can't put a timer on an artist, you know?" says Sherilyn Fenn. But while public pressure certainly didn't hurt, it might not have been necessary; from the start, Showtime's leaders were eager to resolve the impasse. "David Lynch has an incredible sweet tooth, so I remember bringing homemade macaroons from our Passover Seder that my wife would make," recalled Gary Levine. "Over chocolate macaroons, we hashed it out, and ultimately, [Showtime] folded."

The proposal was a deviation from the way Showtime typically did business. What Lynch needed, he and Sabrina S. Sutherland made clear, wasn't a set budget per episode: it was a single budget to make whatever number of episodes it took to make the *Twin Peaks* revival the way he wanted to make it. "We didn't bring up eighteen episodes, or any number of episodes," says Sutherland. "We just said there were more than nine. We didn't know how many more, but there would be more. And, you know: Take it or leave it."

They took it. It was unconventional, but Gary Levine knew, from experience, that Lynch could be trusted. "David, for all his eccentricities, is an excellent producer. He's a great director, but he's also an incredibly responsible producer," he said. "He is on schedule, he is on budget, and he will not let any actors . . . there are no prima donnas in David's ensemble, and everyone wants to work with him; he gets enormous loyalty from actors."

Nevins agreed. "We bobbed and weaved with him; we were patient when we had to be patient," he said. "It turned out not to be very complicated." Even when it was revealed, one week later, that Lynch estimated it would take eighteen episodes to tell the story in full—doubling, appropriately enough, the nine-episode order that had been originally announced—Nevins deferred to the director's wishes. "I expect it to be more than nine, but it's open-ended. I know what the shooting schedule is and then we'll have him cut into it however many episodes it feels best at," Nevins said. "It's ultimately going to be in their control . . . Bottom line is I'll take it when they're ready with it." Lynch would get to make *Twin Peaks* as he intended. It was everything he'd asked for, and just in time. "If we'd waited a few more years, it never would have happened," said Lynch.

MARGARET LANTERMAN

"One day the sadness will end."

I've done my best in these essays not to conflate the characters with the actors who played them. It is very, very hard to avoid doing that with Catherine E. Coulson. Long before *Twin Peaks* existed, Coulson was a key figure in Lynchland. Married to *Eraserhead* star Jack Nance and credited, officially, as the assistant to the director, Coulson played a variety of roles in the film's lengthy production—even donating money from her waitressing gigs to help keep it afloat. She filmed two scenes, playing two different characters, but both were cut from the movie. Prior to *Twin Peaks*, her only on-screen appearance in a Lynch project was in a brief, relatively obscure short film called *The Amputee*, which was written overnight and existed solely so collaborator Frederick Elmes could test some new film stock.

No matter: Lynch had a vision for Coulson, which he shared during the production of *Eraserhead* with anyone who would listen. It was for an educational, half-hour TV series, starring Coulson, called *I'll Test My Log with Every Branch of Knowledge*. "Her husband has been killed in a forest fire and his ashes are on the mantelpiece, with his pipes and his sock hat. He was a woodsman," explained Lynch in the interview book *Lynch on Lynch*, adding:

> But the fireplace is completely boarded up. Because she now is very afraid of fire. And she has a small child, but she doesn't drive, so she takes cabs. And each show would start with her making a phone call to some expert in one of the many, many fields of knowledge. Maybe on this particular day she calls a dentist, but she makes the appointment for her log. And the log goes in the dental chair and gets a little bib and chain and the dentist X-rays the log for cavities, goes

> through the whole thing, and the son is also there. Because she is teaching her son through his observations of what the log is going through. And then sometimes they go to a diner and they never get to where they're going.

If this eccentric-sounding series wasn't exactly PBS-ready, it was, at least, a central image that Lynch couldn't shake: Catherine E. Coulson holding a log. Fearing ABC wouldn't get it, Lynch essentially snuck Coulson into *Twin Peaks* in a brief, wordless cameo that does not appear in the script but earns the biggest laugh in the pilot. "Who's the lady with the log?" asks Dale Cooper. "We call her the Log Lady," deadpans Harry Truman.

For a character who looms so large in *Twin Peaks* mythology, the Log Lady—real name Margaret Lanterman—plays a relatively small role in the show's overarching narrative. She appears in just twelve episodes, and her biggest moment comes early, when she invites Cooper, Truman, Hawk, and Doc Hayward into her cabin and—speaking for her log—offers a patchy account of the night of Laura's murder. Though her connection to the supernatural side of Twin Peaks is undeniable, she seems mainly to be a vessel for the log's power. She gives pointed advice to Cooper, Donna Hayward, and Major Briggs, but she doesn't play a direct role in what happens to them after they've heeded it, and though she offers comfort to Laura herself in *Twin Peaks: Fire Walk with Me*, she can't stop what's coming. "When this kind of fire starts," she tells Laura, "it is very hard to put out."

But any questions about the importance of the Log Lady, at least in Lynch's eyes, were settled in 1993. When Bravo syndicated *Twin Peaks*, Lynch wrote and directed thirty brand-new introductions to be aired before each episode. Each features Coulson as Lanterman, speaking directly into the camera and dropping cryptic, tantalizing references to *Twin Peaks* lore such as pale horses and creamed corn for diehards to obsessively analyze.

All the while, Coulson embraced the Log Lady character wholeheartedly—so much so that the lines between her and Lanterman seemed to blur. "I don't see her as being unusual," said Coulson in a 1990 interview with *People* magazine. "A log is such a solid thing to carry." In the real world, she came to see herself as the log's protector, bringing it onto airplanes as her carry-on item and rebuffing anyone who failed to show it the proper respect. "I tried to pick a little piece off the log once," Michael Horse says. "She punched me." Though Coulson went on to be a well-respected player in the Oregon theater scene, Lynch never cast her in another role. "Sometimes you create a character with an actor, and you never want to see them do anything else," he confessed to the director Richard Green.

Actress Charlotte Stewart recalls attending a *Twin Peaks* event with Coulson roughly a year before *Twin Peaks: The Return* started filming. "She was very weak," says Stewart. "She'd say, 'Charlotte, can you walk with me to the ladies' room?' And she was very unsteady—she couldn't have done it by herself—but we could walk right through this enormous crowd of people, and they'd never know it, because we were arm in arm. She didn't want anyone to know. She didn't want any sympathy. She *especially* didn't want the fans to know. She didn't want to ruin the illusion. And what does that say about Catherine? It's incredible. To the very end, she was devoted."

When *The Secret History of Twin Peaks* was published, it revealed that Lanterman's maiden name had been Coulson, officially (and appropriately) severing the line separating the actress and the character. But while it was impossible to imagine Twin Peaks without the Log Lady by the time *Twin Peaks: The Return* was in production, it very nearly happened. Green's 2025 documentary, *I Know Catherine, The Log Lady*, reveals that Coulson, suffering from terminal cancer, hid the severity of her illness from David Lynch out of fear that he would cut her from *Twin Peaks: The Return*. With Coulson determined to appear but too ill to travel, the production worked out a solution in which she could film her scenes in her own home, with Lynch directing over Skype. He let Coulson choose whether she'd wear a wig. She opted to go without, revealing that the Log Lady, like the actress who played her, was terminally ill.

Coulson's few scenes in *Twin Peaks: The Return* are some of the show's most powerful—in part because the already-tenuous divide between the actress and the character had, for all practical purposes, at last been completely erased. "I think it's one of the more amazing performances, given the circumstances, that I can recall ever seeing," says Mark Frost. In a series of phone calls with Deputy Hawk, Lanterman offers her final bits of guidance before musing on death itself. "You know about death—that it's just a change, not an end," she says. "There's some fear, some fear in letting go." Coulson died four days later. "It hit us like a thunderbolt," says Frost. "But in another way, it didn't seem a surprise, because I think she'd been holding out for that."

Though out of necessity, Michael Horse filmed his side of this conversation later, he recalls an intense feeling of connection with Coulson he still can't quite explain. "I was talking to her spirit," says Horse. "I'm the most un–new age guy you'll ever meet . . . but I was talking to her."

Chapter 10

IT IS HAPPENING AGAIN

On an autumn evening in 2015, just a day before a planned shoot at Snoqualmie Falls, Mark Frost—always, as his social-media followers can attest, a political animal—made David Lynch a promise. "'Look, I'll be Joe Biden here,' he recalls saying. "'I'm your wingman. *You* go do this.'"

For years, the two men had worked in tandem on the massive script for the revival that eventually premiered, a year and a half later, as *Twin Peaks: The Return* (a title that was Showtime's idea, not Lynch's or Frost's). But it was time, Frost knew, to relinquish primary creative control to Lynch. "For David, it was a magnum opus as a director, to have an eighteen-hour canvas to work in. I think he deserved that," Frost says.

At the end of a messy, high-stakes public standoff with Showtime, David Lynch had triumphed: He would get to make *Twin Peaks: The Return* his way. But his victory presented a new conundrum: What was it going to take for David Lynch to make *Twin Peaks: The Return* his way? "The problem, of course, was that we had a finite budget," says Sabrina S. Sutherland. "It didn't matter how many episodes we did. We still had to deliver based on that budget." By necessity, the shooting schedule was aggressive: After beginning production in September 2015, *Twin Peaks: The Return* would be wrapped by the following April, with a similarly accelerated post-production to ensure it would be ready to air on Showtime in early

2017. "We were making nine two-hour movies in one year. That's how you had to look at it," says Duwayne Dunham.

How do you begin wrangling such an unwieldy project? With a tremendous amount of coordination. "We had a tight budget, we had a very interesting schedule, and we had a different way of working. We shot everything like a film, rather than an episodic," says Sutherland—meaning that steady rhythms of a traditional weekly series, in which each episode is its own mini-production, were abandoned in favor of a sprawling shoot in which the entire series was tackled at once. The cast, like the crew, had to be fully on board with Lynch's idiosyncratic process and vision. "There were times that schedules didn't work out, and there were some people who didn't want to do it because they didn't like it or didn't understand it or whatever. I don't know what their reasoning is," says Sutherland. "But the majority of people would try. A lot of people changed their schedules and really worked it in."

As they worked their way through the lengthy list of characters from *Twin Peaks'* original run—and tried to game out where they'd be twenty-five years later—Lynch and Frost had already decided who *wouldn't* be returning. Though *Twin Peaks* had ended with Cooper asking "How's Annie?" they ultimately decided *The Return* wouldn't give fans an answer. "It felt like you had to do either her or Audrey, but not necessarily both," says Frost. Poor FBI Special Agent Chet Desmond, who disappeared a half hour into *Fire Walk with Me*, will apparently remain lost forever: "Chet was discussed, but we found no easy way to bring him back from wherever he is," said Frost. And though Piper Laurie was one of the only cast members to be nominated for an Emmy for *Twin Peaks*, they found no room for her, either—a casualty of *The Return*'s general lack of interest in the night-soapier side of the original series. "I made it very clear to David and the team that I would be delighted to come back," said Laurie. "I'm surprised and I have no idea why I haven't been called back."

But on the whole, the roster of actors who returned was impressively comprehensive. A little more than a year before the premiere of *Twin Peaks: The Return*, Showtime revealed a list of 217 actors who would appear in the series, including some so unexpected they felt like pranks the network had slipped in to see if anyone would notice. (Jim Belushi? *Eddie Vedder?*) Thirty-seven of the actors had previously appeared in *Twin Peaks* and/or *Fire Walk with Me*, and most found out they'd be coming back when Lynch personally called and cheerfully told them he was getting the gang back together. "These people are like family, so it was so beautiful calling them and talking to them again and getting together like for a family reunion," said Lynch. "We all knew we were doing something special, and we all did it for far less money [than normal]," says Michael Horse. "You just don't get a chance to do art on television. If I never worked again, being part of that television icon is enough for me."

Some of the returning actors, including Kyle MacLachlan, David Duchovny, and Miguel Ferrer, had worked steadily since *Twin Peaks* went off the air. Others, including Harry Goaz, Wendy Robie, and Al Strobel, had rarely acted in the decades following the show's abrupt ending. Long retired, Everett McGill proved so hard to track down that Lynch had eventually resorted to sending out a tweet asking if anyone knew how to reach him. A *Twin Peaks* fan was able to pass along a phone number to a house belonging to McGill's family, which Lynch serendipitously dialed on one of the rare occasions when McGill was around. "I hadn't been in touch with him in twenty years," said McGill. "He called me at a telephone number that's not been used. The phone still exists, but it's my mother-in-law's house which has been empty for seven or eight years. I was down there checking on something. Phone rang there, I don't know how he got that number."

Not everyone accepted Lynch's invitation to return to *Twin Peaks*. Just as she had declined *Fire Walk with Me* back in 1992, Lara Flynn Boyle turned down an invitation to return as Donna Hayward. "In preproduction, she came in and talked and decided not to," says Sutherland. "I don't remember that we had a lot going on for Donna, and I was not at all surprised that she turned it down," says Mark Frost. Was Moira Kelly, who had previously stepped into the role of Donna Hayward when Boyle demurred, ever considered? "There was a discussion about that," concedes Sutherland. "But it obviously didn't go anywhere, beyond the discussion." Though Kelly didn't expect to get a call—"I figured it'd be Lara Flynn Boyle, because she's the Donna after [*Fire Walk with Me*]," she says—the announcement of *Twin Peaks: The Return* did make her reflect on what might have happened to Donna in the intervening years. "I actually had an interesting thought," she says. "I said, 'You know what? If he *does* bring Donna back, he should bring her back as Don. She went off, had a sex change, and came back as a man."

Michael Ontkean, who had retired to Hawaii several years earlier, proved more complicated. Though the actor originally planned to return—even enlisting Brad Dukes, the author of the *Twin Peaks* book *Reflections: An Oral History of Twin Peaks* to help him track down an acceptable substitute for Sheriff Truman's original jacket—he abruptly changed his mind shortly after filming began. (Neither Ontkean nor anyone who worked on *Twin Peaks: The Return* has publicly disclosed his reason.) That disappointment, at least, came with a silver lining: the opportunity to cast Robert Forster, some twenty-five years after he declined the chance to play Harry in the *Twin Peaks* pilot, in Ontkean's place. "My agent said, 'You're going to get a call from David Lynch,'" recalled Forster. "Two minutes later, the phone rang and David was on the other line. He said, 'You remember how you weren't in the first *Twin Peaks*?' I said yes. And he said, 'Well, I'd like you to be in this one.'" Scenes written for Harry were quickly reworked to instead center Frank Truman (Robert Forster), Harry's elder brother, and Lynch wrote a new scene to fill in Frank's backstory. "It really didn't involve that much work," says Frost.

For the returning actors facing medical crises, Lynch filmed with speed and urgency. The first scene shot for *The Return* was Doc Hayward's brief appearance on a Skype call, describing his encounter with Mr. C shortly after the events of the season two finale—a scene shot when Frost was on the east coast visiting his father, who died before *Twin Peaks: The Return* premiered. "My dad was getting close to the end, and I told David I didn't think we'd have much time—but if we wanted it, my dad really wanted to do it," says Mark Frost. David Bowie was intended to reprise the role of Phillip Jeffries but died of complications from liver cancer in the middle of the show's production. "We had every intention of bringing him back, and we would have had him. And that would have been sensational," says Frost. "We told him it would probably just be one day's work, but as it turned out, he was gravely ill. With his blessing, we were able to hire a voice double."

Of course, the *Twin Peaks* veterans were just a small part of the story Lynch and Frost had crafted. In addition to the thirty-seven returning actors, there were 180 new roles to be cast, and—just as he had on the original series—Lynch tasked Johanna Ray with finding the right actors to play them. "David usually notifies me at the very last minute," says Ray. "It was awful. I had to go to his house and read the script, which was, like, four hundred pages long. It took a couple of times, going up there to read it and making notes on what actors might be right for it. But by the time I went back to my office and was actively casting, I could barely remember any. It was very frustrating."

The dynamic from the original series had shifted a generation; now the actors who had played teenagers on *Twin Peaks* were the series veterans, and the next generation of young actors were buzzing about their opportunity to join Lynch and Frost's world. "Every actor in town wanted to be considered," says Ray. "They weren't supposed to know that it was David's project, but that got out."

They didn't get every actor they wanted. Initially reported as being part of thc cast, Peter Sarsgaard never appears in *Twin Peaks: The Return*, though he conceded the rumors were "not founded on nothing." And Paul Giamatti revealed that, due to scheduling conflicts, he had reluctantly turned down an offer to star as one of the Mitchum brothers, who were ultimately played by Jim Belushi and Robert Knepper. "It just logistically couldn't work out, which was heartbreaking to me," said Giamatti. "I couldn't watch it because I was so disappointed I couldn't be in it."

"David decided he wanted to cast a different way this time," says Ray. "He didn't want to meet the actors. He wanted *me* to talk with the actors. And he would then look at the taped conversations of all the actors and make his choice." For those auditions, Ray set ground rules in advance. "I said, 'Please don't talk about the business,'" she recalls. "Just find something interesting in your life to talk about." She also wasn't interested in seeing actors read lines. "I never trusted it, because they could really just be doing a monologue they'd done a thousand times. It didn't tell me anything," she says.

One such actress was Madeline Zima, whose dangerously curious coffee shop employee anchors much of the two-part premiere episode. A breakout child actress for her role in the '90s sitcom *The Nanny*, Zima had also costarred opposite *Twin Peaks* alum David Duchovny in Showtime's *Californication*—but she'd never experienced anything quite like this. "There were code names upon code names," Zima says. "It was the most clandestine audition process I've ever been involved with." She met with Ray and her fellow casting director, Krista Husar, for under ten minutes. "I didn't know if it was *Twin Peaks* or just some kind of top-secret David Lynch project," says Zima. "It just kind of felt like a strange dream, like I feel like a lot of people experience when they enter this sort of David Lynch universe." Zima didn't find out it was *Twin Peaks* until she received her contract, which included an NDA with a strict legal clause that could be exercised if she spoke to anyone about the project.

Actress Nicole LaLiberté, who was eventually cast as Mr. C's doomed associate, Darya, had a similar experience. "I went in to meet with Johanna, and I remember it seemed to me to be a really random place to do an interview," she says. "I sat down on a couch and Joanna was like, 'We're just going to chat. David's not here, but we're going to pretend that he's here. And there was a weird pane of glass behind her that felt a little bit like a police station. So I was like . . . *Is he back there?*" (He wasn't.)

Given the instruction to talk about anything other than working in Hollywood, most of those who auditioned naturally gravitated toward a subject they were passionate about. Zima recalls talking about the Kurt Vonnegut book she was reading; LaLiberté gushed about her recent interview with another literary idol, Karl Ove Knausgaard. Others found themselves getting personal. Adele René, who was cast as Lieutenant Knox, spoke candidly about being a caretaker for her brother, who had recently passed away from ALS. "But I also laughed through my interview," she says. "I was talking about the very joyful moments. And—come to find out later—that's what people say about David: that he finds the light in the dark."

In the massive *Twin Peaks: The Return* cast list that Showtime released, there were two names that immediately stood out to David Lynch fans: *Wild at Heart* star Laura Dern and *Mulholland Drive* star Naomi Watts. Though neither had appeared in *Twin Peaks*, their presence gave the sense that *The Return* was something of a grand career retrospective for Lynch, drawing elements from everything he'd directed before it.

Dern had first met Lynch decades earlier while auditioning for *Blue Velvet*, though she knew nothing about the movie except the title. She recalled their first encounter as a "magical moment" interrupted by Lynch's admission that he needed to pee. Lynch later invited her to join him and Kyle MacLachlan for lunch at Bob's Big Boy—curious, she guessed, to see if she and MacLachlan had chemistry. "We ordered malts and French fries and David was doodling on napkins while Kyle was doodling with a knife into his ketchup," said Dern. "And I mean, a girl either goes, *These are really bizarre men and they are twin souls*, or *I am in love with both of these people and want to spend the rest of my life with them*, which is how I responded." Like most of the closest actors in Lynch's troupe, she found out she would be in *Twin Peaks: The Return* when Lynch called and told her. "I don't know if I'm the luckiest person in the world or he's not gracious at all with me, because he doesn't ask me," said Dern. "He just goes, 'And then *you're* going to be there.'"

Naomi Watts, too, required little convincing. "You just trust him. And even if it doesn't turn out great, there's no question that it's going to be a really fun experience. That's what you live for," she said. "I didn't know anything about the whole story. I tried to piecemeal things together or quiz David and even Kyle, but they don't give much away. But, it doesn't matter. Once you release yourself from that, you just get caught up in the experience of it. You trust David and you're just all in."

There is no easy plot summary of *Twin Peaks: The Return*. Over its eighteen episodes, the show zigzags not just through Twin Peaks, but between locations as far-flung as New York City, New York; Buckhorn, South Dakota; Las Vegas, Nevada; White Sands, New Mexico, circa 1945; Odessa, Texas, in a (pointedly) unknown year; and a variety of mythological locations, including the Black Lodge. Plotlines emerge, then spin off into unexpected directions or their own narrative cul-de-sacs. Key information is parceled out selectively; at times, the identities of major characters will only be clear to those who bother to read the credits at the end of each episode. *The Return*'s closest predecessor isn't the original *Twin Peaks* or even *Fire Walk with Me*. It's *The Missing Pieces*: a series of *Twin Peaks* vignettes—sometimes interlinked by plot or characters, sometimes by tone or theme—that, when taken as a whole, add up to a story that could never be told in any other medium in any other way.

The breadth and complexity of the storytelling raised a challenge—especially in the opening hour, which needed to meet the nearly impossible bar set by *Twin Peaks* fans who had been waiting for decades to see the story continue. "We were trying to figure out how to structure and open the thing," says Dunham. "We tried a lot of different things, and nothing was really working. We spent a lot of time on it. Sabrina got pretty, pretty nervous."

For a while—after a Red Room preamble and the new opening credits—the series would have opened not with a return to Twin Peaks as viewers

Cooper and Laura, reunited in the Red Room

ultimately experienced, but with the pitch-black reintroduction of Cooper's Black Lodge doppelgänger, Mr. C. Scored to a bracingly slowed-down version of Muddy Magnolias' "American Woman," which was remixed by Lynch himself, the scene follows Mr. C as he drives through the woods and meets with a group of strange, moonshine-swilling compatriots. In his first minute on-screen, he throws two vicious punches and says one word.

It is, needless to say, a departure from MacLachlan's performance as Dale Cooper. "I've been doing this a while, and I feel pretty capable I can handle anything that comes along. Except when I read Mr. C," said MacLachlan. "I knew, *I've got to find this person in me*. Because if it didn't work, I knew the show wasn't going to work."

Working in tandem with Lynch, MacLachlan constructed Mr. C "from the outside in," right down to his black leather jacket. Mr. C's hair was designed to be "a little bit off, a little bit awkward," said MacLachlan. "Almost as if the character was putting on something that he had seen but wasn't actually that conscious of." The black contact lenses were MacLachlan's idea; he felt that Mr. C should resemble a shark. Even for the actors who knew him, the effect was jarring. Arriving on set, "I'm thinking, *Well, I don't know how everybody's going to be, and Kyle's a big star,*" says Michael Horse. "First day, he comes out of the woods in this dark makeup: 'Michael! How are you? How is everything?' And I'm looking at him going, 'Ooooookay.'" It was a challenge for MacLachlan as well. "Oftentimes when I'm working, I can sort of take off the character," said MacLachlan. "But this guy, he was always with me—not a hundred percent, but I carried at least fifty percent of him. I would be quite happy when I was finished for the day to be able to take off the clothes and leave them in the trailer."

Beginning with MacLachlan's introduction as Mr. C would have sent nostalgia-fueled viewers a bracing message: This is not the *Twin Peaks* you remember. But even Lynch agreed that this opening was too jarring for viewers who tuned in to *Twin Peaks: The Return* expecting, you know, *Twin Peaks*. "He was experimenting, experimenting: 'How do I blend these two worlds?' says Dunham. "And I think that's when we realized, or he realized, it wasn't going to work."

Instead, they settled on a pair of opening scenes that would give viewers a small taste of what happened to Twin Peaks, and the characters they remembered from it, in the intervening five years. In the final version of the episode, we're reintroduced to Dr. Jacoby, Ben and Jerry Horne, and Lucy Brennan—who informs an insurance man, and the audience, that there are now two Sheriff Trumans—before we get our first glimpse of Mr. C.

The tension between *Twin Peaks* as fans expected it and *Twin Peaks* as Lynch and Frost had reimagined it would define much of *The Return*'s run, and much of the conversation around it. In one early, shocking shot—a harbinger of where the series is going—Lynch suddenly cuts across the country to the glittering skyscrapers of Manhattan, where a character we've never met has been tasked with guarding a mysterious glass box. Just as in *Fire Walk with Me*, Lynch is kicking off his story with something that can easily be read as a metaphor for television; once again, he doesn't take long before blowing it up—though not before a horrifying monster pops through and shreds the faces of the young lovers unlucky enough to be in the room when it emerges.

When the show *does* return to Twin Peaks, Washington, we find a town badly scarred by the events of the intervening years—a place that notably resembles the decline of untold thousands of real small towns across the United States in the years since *Twin Peaks* went off the air. With the sawmill permanently closed, it's unclear what, if any, the town has as its local dominant industry. Ben Horne spends his days puttering around the Great Northern; though we never cut to Horne's Department Store, it's hard to imagine he's somehow escaped the decline of similar stores all across the country. Crime must be up, because the Sheriff's Department seems to be thriving, with a cartoonishly large monitoring station to field calls as they come in. But expansion has degraded the quality of law enforcement officers; where the department was once led by Truman, Hawk, and Andy, *The Return* has the sneering, almost openly corrupt Deputy Chad Broxford (John Pirrucello) gumming up the works. Even the breakout success of the Double R Diner is a cautionary tale; Norma's friendly mom-and-pop joint has attracted the attention of a businessman with eyes on leveraging and franchising the Double R brand in a way that does not seem conducive to maintaining the quality of the service or food. That's right: In this Twin Peaks, even the Double R's coffee and pie isn't necessarily something one can rely on.

Was this what *Twin Peaks* fans had been waiting for all these years? Duwayne Dunham had his doubts. "It was just a different, different thing. There was some really brilliant work in there, but it was just different," says Dunham. "I, personally, felt there wasn't enough Twin Peaks. People wanted Agent Cooper. They wanted the music of *Twin Peaks*. I remember putting some of the original music in the first scene with Andy and Lucy, and David was like, 'No. I don't want that music.' And we never revisited it." But he was also committed to doing whatever he could to facilitate Lynch's directorial vision to the letter. "I made a decision when, when I went back and helped him put the reboot together," says Dunham. "I said, 'David, you've taken enough beating through the years of people who don't understand your stuff. I'm not going to argue with you. You should be able to do this one exactly the way you want.'"

It's hard to argue with anyone who'd rather spend a little more time in Twin Peaks, or hear a few more bars of Angelo Badalamenti's legendary score. But Lynch's restraint in relying on the show's old habits does have the effect of making *The Return*'s few nostalgic indulgences all the more powerful. "Laura Palmer's Theme" doesn't play until *The Return*'s fourth episode, when Bobby—revealed to have become a sheriff's deputy, in a nod to Major Briggs' vision of a brighter future for his troubled son—sees Laura Palmer's picture for the first time in years. As the soundtrack swells, his eyes well up with tears. "Brings back some memories," he finally says.

Though *The Return*, by design, never wallows in *Twin Peaks* nostalgia, it takes a small dip into it every so often. Even some of the original show's least popular storylines get belated resolutions. After all the hand-wringing over whether Andy or Dick was the father of Lucy's baby in *Twin Peaks*' second season, we're finally introduced to Lucy's baby: a roving, poetry-spewing biker named Wally Brando. Played by Michael Cera and dressed in a nearly one-to-one replica of Marlon Brando's costume from *The Wild One*, Wally pops in for a single scene to deliver a lengthy, deadpan monologue about Lewis and Clark, his own shadow, and the emotional process by which he came to accept that his parents are turning his bedroom into a study. It has, needless to say, almost no relevance to the plot. "I think I ruined a take, I was laughing so hard," says Mark Frost. "I know that scene rubbed some people the wrong way, but I would watch it every day for two weeks and be very, very happy."

The handful of comedic scenes that take place in Twin Peaks—which also include a wild drug trip in the woods for Jerry Horne and Dr. Jacoby's reinvention as a scammy shock jock called Dr. Amp—play out in tandem to the main plot, which unfolds in both South Dakota and Las Vegas. The deaths of Sam (Ben Rosenfield) and Tracey (Madeline Zima), the young lovers in New York, aren't the only horrifying acts of violence in *The Return*'s opening hours. Just as the original *Twin Peaks* began in the immediate aftermath of a murder, the early hours of *Twin Peaks: The Return* unfold against a backdrop of inexplicable violence and the people trying to figure out what caused it. The crime, this time, is a stranger one: the murder of a South Dakota librarian named Ruth Davenport (Mary Stofle), whose severed head has been ritualistically positioned over the headless corpse of an older man. It's in the aftermath of this crime that the FBI, and the audience, end up following Mr. C as he tries to avoid being pulled back into the Black Lodge.

At the same time, the real Dale—or, to borrow Annie Blackburn's phrase, the "good Dale"—is finally being set free from his twenty-five-year Black Lodge prison. But he doesn't return from the Black Lodge unscathed. Taking the place of another double manufactured by Mr. C, Cooper emerges and slips into the life of Dougie Jones, a sleazy Las Vegas insurance agent married to Naomi Watts' Janey-E. The experience has fried his brain, and he spends much of *The Return* wandering around in an addled haze, bumbling through *Forrest Gump*-like scenarios in which he inadvertently makes the world a better place by winning hundreds of thousands of dollars on

Janey-E and "Dougie Jones"

slot machines or palling around with a pair of surprisingly good-hearted mafiosos. MacLachlan's performance—inspired by Peter Sellers in *Being There* and Jeff Bridges in *Starman*—is hilarious and surreal. "I don't know what type of person, but there must be a lot of them that just love Dougie," said David Lynch. "You want to have a Dougie at home, to take care of and sit with and have cake and stuff."

It is fair to say that not everyone loved Dougie. For a vocal contingent of *Twin Peaks* fans, who had waited decades to see what would happen if and when Cooper escaped from the Black Lodge, Dougie Jones proved frustrating. Kyle MacLachlan has revealed, reluctantly, that there were drafts of *The Return* in which Cooper emerged sooner. "I don't want to speak too much about this—but there were other things that were in place in the script that were more of . . . let's just say Cooper was a little more present," he said. "I mean, look: It didn't happen fast enough for some people. I'm sure for others it was just fine," says Mark Frost. "I thought Kyle was absolutely hilarious. It's a brilliant performance, so what can you do? If you want fast storytelling, go watch a network show. That's not what we do here."

For Michael Horse, the solution to appreciating what *The Return* was doing was something he had learned while filming *Twin Peaks* decades earlier. Working alongside Robert Forster, he watched, amused, as the new Sheriff Truman tried to wrap his head around everything that was happening. "On the second day, he finally went, 'Hey, Michael. I don't get this,'" says Horse. "And I said, 'You're not gonna get all of it. Just relax and enjoy.'"

DIANE EVANS

"Fuck you."

Who else could it have been?

Twin Peaks fans had wondered about the identity of Diane—the mystery woman to whom Cooper addresses his many, many cassette tapes—from the very beginning. Was she a secretary or a fellow FBI agent? A sister, a friend, or a lover? The name of his tape recorder? Like most of Cooper's backstory, the most complete information fans had for years came from Scott Frost's *The Autobiography of Special F.B.I. Special Agent Dale Cooper*, in which Cooper describes Diane, his newly appointed secretary, as "an interesting cross between a saint and a cabaret singer." They go on at least one date—she's a big fan of the restaurant's Peking duck—and the fact that that extremely mundane piece of trivia has lived on for decades tells you just how hungry *Twin Peaks* fans were to learn more about this woman. "Diane, I hope that you will not mind that I address these tapes to you even when it is clear that I am talking to myself," he remarks at one point. "The knowledge that someone of your insight is standing behind me is comforting."

Who is this woman for whom a man as enlightened as Dale Cooper has such singular respect? As Mark Frost recalls it, the original plan for Diane was more prosaic. "Writers are always trying to find an interesting, fun way to bury exposition," says Frost. Cooper's tapes were, more than anything, a convenient excuse for the FBI agent to pass necessary information to the audience. But the curiosity around Diane was enough that, at the height of *Twin Peaks* mania, newspaper columns ran with the rumor that actress Carol Lynley, best known for the 1972 disaster movie *The Poseidon Adventure*, was set to join the *Twin Peaks* cast as Diane. ("Never happened, never discussed it," revealed Mark Frost in 2014.)

There was, however, one actress who both Lynch and Frost had in mind, from the very beginning, if they ever decided to bring Diane into the *Twin Peaks* fold. "Honestly, you know, Kyle was dating Laura Dern at the time, and she was actually even up visiting while we were shooting the pilot," says Frost. "So I think we were both thinking if we ever wanted to show Diane, that Laura would be the obvious choice."

It was worth the wait. Diane's reveal at the end of "Part 6" of *Twin Peaks: The Return* is one of the show's big fist-pump moments—the perfect answer to a decades-long question. Dern, who starred in Lynch's films *Blue Velvet*, *Wild at Heart*, and *Inland Empire*, was the perfect actress to fill in the blanks of one of *Twin Peaks*' longest-standing mysteries. "It's the only time I've ever had this outrageous gift of playing someone who means a lot in terms of storytelling in people's minds but there are no visuals. That's such a cool thing to walk into," said Dern.

"I know where she drinks."

Working in tandem, Lynch and Dern developed Diane's distinctive look together—precisely enough, said Dern, that Lynch eventually collaborated with the show's makeup artist to develop a unique Diane lipstick shade when he couldn't find an existing color that matched what he had in mind. "Every aspect of her was so specific, so it was an unbelievable blast to find every detail of her," said Dern.

Given Cooper's affectionate, chatty way of speaking to Diane through mere cassette tapes, it was easy to imagine her as the perfect confidant: warm, trustworthy, nonjudgmental. That is not the Diane we meet. Hard-drinking, chain-smoking, and caustic to nearly everyone she meets—a significant chunk of her dialogue is just saying "fuck you" to people—Diane reluctantly accompanies Albert Rosenfield, Gordon Cole, and Tammy Preston to South Dakota, where they ask her to interview the prisoner who seems to be the long-missing Dale Cooper.

It's here, for the first time, that Diane seems vulnerable. "When did we see each other last?" she asks Mr. C. "Are you upset with me, Diane?" he replies. When she asks again, he replies, slowly and smugly, "At your house." The implication is both clear and disturbing, but it's not until much later in *The Return* that Diane confirms what Mr. C implies: Soon after he left Twin Peaks, he turned up on her doorstep and raped her. But even before we have that information, her behavior is a puzzle. Though she seems disgusted whenever she's in Mr. C's presence, she spends much of the season helping him, sending him information on the FBI investigation she's been drawn into.

Why would Diane betray her former allies to aid a man who caused her so much pain and sorrow? The answer, which we learn late in the season, is another tragic one: She isn't Diane at all. As it turns out, we *still* haven't met Diane. While she possesses all Diane's memories, the character we've known as Diane is actually a tulpa, created by the doppelgänger as a sleeper agent to do his bidding at critical moments. "I'm not me," she cries, aware that something is horribly wrong, drawing a gun before Albert and Tammy shoot her.

When the real Diane emerges, at last, from the Black Lodge, she's sporting red hair and black-and-white nail polish. It's a critical moment—the one *Twin Peaks* fans have been waiting for since 1990—and David Lynch marked it with something he employed only sparingly: actual, concrete backstory for the actors to consider. Behind-the-scenes footage reveals that Lynch told MacLachlan and Dern that Cooper and Diane had been in a secret relationship, unknown even to their closest FBI colleagues, before they both disappeared.

It seems likely that this behind-the-scenes revelation—never actually intended to be heard by the show's audience—was designed, primarily, to conjure up the necessary emotions for MacLachlan and Dern. (Among many problems: Unless you believe Cooper was so good at disguising his caddishness that the *audience* didn't know about it, it's basically impossible to square the idea of a Cooper/Diane relationship with his courtship of Annie Blackburn.)

But whatever the truth of Cooper and Diane's romantic past, the brief time we spend with them—at long last, the *real* Cooper and Diane—is fraught with strangeness and pain. Reunited after so much time, Cooper and Diane journey across a threshold to another world. Diane has her doubts. Cooper—who once valued Diane's opinion so much that he mailed her cassette tapes chronicling nearly every detail of his day-to-day experiences—cuts her off mid-sentence, before she can even finish expressing her concerns.

Whatever this relationship was before, it seems to be something different now. And even with her tulpa gone and her rightful place in the world restored, Diane's identity has become too fractured to return to normal—something underlined, cryptically, when Diane witnesses her own doppelgänger lurking outside the motel where she and Cooper book a room for the night. "I loved the idea, or it felt to me, that what had evolved in her was the awareness that there were other sides of him and not knowing what would be on the other side of following him," said Dern. "In letting herself love him, in following him on this journey, and that she didn't know which side of him she'd get, I think is very true of any love story." This one, as it turns out, is over. After a very fraught sex scene, Cooper wakes up the following morning to find a Dear John note, asking him not to try to find her, signed by Linda. Whatever her life will be after this, Cooper is not privy to it, and neither are we.

There is little joy to be found in Diane's story, but plenty of courage. In the end, it's her—not Audrey, not Annie, not Truman—who joins him on the other side of the threshold. Maybe that's why one of the most iconic images to emerge from *Twin Peaks: The Return* is Cooper, Diane, and Gordon Cole—or, if you prefer, *Twin Peaks'* cocreator, flanked by two of his most beloved actors—emerging together from the dark.

But with apologies to the real Diane, who waited so long to take her rightful place on *Twin Peaks'* stage, it's the tulpa whose story I'll really remember. Drawn back into the Black Lodge after her FBI companions gun her down, she ends up perched on a black leather chair in the Red Room—cross-legged and clearly unimpressed—as Mike tells her, bluntly, that she was created by the Black Lodge. It's an unsentimental ending for one of *The Return*'s most memorable characters, and she takes it with a characteristic lack of sentiment, even as she recognizes she's doomed. When your maker is just moments away from obliterating you forever, what else is there to say besides, "Fuck you"?

Chapter 11

GOTTA LIGHT?

One of the joys of watching *Twin Peaks: The Return* in real time over the summer of 2017 was the sense that you never knew what you were going to get. The premiere had already set an anything-is-possible-here tone with its extended trips to New York City and South Dakota. Subsequent episodes were released untitled, with nothing more than a brief, cryptic quote from each episode released in advance to tease viewers about what they could expect: "The stars turn and a time presents itself" or "There's a body all right." The show's eccentric, leisurely structure—which made it feel like Cooper might suddenly snap out of his Dougie spell, or Audrey Horne could suddenly walk into a scene, at any moment—only increased the sense of anticipation.

But even by those heightened standards, it's almost impossible to distill what it felt like to tune in to "Part 8" expecting a normal-weird episode of *Twin Peaks: The Return*, and watching what would soon be widely hailed as one of the greatest hours of television ever made. "It's one of the things I'm proudest of ever having been a part of," says Mark Frost. "Structurally, the week before, we had done maybe the most *Twin Peaks* old-style episode. I just felt it was the right time for a sucker punch. People were getting used to a rhythm, and a way of the story moving along, and I said, 'Well, let's just disrupt that and hit them with this and then see what happens.'"

Where does evil come from? In *Twin Peaks*, that's not an abstract question. Sheriff Truman described the evil in the woods. Albert Rosenfield described the evil that men do. When asked what he feared most, Major Briggs replied, "The possibility that love is not enough."

All those answers imply an evil that's ancient, or maybe even eternal. That's certainly one way to read the opening scenes of "Part 8," in which Mr. C's double-crossing associate Ray tries, with apparent success, to kill him at the behest of someone he believes is Phillip Jeffries—only to watch in horror as a group of woodsmen emerge and bring him back to life. "Four weeks into shooting I hadn't really designed those woodsmen yet, and David and I hadn't really talked tremendously about them," said makeup artist Debbie Zoller. "As we were shooting, I looked around in the areas where we would be filming in Washington and would take colors with me—a certain color in the tree bark or a purple mushroom that was growing wild, different colored mosses, all different tones. I matched those colors to makeup colors that we would airbrush onto the woodsmen, working with layering and texturing and different kinds of mud. Then they were looking too matte, so I put yellow Snack Pack pudding that I got at the grocery store in their beards and hair. At night when we were filming them, you would see the reflection from the lights so that they came alive. And then I brought out different paints and brushes, and David would take this black paint and paint a layer on top of everything that we did."

The end result was disturbing enough that it rattled even the crew. "Although we had shot the woodsmen before in the show, their environment there was very striking, and I think that maybe more than one person on the crew was struck with an imagery that night that they weren't too comfortable with," said director of photography Peter Deming. "It was a joyful working experience," said MacLachlan. "Even, you know, late nights covered in blood, being massaged by large bearded men, lying on the cold ground. I'm like, 'I'm so happy to be here.'" Just as Windom Earle learned, the Black Lodge seems to play by its own rules (which, conveniently, dovetail with the rules of dramatic television); Mr. C is simply too powerful to be gunned down in the middle of the series by a henchman without the Black Lodge immediately correcting it.

After a Roadhouse performance by "the" Nine Inch Nails, Lynch delivers a cut that's even more startling than the premiere's sudden shift to New York City: a title card that reads "July 16, 1945. White Sands, New Mexico. 5:29 AM (MWT)." To the discordant sounds of Krzysztof Penderecki's 1961 string composition "Threnody to the Victims of Hiroshima," we watch as the world's first nuclear bomb is detonated, unleashing untold horrors into the world. *Twin Peaks* fans had long wondered where BOB came from; as it turns out, we're the ones who let him in.

"We needed an origin story for the evil that we had been depicting in this area," said Frost. "I had mentioned the atomic bomb and White Sands. It's all metaphorical, but what if something ripped a hole in the space-time continuum? It opened Pandora's box. And things unanticipated and strange came out of the box. Just like in the myth."

The entirety of "Part 8" took up a slender twelve pages in Lynch and Frost's behemoth of a script. "We worked on that diligently," says Frost. "I said, 'You know, this may turn into an entire episode that's stand-alone.' It was almost an interlude. A reset button, you know? A bridge back into the mystical world that we had created." It was important enough to both men that, for a time, Lynch and Frost's working title for the revival was *Twin Peaks: Jornada del Muerto*, which translates as Dead Man's Journey—a nod to the desert where the Trinity test was held. "It was something I spotted on a map. It literally led us right to it," says Frost.

"It is in our home now."

The detonation of the bomb gives way to a variety of Lynchian images. We see, almost simultaneously, the emergence of BOB—an orb containing the image of the late Frank Silva, spewed from the mouth of the same creature who killed Tracey and Sam—and an apparent counterpunch from the White Lodge, the Black Lodge's virtuous counterpart: the creation of an orb containing the face of Laura Palmer.

The latter was engineered by a character—credited as "???????" in "Part 1" and "Part 8," and credited as "the Fireman" in "Part 14" and "Part 17"—who *Twin Peaks* fans will recognize as the Giant. Actor Carol Struycken never asked why the character's name was changed, or even if it was the same character at all. "I have no idea. I never really cared," he says. "To me, it was the same character. That's all I can say." According to Mark Frost, the Giant and the Fireman are intended to be one and the same: "In the cosmos of the world, he was the Fireman," says Frost. "He was, in fact, the Fireman all along." When asked directly about the Fireman's place in the cosmic order, Frost is more circumspect: "The Fireman has his own reasons which are almost certainly too abstract and unfathomable for us to grasp." But Struycken is willing to hazard a guess: "I saw it as somebody who tries to salvage things, right? And that's why I summoned Laura Palmer to come down. I was kind of like the fire hose, to put out the fire that Bob is starting."

A second side effect of the bomb's detonation is the appearance of a gang of woodsmen at a convenience store—a place, as Mike once revealed, that he and BOB used to live above. A lumberjack had appeared in the surreal meeting of Black Lodge denizens in *Twin Peaks: Fire Walk with Me*, and Lynch had clearly maintained a fascination with woodsmen in the years since the film's release. In *Woodcutters from Fiery Ships*—a little-remembered, ultimately unrealized CD-ROM game Lynch worked on for the Japanese developer Synergy, Inc. in 1998—"certain events have happened or are sort of happening in a bungalow which is behind another house in Los Angeles," said Lynch. "And then suddenly the woodcutters arrive and they take the man who we think has witnessed these events, and their ship is . . . uh, silver, like a '30s sort of ship, and the fuel is logs. And they smoke pipes."

Not *all* of those ideas show up in "Part 8," but when the episode skips ahead again—to a sequence set on August 15, 1956, and shot entirely in black-and-white—the woodsmen do descend from the heavens. "Just before the sun went down, we did the scenes where we dropped out of the sky, or Mars," says actor Robert Broski. "Who knows where we were from? Probably atomic waste from the bomb, and we were floating down with the ash, I guess."

Like most of the actors cast in *Twin Peaks: The Return*, Broski had no idea what he was signing up for. "It was really pretty much a mystery," says Broski. "I did know it was for David Lynch." After a career working in construction, he had made an unlikely career pivot into acting when someone noted his remarkable resemblance to Abraham Lincoln. Donning a black suit and a stovepipe hat, he built a second career playing the sixteenth president at parades, school assemblies, Civil War reenactments, and local commercials. Prior to *Twin Peaks: The Return*, his acting credits included Abraham Lincoln in the Nickelodeon sitcom *The Haunted Hathaways*, Abraham Lincoln in the Netflix movie *Pee-wee's Big Holiday*, and Abraham Linclone in *Linclone*, a sci-fi comedy short produced to promote Heineken beer. For *Twin Peaks: The Return*—a literally unprecedented non-Lincoln role—Broski auditioned remotely, over Zoom, outside a hospital where his wife was receiving medical treatment. It was mere days later when he got the call to come out to the Mojave Desert.

The Return was produced with as much secrecy as possible, but even by those elevated standards, Broski and the handful of other actors who had been cast as woodsmen were truly in the dark. It wasn't even decided he would have a speaking role until he had arrived on set. "We showed up in the afternoon, 'cause we were waiting for the sun to set," says Broski. "We were out in the middle of the desert, and we didn't know what the heck we were doing. We didn't know anything about the atomic bomb." Fortunately, he recognized two fellow actors, Christian Calloway and Stewart Strauss. "All of a sudden, they put us through wardrobe," says Broski. "They start spraying us, painting us. On our ears, in our noses, in our mouths—every orifice you can think of, they sprayed us in black. And we *still* didn't know what was going on."

The answer, they eventually learned, was a scene right out of a 1950s horror movie, in which they'd be playing monsters. "We talked a little about the fifties . . . not horror films, but sort of genre films. As usual with David, you never pick out any movie. It's just sort of a feeling," said Peter Deming. "The first movie we did together, I asked him about referencing things, and he said, 'No, this movie is going to look like this movie. Forget about all the other movies and just make it look like this movie.' That's the mindset, on whatever it is, so the fact that he actually referenced something, I was sort of surprised."

In the episode's nightmarish coda, the woodsmen descend on a small desert town, scaring or killing anyone who gets in their way as they stalk toward a local radio station. "I loved how Lynch directed," says Broski. "Most of the direction he gave me was 'Slow down your movement' or 'Slow down your speech.' He would tell you what he was looking for and he'd leave it at that. He didn't micromanage. I didn't ever see him scratch his chin and go, *I wonder if we should do it this way or if we should do it that way.* He knew what he wanted, he got it, and he moved on."

For this pivotal scene, the production spared no expense, spending some $250,000 to construct a purpose-built radio station for Broski's woodsman to terrorize. "That radio station was *authentic*," says Broski. "Even Mr. Lynch commented about it—how much money they spent on the radio station, just for one scene. But you walked in and it put you right in the mood of what you were doing: the era and the time of day." As Broski played the woodsman, killing the radio staff so he could broadcast his own message, Lynch was characteristically hands-on: "We could only do one take," says Broski. "When I was squeezing the secretary's head, David himself was pouring the Hershey's syrup over her head. He wanted it done the way he wanted it done."

As he recalls it, Broski received the poem that would make the woodsman another iconic character in the *Twin Peaks* pantheon just ten minutes before filming the sequence. Ripping the Platters single "My Prayer" off the turntable, he recites a poem that recalls the original series' exhortation to "fire walk with me": "This is the water, this is the well. Drink full and descend. The horse is the white of the eyes, and dark within."

Repeating it over and over, the woodsman puts listeners across town under a strange trance.

"I was saying it slowly and methodically, so I had time, I guess you can say, to think of saying it a little bit differently the next time," says Broski. But he was given no special insights into what the poem actually means. "It ties in with some scenes before, and I think it ties in with *Fire Walk with Me*," he says. "But when I think of David Lynch, and the things he's done, my interpretation is that it's kind of like when you walk into a museum. Each room is different, and each room has its own impact, and it all has its own meaning. But it's still in the same museum of art. It's all separate, but it all comes together."

The woodsman's most notable victim is a young woman walking home with a boy after a first date. When she finds a penny—heads up, showing Lincoln's face—she wonders aloud about the good luck it might bring.

Later, as the young girl sleeps, a creepy creature called a frog-moth, which has slithered up from the desert, crawls up to her mouth, which becomes unnaturally distended as it slides down her throat.

It's a disturbing, violating image. It's also one that's unusually personal to David Lynch. The frog-moth—Lynch revealed, passingly, in a video about how to make quinoa—originated from an experience he had on a train trip from Athens to Paris. When he disembarked to buy a sugary beverage from a man in a tent in a dusty region of Yugoslavia, he says, "moths were flipping and flying like frogs. Frog-moths were pulling themselves out of the Earth and flying up in front of the stand." It was a memory that had stayed with him for many years, and now he had occasion to use it. "Things just sort of show up in the world of Twin Peaks," he said.

There was one more series-altering revelation left buried in the closing moments of "Part 8," though—owing largely to Lynch's desire to avoid spelling anything out too cleanly—many viewers missed it until Mark Frost wrote about it more plainly in *The Final Dossier.* The girl who swallows the frog-moth is Sarah Palmer, who unwittingly carries the creature with her when her family moves to Twin Peaks. "That's what I pitched to [David]," says Frost. "I said, 'I think if we're looking for a way to find a unified field theory of BOB, it's a twist to have it actually come through Sarah.' We never wanted to hit the nail right on the head with people, but I think all the clues were there."

SARAH PALMER

"What is going on in this house?"

Imagine, if you can, enduring what Sarah Palmer endures over the course of *Twin Peaks*. It's Sarah who first discovers that Laura is missing, making a series of increasingly frantic phone calls in a desperate attempt to track her down. It's Sarah who watches in grim chain-smoking horror as Leland deteriorates in the wake of Laura's murder: leaping onto her casket at the funeral, dancing manically with Laura's homecoming portrait, and ending up in jail after sneaking into the hospital and murdering Jacques Renault. When Leland/BOB is revealed as the killer—having regularly drugged Sarah to commit his crimes while she was unconscious—she learns, simultaneously, that Leland raped and murdered their daughter and that he is dead. Though Cooper tenderly consoles her on the morning of Leland's funeral, she departs the show immediately after, only returning for a brief, cryptic appearance in the season two finale.

One has to assume that for the rest of the time—and for the twenty-five years that followed—Sarah lived alone in that empty house as the last surviving witness to unspeakable horrors, like a ghost that haunts a vacant home. It's a bitter outcome for a bitterly tragic and disappointing life—one that Sarah expected, on some level. "Of course she knows Laura is already dead when she gets the call from Leland," wrote actress Grace Zabriskie in 2020. "She's been waiting for this call and for too many others all her entire lives."

In *The Secret Diary of Laura Palmer*, Laura repeatedly expresses a sense of unique kinship with Sarah. "Sometimes I think Mom and I think the same thoughts, have the same dreams," she writes. After attending one sex party, she daydreams that Sarah once had her own strange sexual experiences in the woods, and that she would be so proud of Laura that she'd call all her friends and brag about it. "Sometimes I think that my mom and I could be the best of friends," Laura writes in another entry. "Every once in a while I will look into her eyes and think, I wonder if Mom has ever felt anything that I'm feeling . . . ? I sense that some of my experiences are ones that she would understand, but she comes from a family and a generation that doesn't really like to talk about things that make them uncomfortable."

Later in the book, there's an otherwise unexplained, similarly revealing moment that plays very differently with the context of *Twin Peaks: The Return*. As she heads up to her bedroom, Laura senses her mother staring her down—"pure jealousy at my back."

Twin Peaks makes it clear, from the very beginning, that there's something strange about Sarah Palmer. "Laura used to say her mother was kind of spooky," Donna tells James in one early episode. "She used to see stuff; she'd have dreams." The pilot episode ends with Sarah waking up, screaming, after an (entirely accurate) vision of a gloved hand pulling Laura's necklace from the hole where Donna and James buried it. When drugged by Leland, she has visions of pale, spectral white horses. But her supernatural powers seem to run deeper than those connected to her daughter's murder. In the season two finale, Dr. Jacoby brings Sarah to the Double R to speak with Major Briggs. In a trance, she tells him, "I'm in the Black Lodge with Dale Cooper. I'm waiting for you."

What has possessed Sarah Palmer? An answer comes, at last, in *Twin Peaks: The Return*. Among the victims of the strange events following the Trinity test in "Episode 8" is the young woman played by Tikaeni Faircrest, credited only as "Girl (1956)." In *The Final Dossier*, Mark Frost makes it clear that this unnamed girl is Sarah Palmer. Like much of "Episode 8," this new information represents a radical reworking of *Twin Peaks*' previously understood mythology. What does it mean if Sarah—like Leland, a victim targeted during childhood—was possessed by a creature from the

Black Lodge decades before the events of *Twin Peaks*? *What was going on in that house?*

What *did* Sarah know? Just as with Leland, it's an unsettling question *Twin Peaks* never concretely answers. Leland's habitual drugging seems to offer a reason that Sarah didn't know about the sexual abuse happening under her roof. But in *Fire Walk with Me*, as Leland menacingly insists that Laura wash her hands, Sarah is fully conscious of Leland's abusiveness, pleading with him to stop, but not doing anything to stop him. One has the sense she's seen Leland act like this before. It's hard to believe Sarah didn't know *something* was going on in this house; whatever she knew, she did nothing to stop it.

For the 2014 Blu-ray set *Twin Peaks: The Entire Mystery*, David Lynch wrote and directed a very unusual special feature: a short film, titled *Between Two Worlds*, that represented the closest thing *Twin Peaks* fans had to an official sequel until the premiere of *The Return*. The film takes the form of a conversation between Lynch and the Palmer family, with all three actors reprising their roles from the original series. Laura and Leland are, necessarily, speaking from the afterlife; Sarah, the surviving Palmer, speaks candidly about what it's like to live alone in that house in Twin Peaks. "I can still make 'the happy face' when I go to get my hair done, or to the grocery store," she says, smiling and breaking at the same time.

By the time *The Return* rejoins Sarah, the ugliness of her past life has festered even further. She is no longer making "the happy face" at the grocery store. She spends her days drinking like a fish and smoking like a chimney, watching a looping video of animal slaughter on her TV for entertainment. When Hawk shows up at her door, expressing concern, she turns him away. When a cruel stranger threatens her at a bar, she literally opens her face up, revealing a mouth that bites his throat open, before closing it and feigning distress that a strange man is bleeding to death in front of her.

There are mythological explanations for what's happening to Sarah Palmer. It is strongly implied that the dark spirit possessing her is Judy, or "Jowday," who *The Return* belatedly reveals to be the reigning evil of the Black Lodge. But even as *The Return* introduces eldritch undertones and split time lines to the *Twin Peaks* narrative, it remains compelling to look at what's happening, day to day, through Sarah's eyes. Whichever way you look at it, she is, after all, wearing a face to conceal the horrors underneath—even as the real thing occasionally pokes through. "Something happened to me. Something happened to me!" Sarah cries during one breakdown in *Twin Peaks: The Return*. It's a moment of great horror, but also of great pain—a reminder, even decades later, that she has been a victim, witness, and perpetrator of unfathomable wrongs. As Sarah says, practically choking on her own words, in *Between Two Worlds*: "The house is still the same."

Chapter 12

PEOPLE ARE UNDER A LOT OF STRESS

The hottest concert of 2016 was held at a soundstage in Pasadena. For two straight days, and well into the night, an elderly emcee introduced a fascinating and eclectically curated series of musical acts—Chromatics, the Cactus Blossoms, Sharon Van Etten, Au Revoir Simone—to an invitation-only crowd. "David does create a vibe," says James Marshall. "And as soon as you got there, you felt the vibe."

He should know; he was, of course, one of the performers. Interspersed among acts such as "the" Nine Inch Nails and Edward Louis Severson III—you might know him better as Eddie Vedder—were performances by James Hurley, Audrey Horne, and famed *Twin Peaks* chanteuse Julee Cruise. While Marshall was disappointed Lynch wanted him to play to the original track of "Just You" instead of performing a new version of the song—"That way, it could have had at least had a different feel," he says—he took comfort in knowing that this crowd, at least, would be extremely receptive to his performance. "They said 'This is our family and friends unit. We're not having anybody else come here,'" recalls Marshall.

In *Twin Peaks'* original run, the Roadhouse was the location that repeatedly brought the show's different characters and plot threads together—so it was appropriate that *The Return*'s Roadhouse shoot was also the production itself in microcosm. If the atmosphere was warm, convivial, and celebratory, it was also a little dizzying: packed with star power, overloaded with storylines, and produced on a necessarily frantic schedule. It was also distinctly Lynchian—more so, even, than the rest of *The Return*. "David did that," says Mark Frost. "Those interstitial scenes of people in the Roadhouse, who you didn't really know, before you'd hear a song. He asked me if I wanted to write them, and I said, 'You know, honestly, if you were working on a TV show, that's the kind of thing you'd give to a staff writer to fill out for you.'" Busy writing *The Secret History of Twin Peaks* and *The Final Dossier*—which were also being produced under an exceedingly tight deadline—Frost passed.

David Lynch was having the time of his life making *Twin Peaks: The Return*. "He hadn't been on set, in earnest, for a very long time," says Harley Peyton. "I still remember Mark calling me from location to say, 'You know what? He's like a great pitcher who hasn't lost his fastball.'"

The time and budgetary crunch, however, was constant. "The whole idea was that David was going to shoot the whole thing himself and I was going to cut the whole thing by myself," says Duwayne Dunham. "At the start of September, he started shooting and I started cutting, and by Thanksgiving I already had six hours of cut footage on the shelf. So we both know this is *way* longer than we ever thought. By Christmas, I had about twelve hours on the shelf. He was about halfway through shooting, and we had to deliver the entire show, locked, on September fourth. I finally said to David, 'How etched in stone is this delivery date? Because I don't even know how many episodes it's going to be.' And he said, 'It's etched in granite,' in the tone that I know, from David, means he's dead serious."

"One of the things he went into the show with, that he was a little bit frustrated about, was he wanted to be able to experiment every day," says Sabrina S. Sutherland. "Everything he did, he wanted to have time to experiment. I tried to give that time to him, but, unfortunately, a lot of the days, there wasn't room to experiment, because we were on such a limited budget. We really were."

One constant, of course, was Lynch's meditation schedule. "He always made sure he meditated twice a day," says Sutherland. "He meditated before we picked him up, and he meditated when we broke for lunch and then ate his food, quickly, while they were lighting." Another regular occurrence was "gather-rounds"—a round of applause, introduced over a bullhorn by Lynch, for every single actor who completed their work on the series.

To say it was a happy set does not mean it was not a challenging set. In a moment captured during the show's behind-the-scenes footage, we see Lynch decide there should be three detectives named Fusco, not two. As the final episode shows, Sutherland dutifully rounded up a third. When asked if she recalls any comparable situations, Sutherland laughs. "Every day, there was something," she says. "My job is to bring David's vision to the screen. I'm supposed to try and make sure that everything that he wants happens in such a way that what he sees is what he wants. You just have to work and go with the flow, and figure out whatever he wants, and do the best you can. He'll adapt, but he doesn't compromise. It's not like he'll say, 'Well, I'll go with a lesser thing.' He will come up with a different idea, 'If we do it *this* way, that will work as well.'"

This philosophy is how—due to the absent Michael J. Anderson—the Man from Another Place can simply be reborn as a talking electric tree, or how David Bowie's terminal illness meant that Phillip Jeffries could reemerge, instead, as a giant metallic spout spewing steam and numerical coordinates. Lynch's famous penchant for "happy accidents" had been fully integrated into his creative process. It was the ideal attitude for a show being produced under such tight conditions; whenever the production ran into what seemed to be a dead end, enough creativity and flexibility ensured that a path out could be found. *The Return*'s happy accidents were abundant. A tense standoff between Richard Horne and Red, a menacing drug dealer played by Balthazar Getty, was originally scripted to take place in the woods. When heavy rainfall made shooting outdoors a practical impossibility, the scene was hastily reconfigured to take place in a nearby location that was immediately available: an indoor batting cage. "I said to David, 'This is such a great set,'" recalls Dunham. "I thought it was so interesting. *Who made all these holes in the wall?*" The reality—just as it had been with the flickering light during Laura's autopsy or the deer's head on the table—was that the most interesting answer had naturally presented itself, and Lynch had been wise enough to take it.

The production of *The Return* had required compromises from the very beginning, but they'd largely been manageable ones. When Michael Ontkean dropped out, Harry Truman became Frank Truman fairly seamlessly; when Catherine E. Coulson's illness necessitated rewrites, the script was already written in such a way that Margaret Lanterman being homebound barely affected the story. "We had written, I think, only one or two scenes where she was outside of her house," says Mark Frost.

There was, however, one major rewrite that threw the production an unwelcome curveball: the role of Audrey Horne. Always a fan favorite, Audrey was slated for a relatively prominent role in *The Return*, which would have brought her into the story much earlier than her eventual appearance two-thirds of the way into the season. "We had written a storyline for Audrey, which [Sherilyn Fenn] rejected while we were already shooting," says Mark Frost. "I just remember that she came in to read those pages, she got angry, and she left. I don't know what she thought. I was not privy to those conversations. But it was a substantially bigger role. I was shocked when she turned it down, honestly."

"I get called to an office, and David is just sitting there, and I go and read these pages," says Fenn. "And they're ridiculous. It was such shit. She's working in some hair salon, and she has this son that's a real asshole."

"And I just couldn't. I said, 'You don't even have a scene with Cooper.' Not even, 'They drive past each other and connect eyes.' And [David] goes, 'Oh, Sherilyn Fenn, you had a dream.' And I said, 'I didn't have a dream. Your fucking fanbase has a dream.' I was, literally, crying. Couldn't even talk. I was whispering at the end. I was just like, 'I don't even know what this is. I don't see her.' And I just ran out."

What did Fenn find so upsetting? Fans have long speculated that one of *The Return*'s most brutal scenes—in which Audrey's son Richard ties up his autistic uncle Johnny, berates and strangles his grandmother Sylvia, and leaves in a fury after stealing money and other valuables—was originally written with Audrey, not Sylvia, as the target of Richard's abuse. According to Mark Frost, that was never the case. "It was not her being attacked," says Frost. "I think she might have been a witness."

What *is* accurate, says Frost, is that Audrey's scenes would have taken place in Twin Peaks proper, not in the limbo of her strangely apathetic husband Charlie's office and the Roadhouse. "David came up with another way to do it. Maybe even a little bit better than what we'd had," says Frost. "A lot of it, in my opinion, was fueled with his anger with me. And that's okay," says Fenn.

The show's fundamental strangeness, abandonment of typical TV structure, and lack of traditional narrative payoffs led some viewers to find meaning when meaning wasn't actually there. After "Part 7" aired, fans spent weeks arguing over whether a strange inconsistency during the closing credits—in which a variety of Double R patrons seemed to be switching seats between cuts—was actually a deliberate hint that *The Return* was unfolding across parallel universes or multiple time lines. (For the record: "No," says Duwayne Dunham.)

On almost any other show, this detail, if noticed at all, would be recognized for what it was: a simple continuity error. But Lynch's reputation as a genius who obsessively considered and controlled every aspect of the production made it difficult for some to believe that anything about *The Return* was accidental. Debates that took place on alt.tv.twin-peaks during the original series were now held on Twitter and Reddit, which hosted a proliferation of multi-thousand-word theories and counter-theories about how all these seemingly disconnected plot threads and non sequiturs would, or wouldn't, seamlessly tie together by *The Return*'s end.

The downside of writing *The Return*'s script as a single massive feature was needing to figure out, retroactively, how to break the show into discrete episodes while ensuring that no individual story got lost in the mix. "I worked on color-coded index cards," says Dunham. "I put them up in an entire room, three hundred and sixty degrees. You could stand in the middle of the room and figure out where you were. Something important would happen in hour three, and I'd turn to David and say, 'You see that colored card way over there? *That's* when we come back to this.'" Flexibility, again, proved essential. "Everything was kind of modular for David," says Sutherland. "Scenes and different things could be put anywhere, in a way."

Take, for one representative example, the story of Becky Burnett. Played by Amanda Seyfried and introduced in "Part 5," Bobby and Shelly's troubled daughter is living in a trailer with her husband, Steve, a sketchy addict played by Caleb Landry Jones. Becky seems to be trapped in an echo of her mother's abusive first marriage to Leo Johnson, and the character's sudden prominence—as well as the relative star power of the actress playing her—seems to be setting her up for a major role in *The Return*.

But after an introduction that includes one of the most memorable shots in the entire series, Becky disappears for five episodes. Returning in "Part 10," Becky is furious when she realizes Steve is cheating on her with an ex-girlfriend. (His affair is, of all people, with Donna Hayward's little sister Gersten, played by Alicia Witt—a character even *Twin Peaks* fans may strain to recall from the original series.) As Steve hides in the woods with his lover and his gun in "Part 13," it's strongly implied that he may have killed Becky off-screen—"I did it," "No, *she* did it," he and Gersten argue—while trailer park manager Carl Rodd looks, ominously, at the couple's trailer, where a window is conspicuously broken.

This would seem, at the very least, to be a major development for Bobby and Shelly—two of the characters *Twin Peaks* fans had been most eager to check up on. But we never see their reaction, because *The Return* never returns to this story again. It's only in *The Final Dossier*, which was published after *The Return* concluded, that Mark Frost revealed—to the surprise of many—that, despite the obvious implication of Steve's final scene, Becky Burnett was alive and well. "I was so happy that Amanda Seyfried came on board, because she's an incredible talent," says Frost. "I think maybe I just liked her so much that I didn't want her to die."

The Becky subplot isn't the only one that defies television's traditional narrative storytelling structure. *The Return* is loaded with an ever-expanding array of law enforcement officers, government officials, and shady underworld players, most of whom get one or two scenes before they disappear from the story for good. Some are given tantalizing pieces of backstory that a more traditional TV show might follow up on. Mr. C expertly manipulates Dwight Murphy, the prison warden played by James Morrison, by making a series of references that clearly terrify him: "Mr. Strawberry," "Joe McCluskey," "The cow jumps over the moon." Fans and recappers spent weeks theorizing about the identities of these mysterious men and when they might emerge.

But *The Return* had already moved on; Warden Murphy had served his purpose. Morrison, as part of his acting process, had worked out his own answers for what all of it meant—but he never asked for, or received, any information about what dark secrets Murphy was harboring. "I didn't talk to Lynch about that," he says. Instead, he recalls, Lynch was focused on the present, ensuring that Morrison's performance fully conveyed just how disgusting it was to be in Mr. C's presence. "The only real direction I got from him was, 'He makes you want to vomit,'" recalls Morrison. "'When you're with him, you just feel like you're going to be sick to your stomach. Okay, let's do it.'"

Some of *The Return*'s most puzzling plot threads unfold *entirely* off-screen. Throughout the series, there are regular references to a man named Billy, whose misadventures are described secondhand by a number of characters, including Audrey Horne. Billy is referenced so frequently that anyone familiar with even the basic principles of storytelling probably assumes he'll turn up at some point—maybe, after all that buildup, to play some key role in the show's climax. But if we ever meet Billy—fans, of course, have their theories about who he might be—we're never formally introduced to him.

And some of the flourishes seem to play with time itself, luxuriating in the freedoms afforded by eighteen hours on premium cable. At one point, Lynch devotes two and a half minutes to a static shot of a janitor sweeping up cigarette butts at the Roadhouse while "Green Onions" plays over the soundtrack. It is far, far longer than audiences have been trained to expect, and the scene becomes strangely suspenseful simply because your brain can't figure out why the show is spending so long on a man sweeping a floor. By depicting something so mundane for so long, the effect, paradoxically, is to make the audience sit up and pay attention. "In American filmmaking, it's like, 'How can I entertain them as much as possible in these eighty minutes?'" said Laura Dern. "And I think there's something radically brave and inventive that David plays around with [time], and it takes our own willingness to go with it."

The Double R, as beloved as ever

All these unusual creative swerves come from the deal Lynch fought Showtime so hard for up front: total creative control and a budget to make as many episodes as he saw fit. Lynch doesn't need to lock in on a single character, as he did with Laura Palmer for *Fire Walk with Me*; he can follow all these stories and ideas wherever they take him. It's not hard to imagine a tighter, more focused edit of the series—maybe even the nine hours Showtime originally imagined—that zooms in on the central stories of Dale Cooper and Mr. C and the town of Twin Peaks. But then, of course, it wouldn't be *Twin Peaks: The Return*.

There's another powerful side effect of subverting the medium's norms: how much more impactful it is when you *do* give the audience what they want. Before the one-two punch of its final two episodes, *The Return* offers one of its few truly unadulterated bits of fan service when—after literal decades of longing for each other from afar—Norma Jennings and Ed

Hurley finally get together, and make a plan to get married, while Otis Redding's "I've Been Loving You Too Long" plays over the soundtrack. "David and I both said, 'That's gotta happen.' That's been the slowest burn in history. They were old lovers when we met them in *1990*," says Mark Frost. "These sweet people, these beloved characters... let's give them a fucking break. You can't always have happy endings. But I think you should have a few."

AUDREY HORNE

"One of these days, before you know it, I'm gonna be grown-up and on my own. And you better watch out."

Everything you need to know about Audrey Horne can be pieced together from her opening scenes in the *Twin Peaks* pilot. Driven to Twin Peaks High School in a fancy town car, she climbs out of the car wearing a pair of black-and-white saddle shoes. Arriving at her locker, she pulls out a pair of bright-red pumps, slipping them on and dumping the saddle shoes back into her locker.

In a show filled with characters immersed in double lives, the implication is obvious. Audrey wears the saddle shoes to school so her parents will think she's a good girl; she changes into the red heels among her peers, lighting up cigarettes in the bathroom of Twin Peaks High School, so her classmates will think she's a bad girl. (The black-and-white/red resonance with the Red Room, still to be introduced a few episodes later, is interesting but apparently unintentional.) This specific sartorial choice was important enough to Lynch to pause on the third day of production until it was just right; those saddle shoes, Sherilyn Fenn says, were so out of fashion that the costumer had no choice but to buy Oxfords and paint them to suit Lynch's vision.

It's an arc not entirely dissimilar to Laura Palmer, but in reverse. The difference is that Laura hides her sex-and-drug-fueled double life behind the veneer of radiant goodness. Audrey, somewhat less convincingly, hides her innocence behind a teenage girl's impression of a worldly, sexually adventurous young woman. Her famous solo dance at the Double R Diner—the moment, for many, at which Audrey became *Twin Peaks*' breakout heroine—was unscripted and conceived by Lynch on the day it was shot. "He said, 'Everybody go get a cappuccino. You can leave,'" says Fenn. "'We're rewriting the scene and Sherilyn Fenn, you're going to dance.' I was like . . . 'What? Why am I dancing?' 'Because we wrote you a song.' I was so scared I called my acting coach. And he said, 'Sherilyn, you're with David. He's an artist. This is somebody you can trust. Just do what he says.'

"If you look closely enough, my hands are just a little bit shaky. It was hard for me to understand in any logical way, and I was just beginning to understand David's world," says Fenn. But unplanned as it was, Lynch's impulse was the right one. The essence of Audrey is there: confident, captivating, and free.

You can spot the gulf between who Audrey pretends to be, and who she actually is, in the arc that plays out across *Twin Peaks*' first season, which plays a little bit like *Nancy Drew and the Secret of the Brothel She Absolutely Should Not Have Taken a Job At*. While undercover at One Eyed Jack's, she borrows the name Hester Prynne from the heroine of *The Scarlet Letter*—a teenager's idea of a fallen woman. Blackie, the brothel's proprietress, instantly recognizes that Audrey had no idea what she's doing: "I read *The Scarlet Letter* in high school too, honey," she sneers. Audrey wins her over with the most famous of *Twin Peaks*' sexual provocations: a lengthy scene in which she twists a cherry stem into a knot using only her tongue.

This, too, is a performance. As Audrey reveals much later in the series: She was a virgin until her brief affair with John Justice Wheeler (Billy Zane), a dashing Ben Horne protégé who promptly zips off to Brazil in his private jet. No matter: One has to imagine that Audrey—a budding activist with designs on taking over the family business—wouldn't have wasted much time awaiting the return of this blandly handsome cipher. Even Audrey seems to recognize this: The show's final line on Wheeler, from Audrey's own mouth, is that she hopes it won't hurt so much in a week.

But even as *Twin Peaks* works overtime to establish Audrey as a secret innocent, it puts her through a litany of traumas that suggest—if Laura Palmer and Ronette Pulaski weren't proof enough—that Twin Peaks is an especially awful place to be a teenage girl. Her father, we know from the start, either ignores or belittles her; her mother, it's revealed in a deleted scene included in the *Twin Peaks* DVD sets, openly blames her for her brother Johnny's condition based on an incident that happened when Audrey was a toddler. By the end of the first season, still undercover at One Eyed Jack's, Audrey is wearing a mask and retreating from her father, who doesn't recognize her as the teenager he's trying to have sex with. Though she manages to fend him off, she ends up as a hostage to Jean Renault and his cronies, who keep her compliant by injecting her with heroin. "In season two, I had this dress—black and double-breasted—and I was like, 'That's my Special Agent Audrey dress,'" says Fenn. "That's who I thought she was. *I'm going to become a special agent like Dale Cooper.* I pictured them like Nick and Nora. That's who I wanted her to be." Could anyone blame her for dreaming of a better life solving crimes on the road with Agent Cooper?

The cancellation of *Twin Peaks* left a number of characters in limbo, but none, apart from Cooper, as tragically as Audrey. We don't need to imagine where else the character could have gone—we already know. A nascent version of what eventually became David Lynch's film *Mulholland Drive* was conceived as a possible spinoff for Audrey, who would abandon Twin Peaks for the glamour of Hollywood and end up at the center of the kind of mystery she hoped to solve with Cooper.

Instead, she ended up as an unlucky victim: in the wrong place, at the wrong time, when Thomas Eckhardt manipulated Andrew Packard into triggering a bomb at the Twin Peaks Savings and Loan. While Audrey's fate was, technically, in question at the end of season two, nobody truly believed that the show would kill off a fan-favorite character so unceremoniously, and Fenn later confirmed that Audrey was intended to survive anything the town could throw at her. Still: It wasn't until the publication of Mark Frost's *The Secret History of Twin Peaks* that it was revealed that Audrey had survived, with the late Pete Martell shielding her body from the worst of the explosion.

It is, the subsequent record shows, the last kind thing anyone does for Audrey Horne. *The Return*'s introduction of Richard Horne comes with a dawning horror: If this is her son, there's only one explanation for it. But it's not until Richard's death late in *The Return*, when Mr. C says, "Good-bye, my son," that an awful, widely speculated theory is finally confirmed: While pretending to be Dale Cooper in the weeks after the events of the season two finale, Mr. C went to the hospital and raped the comatose Audrey, impregnating her with the son who will go on to terrorize Twin Peaks. It's an especially vindictive betrayal of the love and trust Audrey had for the real Dale Cooper, who gently turned her down when she showed up in his bed naked.

Where does that leave Audrey? It's here that the actual production problems make her story harder to parse. When Fenn rejected the storyline that had been written for Audrey for *The Return*, Lynch wrote a different one that—like the scenes he wrote for the various characters at the Roadhouse—hinges, frustratingly, on characters we barely know. As Audrey rants and raves about her lover Billy, to the apparent indifference of husband Charlie, she insists that she wants to go to the Roadhouse, but shrinks away from the idea whenever it seems like Charlie is actually willing to take her. Is Audrey's marriage to this condescending bore even real? Is it some kind of therapeutic game, or a bleak comatic fantasy, or even some kind of cosmic nightmare realm? When Charlie suggests he might need to end Audrey's story, she replies, "What story is that, Charlie? Is it the story of the girl who lived down the lane?" It's a question repeated, unnervingly, by the former Man from Another Place, now called the Evolution of the Arm, in the finale of *Twin Peaks: The Return*. Whatever is happening to Audrey, the Black Lodge seems to be a part of it.

When Audrey does, at last, arrive at the Roadhouse—a place we know, through other plotlines, is entirely real—events still unfold with the uncanniness of a dream. As she and Charlie toast over martinis, the emcee makes an announcement: "Ladies and gentlemen: Audrey's dance." The crowd lines the dancefloor, swaying slowly, as Audrey takes center stage and begins dancing to Angelo Badalamenti's iconic score. For longtime *Twins Peaks* fans, it's a moment of almost weapons-grade nostalgia—until a fight breaks out, Audrey asks Charlie to get her out of there, and the scene suddenly cuts to Audrey, alone and afraid in a white room, staring horrified into a mirror. "I was really saying, for some weird reason, that I wanted her to go mad. I don't know why. Like she'd been hurt too much," says Fenn. "And after the last take, David said, 'Sherilyn Fenn, come over here. I need to talk to you.' And he just . . . said he was sorry. 'You were right. You were right. We're going to do what you said. Take off some of your makeup, and we're going to do one shot of you looking at your mirror.'"

Where has Audrey ended up? However it's interpreted—a mental-health facility, a comatose fever dream, limbo itself—it's a haunting end for one of *Twin Peaks*' most memorable characters. Audrey deserved better, and fans had hoped for better, but a series that doled out relatively few happy endings didn't find one for her. Maybe that's why I prefer not to focus on the white room at all. When I look back at *The Return*, I'd rather leave Audrey in the one happy moment the show managed to find for her: dancing at the Roadhouse, confident, captivating, and free.

Chapter 13

WHAT YEAR IS THIS?

Twin Peaks had never received a proper ending. Though the closing scene of the season two finale was unforgettable, it was also an accident. Neither Lynch nor Frost ever planned to end *Twin Peaks* with Cooper cackling in a mirror with BOB smiling at him. That was, they knew, the beginning of another story—one that it ultimately took twenty-five years to tell.

Now, in its closing hours, *The Return* promised something that had never happened before: a conclusion to the story of *Twin Peaks* told entirely on Lynch's and Frost's terms. This time, the show's cocreators would write an ending together—one that could plausibly serve as the final word on *Twin Peaks* as a whole. "We went back and forth on the ending for quite a while. We had two or three different endings we were playing with," says Frost. "I think, in a way, it reflects the fact that *Twin Peaks* was the written work of two very different personalities. I might have been more inclined to do something more optimistic, and David might have been inclined to do something more pessimistic. And instead, we found something in the middle."

They knew, in broad strokes, that the final episodes would resolve the long-simmering conflict between Dale Cooper and Mr. C. After spending nearly the entire season in his addled Dougie Jones persona, Cooper finally returns to normal in "Part 16." It was everything *Twin Peaks* fans had been waiting for. As Angelo Badalamenti's "Twin Peaks Theme" swells on the soundtrack, Cooper calmly assesses the situation, thanks Dougie Jones's good-natured boss Bushnell Mullins (Don Murray) for his kindness and decency, and leaves a note to pass along whenever Gordon Cole calls. As Cooper leaves, Bushnell asks, "What about the FBI?" Cooper turns, smiles, and delivers one of the most famous lines of the series: "I *am* the FBI." Cooper's line "just came out of me," says Frost. "As we wrote that scene, it was like a tennis match. We'd often just bounce lines back and forth. And the minute I said 'I am the FBI,' I knew David was already thinking it. I think we came up with it simultaneously. I just said it first."

For Dougie skeptics, "Part 16" at least offers a retroactive justification for why *The Return* left Cooper unmoored so long: the show would have been very, very short if he'd had his wits about him from the very beginning. With characteristic confidence, Cooper heads back to Twin Peaks to save the day. He's on a collision course with Mr. C, whose own wanderings have finally pointed him to the Twin Peaks Sheriff's Department. But while Andy is thrilled to see the man he believes to be the long-lost Dale Cooper, Mr. C's impression remains an unconvincing one; frankly, everyone should have known something was up when he rejected a fresh cup of coffee.

Even more than the episode that follows, "Part 17" feels like a season finale, bringing many of the show's threads together for a climactic, rousing battle of good vs evil in the heart of Twin Peaks. There needed to be *some* reason to get all these characters into one room: the good Cooper, the bad Cooper, the FBI, the Twin Peaks Sheriff's Department, and the various hangers-on that had accumulated over the course of the season. Fortunately, an answer had already presented itself: the mysterious presence that had loomed over *Twin Peaks*, unexplained, since *Fire Walk with Me*. "The key was Judy," says Mark Frost.

Cooper, Diane, and Gordon, into the darkness

How did a tossed-off reference to Bob Engels' sister-in-law in *Fire Walk with Me*—a movie Mark Frost had no creative hand in—become the lynchpin of *Twin Peaks*' mythology? As he had throughout the writing of both *Twin Peaks* and *The Return*, Frost took it upon himself to impose meaning and structure to an idea *Fire Walk with Me* had never explained. "It's no secret that one of my strengths in storytelling is making a tapestry work. Weaving a lot of things together," says Frost. "I remember thinking, *Well, maybe they misheard 'Judy.' Maybe it was something else*. And then I thought, *Well, what else could it be?* And I guess I pulled a page from the Dan Ackroyd playbook, and said, 'Oh, it's gotta be a Sumerian demon, you know?' And in fact, there turns out to be one named Jowday."

Before *The Return* turns to Jowday, there's Mr. C to deal with. Lucy lands the first blow by shooting the doppelgänger in the back, but when BOB emerges from the corpse as an orb—just as he appeared in "Part 8"—the real fight comes down to the heroism of a truly unexpected character: Freddie Sykes (Jake Wardle), a Great Northern security guard introduced just a few episodes earlier. "He's who the Greeks used to call a deus ex machina, you know?" says Frost. "He's a machine of the gods, who has come down to ren der a service, quite unknown to the bearer of the glove. I think it sort of tickled us both—a green garden glove boxing match."

How did this boyish Englishman end up squaring off with *Twin Peaks'* embodiment of evil? As Freddie explains it to James Hurley, he wandered into a portal after a night of drinking and was greeted by the Fireman, who told him to buy a particular green garden glove, which would grant him superhuman strength. He had a destiny, the Fireman explained, and it awaited him in Twin Peaks, Washington. The green garden glove concept had long been in "David's junk drawer of ideas that didn't fit anywhere," says Frost. "I don't mean to disparage it by saying 'junk,' but it's like—*there's an old pocket knife, there's some change from 1965, there's a ticket to a concert you went to in high school.* When he told the idea to me, I went, 'Well, I've never seen *that* before.'"

Though Lynch had originally conceived of the green glove many years earlier, with Jack Nance in mind to wear it, they ultimately repurposed it for Wardle, who performed accents, on a heavily trafficked YouTube channel Lynch had come to admire. The rest of the characters stand and watch as Freddie pummels the BOB orb until it finally shatters—the great evil of *Twin Peaks'* original run finally, apparently, defeated. "I loved it," says James Marshall. "It was so much fun. Cooper's there, and Gordon Cole's there—all of these iconic characters from the show. And then Lucy comes walking in with a fucking hardcore gun, and this dude's just punching this BOB orb . . . It's kind of awesome. But it is kind of absurd."

It's here, after BOB is finally defeated, that the events grow a little harder to parse. "Now there are some things that will change. The past dictates the future," Cooper warns the people in the room. Naido (Nae Yuuki)—a mysterious, eyeless woman rescued from the woods outside Twin Peaks—is revealed to be the real Diane. They kiss, and Cooper turns to the rest of them room for a *Wizard of Oz*–like address that does, in fact, turn out to be his final goodbye: "I hope I see all of you again. Every one of you." All this unfolds with a strange digital effect of Cooper's head superimposed over the action. "We live inside a dream," he says, echoing both Phillip Jefferies in *Fire Walk with Me* and a verse of the ancient Indian text the Upanishads, which was referenced by Monica Bellucci in a dream Gordon Cole had earlier that season.

All of this sequence is filmed in a way that has led some fans to conclude that the scene, if not the *series*, took place entirely within Cooper's head. Whatever you make of that reading, there's no question that the rest of the series unfolds in a kind of dream logic. In the basement of the Great Northern, Cooper finds a door that leads him, at last, to a meeting with Phillip Jeffries. It's here that Cooper gets what he's been looking for: a chance not just to solve Laura's murder, but to save her from being murdered at all. Transported to 1989, into the woods on the evening Laura was murdered, he witnesses her leap off James's motorcycle but intervenes before she can rendezvous with Leo, Jacques, and Ronette. Initially afraid, Laura realizes she recognizes Cooper from her dream in *Fire Walk with Me* and takes his hand. "Where are we going?" she asks. "We're going home," says Cooper.

"We thought about ending it there," says Frost. "And then we realized we wanted to make it not quite so close-ended—or *seem* close-ended. I mean, Cooper pulls an Orpheus. He goes into the underworld and he tries to retrieve a dead girl. And while that might seem to make good on his quest, it's an act of hubris. David argued, 'Cooper's got to pay a price.' And I didn't disagree."

And so, after a brief, hopeful window in which reconstituted footage from *Twin Peaks* shows Pete Martell embarking on a totally uneventful morning of fishing, things start to feel wrong. A cut to Sarah Palmer—or, perhaps more accurately, Jowday—reveals her maniacally stabbing Laura's homecoming picture over and over as time itself seems to loop. In the woods, Laura screams; when Cooper looks back, she's gone. It was kind that Showtime opted to air "Part 17" and "Part 18" back-to-back; by then, *Twin Peaks* fans had already suffered through plenty of nail-biting cliff-hangers.

"Part 18" unfolds with its own loping, disturbing rhythms, only comprehensible to those who followed the Fireman's dictum to remember certain names, numbers, and phrases. Following instructions given by the Fireman in *The Return*'s premiere, Cooper leads Diane to a mysterious crossing. "Once we cross, it could all be different," he warns, though it's clear that nothing is going to stop him now.

Once they cross, things *are* different. After a joyless night in a motel, Diane leaves Cooper a goodbye letter addressed to Richard and signs her name *Linda*. When Cooper leaves the room, both the motel he checked into and the car he drove have, inexplicably, changed. But he barely seems to notice; he's on a mission to find Laura, and nothing else seems to matter.

"We were trying to think, *What's the antonym to Twin Peaks? What's the other side of the compass?*" says Mark Frost. "And Odessa, Texas, in addition to being a slight nod to the *Odyssey*, at least phonically, felt kind of desolate and appropriate." Spotting a diner called Eat at Judy's, he stops for breakfast—making no comment either way about the coffee—and ends up in a surprisingly brutal fight with a trio of roughnecks harassing the waitress. This was, MacLachlan acknowledged, yet another version of Cooper he was being asked to play. "The way it was described to me, he's just a little harder," he said. "So it was another variation, sort of a subtle variation obviously, compared to the other two, but a subtle variation of Cooper. And so that was that last hour, watching him navigate that."

Cooper's violent standoff at Eat at Judy's leads him to the front door of its absent waitress: an embittered woman named Carrie Page, played by Sheryl Lee. And just as in *Twin Peaks'* original Red Room dream—when a girl played by Lee insisted, despite all appearances, that she wasn't Laura Palmer—Cooper refuses to believe this isn't Laura.

Carrie is in some kind of serious trouble. There's a dead man in her living room with a bullet in his forehead. She doesn't explain, and Cooper doesn't ask. The brief, grim glimpses of Carrie's life were "like showing the boot of the giant onstage, but not the giant," says Frost. "Look where she ended up. Yeah, she was alive—but it was no bed of roses." When Cooper says he wants to take her to Washington, she initially assumes he means Washington DC; still, her circumstances are dire enough that she's willing to get in the car with this stranger if it means getting away.

The drive from Odessa, Texas, to Twin Peaks, Washington is a long one, and Lynch shoots it that way. "I said, 'David, are we going to do this drive in real time?'" says Duwayne Dunham. "I said it jokingly, but David knew I was serious. But see, David likes that. He was fascinated with the infinite. Everything held infinite wonder."

▲▲

Like its opening scenes, *The Return*'s ending went through multiple edits. "It's the nature of editing: You try it a bunch of different ways," says Dunham. "My thought was to move the Audrey stuff to right before Cooper shows up at the Palmer house. So when they came back to Twin Peaks, we were there with *all* of those people, and it felt more like a giant resolution. David entertained it, and we went back and forth for quite a while, but he finally said, 'No, no, we're going to do it the way it was written.'"

Cooper's destination is the Palmer house, which—in the real world—had recently changed owners. Mary Reber and her then husband had purchased the Everett, Washington house—which was used as a filming location for both the *Twin Peaks* pilot and *Fire Walk with Me*—in September of 2014, after their original offer for a different house down the street was rejected. "There were holes in the walls upstairs. It was just kind of falling apart," she says. Two months later, they returned home to find a note saying that an unnamed Hollywood production was interested in filming at their house. Unsure if the project was *Twin Peaks*–related, she was surprised when David Lynch himself turned up—first in January, then in April, then in July, and finally in October to film *The Return*'s closing scene. "When he was here in April, he was writing at the door," says Reber. "I believe he was writing that ending."

There are three major characters in *The Return*'s unforgettable final scene: Dale Cooper, Carrie Page, and Alice Tremond—the homeowner who is played, in a meta flourish, by Reber herself. Reber is quick to note that she's not an actress, but she also believes Lynch not only knew that, but saw that as an asset. "I think he probably figured, 'She's gonna be nervous,'" says Reber. "But how else would you be if an FBI agent came to your house at eleven o'clock at night?"

In the elliptical conversation that follows, Lynch instructed Reber to build in long, languorous pauses before answering each of Cooper's questions: "We can edit time out," Lynch told her, "but we can't edit it back in." Cooper badgers Alice about the home's true owner, only for Alice to calmly insist that she doesn't know the Palmers and that the previous occupant was a Mrs. Chalfont. *Twin Peaks* fans know the names Tremond and Chalfont resonate with *Twin Peaks*' supernatural side; whoever Alice is, it's impossible to shake the feeling that something dark and sinister is happening.

Cooper has traveled through space and time, and reversed death itself, to defeat Jowday. But if the great evil of *Twin Peaks: The Return* is lurking on the other side of that door, Cooper doesn't seem to recognize it. Backing away from the house, he seems to lose his grip on reality together: "What year is this?" he asks, puzzled and afraid. ("David is the one who came up with that last line. Which is a killer," says Frost.) But it's Carrie Page who gets the last moment of *The Return*, as she looks back at the house and hears the spectral echo of Sarah Palmer calling for Laura on the morning her body was found. Faced, apparently, with a sudden flood of Laura's traumatic memories, she screams—and the lights at the house, all at once, go out.

What does it all mean? Has Jowday triumphed or been defeated? Either way, what's the cost? Is this an ending, a beginning, or a loop? Lynch, of course, had no interest in offering any explanations. "Some things came to a conclusion. And some things dangled out there. And that's sort of the way it is in life," said Lynch, in one of his increasingly rare interviews, shortly after the finale aired.

Kyle MacLachlan, for his part, was willing to weigh in. "You realize it's been about good versus evil," he said. "It's been about Cooper trying to save Laura Palmer. It really just boils down to good versus evil, and in this particular case, we were at an impasse. So the cycle is not complete yet. That was kind of my feeling." It was, for him, an ending in which Cooper failed. "All I know is I'm in a place and I'm at a loss. And the Cooper character that we all know and remember I don't think was ever at a loss," he said. "And to see that for the first time was very frightening and disheartening and confusing. That's not what I played, but it's what I saw when I saw it. It was like, 'Oh, now we're in trouble.' You know? And you realize that even the best man—we think of Cooper as the best man—maybe he didn't get there."

Just like the original *Twin Peaks*, the ambiguity and horror of the ending seems to be part of what keeps *The Return* alive, inspiring theories and debates that are, by their nature, unresolvable. "If there's one hundred people in the audience, you're going to get one hundred different interpretations, especially when things get abstract," said Lynch. "It's beautiful.

Everybody's a detective and whatever they come up with is valid in my mind." Frost agrees. "Why would you want there to be only one interpretation to what you do? What is the benefit of that?" he says. "You can't control what people are going to think anyway. So why don't you put it out there, and however people respond to it? That's their part of the bargain."

In that spirit, I have asked nearly everyone involved in *The Return* what they personally took from this ending. It's only fair that I tell you what I make of it.

In Alain Robbe-Grillet's 1953 novel *The Erasers*, Special Agent Wallas embarks on a desperate hunt for a serial murderer, which abruptly ends when Wallas and the reader discover—inexplicably and unsettlingly—that the most plausible culprit is Wallas himself. It's a book that owes a heavy debt to *Oedipus Rex*, the Sophocles play described by some scholars as the first detective story. In that ancient tragedy, Oedipus, the King of Thebes, attempts to ward off a plague by finding and punishing the man who killed the previous king. When Oedipus discovers, to his horror, that *he* is the man who killed the previous king, he stabs his own eyes out, leaving the Greek chorus to deliver the play's ultimate moral: No man is truly fortunate until he is dead.

To be clear: I don't think Dale Cooper killed Laura Palmer. The truth, I think, is something less comprehensible and more troubling. Our hunger for justice can be our undoing. Its purity, in fact, can be the most dangerous thing of all. *Fire Walk with Me* gave Laura peace: a moment of true, cathartic joy, after all the horror of her life, as she sat in the Red Room, when her angel finally arrived. It was Cooper, not Laura, who couldn't let go. Dale Cooper wanted to save Laura Palmer so badly that he literally found a way to go back in time and drag her out of harm's way. When she saw him in the woods, she screamed; though she later took his hand, her first instinct was the right one.

None of this is to say that Cooper's heart wasn't in the right place. It's to say that he was wrong, with disastrous and unforeseen consequences for many, including himself. What did he give up, personally, because he couldn't let go of Laura Palmer? We see, firsthand, in the bonds he forges with Janey-E and Sonny Jim (Pierce Gagnon). Which cases weren't solved—which wrongs weren't righted—because Cooper was so fixated on Laura Palmer that he, like Phillip Jeffries or Chet Desmond before him, went so deep that he ultimately lost himself?

This is, among other things, the nature of TV reboots. A story that continues, as a night soap does, needs to keep escalating, finding new ways to shock and disturb us. We, like Cooper, disturbed the *Twin Peaks* universe with our desire for more. "What year is this?" he asks. We have seen many versions of Cooper, but he's never looked so old or so lost. Bringing *Twin Peaks* back in 2017 wrenched the town and its characters into a darker, harder world—the same one viewers were hoping to escape by revisiting *Twin Peaks*. Everything that happens to them happens because we, like Cooper, simply couldn't leave the past alone. Cooper told Laura he was taking her home; *The Return* knows, in the end, that you can't go home again.

But that's what it means to me. It might mean something different to you. "I can tell you what *Twin Peaks* was about," said Lynch in 2018. "It's about eighteen hours long."

DALE COOPER

"I have no idea where this will lead us, but I have a definite feeling it will be a place both wonderful and strange."

"You know, there's only one problem with you," Audrey Horne tells Dale Cooper midway through *Twin Peaks'* second season. "You're perfect."

At that point in the show's run, it's hard to argue with her. Suit perfectly pressed, hair pomaded into a perfect black helmet, handsome and trim despite consuming massive quantities of donuts and pie—"You must have the metabolism of a bumblebee!" marvels Truman—Cooper is both a preternaturally brilliant investigator and an abnormally kind and enlightened human being. It's no wonder Audrey has him pegged as her Manic Pixie Dream Special Agent from the moment she meets him.

Where does someone like Dale Cooper come from? Scott Frost's *The Autobiography of F.B.I. Special Agent Dale Cooper* is dubiously canonical, but its depiction of an adolescent Cooper was crafted with both Mark Frost's and David Lynch's input. "David said, 'I want you to do something with asparagus and the way it smells when you pee,'" says Scott Frost. "Besides that, it was pretty wide open."

The book's portrait is instructive. Cooper's life seems to be pointing in one direction from the very beginning—a path that will lead him to become, as Harry S. Truman describes him, "the best lawman I've ever seen." The young Dale, we learn, had a poster of Jimmy Stewart in the hagiographic 1959 drama *The FBI Story* in his childhood bedroom; risked life and limb to recover a friend's bicycle that was stolen by a local gang; and—yes—conducted an elaborate experiment, faithfully recorded on his reel-to-reel cassette player, on the effects of various foods on the smell of his urine.

More interesting cases were yet to come, but the truth is that Dale Cooper was a man out of time long before he said "What year is this?"

Everything about Cooper in *Twin Peaks* feels like a throwback to an ultra-idealized version of an upstanding FBI agent circa the late 1950s—a quality that remained true even as *The Return* was airing in 2017. While filming *The Return*'s finale, Kyle MacLachlan suggested to David Lynch that it might make more sense for Cooper to have an FBI lanyard instead of a gold-plated badge in his breast pocket. No, said Lynch—Cooper would do it the old-fashioned way.

In keeping with his status as an unquestionably upright lawman, Cooper's "flaws" in *Twin Peaks*' original run feel a little bit like someone who fills out the "weaknesses" section of a job application with phrases like "works too hard" or "cares too much." He employs strange, definitely-not-FBI-approved investigative techniques that unfailingly lead to fruitful results. Not only does he reject Audrey's advances when she turns up in his bed—he offers to listen to all her problems over malts and French fries, his treat. When he gambles with FBI money on an undercover mission at One Eyed Jack's, he brings back a healthy return-on-investment for the Bureau's coffers. His great regret, we eventually learn, is falling in love with Caroline Earle—as if being the tragic hero in a love story is supposed to make him *less* appealing.

He is, in a word, perfect. Which is exactly why it's so powerful to see what happens to him when he truly, devastatingly fails.

Replaced in the real world by his doppelgänger after the events of the season two finale, the Cooper who emerges from the Black Lodge is a changed man, though not necessarily in the way fans might have expected. Cooper's extended time as Dougie Jones makes the world a better place: like a cross between Mr. Magoo and Amélie, he bumbles through each day, inadvertently improving the lives of everyone around him. But for all the comedy surrounding his exploits, there's also something deeply poignant about Dougie. After all, Cooper spent twenty-five years—nearly half his life—in the Black Lodge, finally emerging as a man in his late fifties. His time as Dougie Jones was a chance, however briefly, to experience something that had otherwise been permanently lost to him: a life as a husband and father.

Cooper—being perfect—doesn't seem to dwell on this loss; instead, he ensures that a Dougie replacement has been manufactured to take his place. Unlike his doppelgänger, he does not ask how Annie is doing. He doesn't seem to care about much of anything, in fact, except saving Laura and defeating Jowday.

There is nothing in Cooper as cruel, sadistic, or evil as Mr. C, who took special delight in betraying those who loved Cooper most. But while we spend relatively little time with Cooper in *The Return*, it's striking how quickly the show discards the Cooper we knew when he's back to normal. "I *am* the FBI" and an enthusiastic request for a pot of coffee aside, *The Return*'s Cooper seems to recognize, on an intuitive level, that putting the Laura Palmer case behind him for good will require him to change as well. "I'll see you at the curtain call," Cooper tells his allies the last time he sees them—a nod to *The Return*'s self-awareness as a piece of drama, but also a sign that the fundamental nature of his relationship with these characters has changed. They're not his friends; they're characters in a story he won't be satisfied with until everyone has played their part.

To be the perfect lawman Cooper can't just push aside the things he used to care about. He needs to strip them out of himself altogether. The Cooper who pushes through to the other side, who Diane addresses as Richard, is a colder, more single-minded man than we ever saw in *Twin Peaks*. "I don't recognize you anymore. Whatever we had once is over," she writes, addressing the letter to Richard.

What would it take, at this point, for Cooper to stop? Losing Diane isn't even enough to slow him down. When strangers pick a fight at the diner in

Odessa, he viciously fights back with minimal regard to the safety of other patrons. And when he tracks down Carrie Page, he drags her back to Twin Peaks to relive the traumatic memories she'd managed to avoid experiencing in this time line. She agrees to go because she's already in trouble in Odessa; one wonders what he'd do if she refused.

It's fitting, in the end, that *The Return* ends with Cooper and Laura together one last time for that long, largely silent road trip. Though they never met in life, their fates have long since become intertwined; Laura can't move on because of what happened to her, and Cooper can't move on because he can't let it go. In that way, he really is the perfect lawman—so committed to solving the case that he'll give up anything, including himself, to see it through to the curtain call. "What year is this?" is a perfect ending, but unlike "How's Annie?" it's hard to imagine where the story could take him next. Cooper has already given up everything, including himself. What's left to sacrifice?

Acknowledgments

Anyone who says you shouldn't meet your heroes has never met Mark Frost. Mark was the first person I approached about this project, and his willingness to hear me out opened the door for everything that followed. Thanks, Mark, for your time, candor, and kindness.

I am grateful beyond words to the dozens of people who worked on *Twin Peaks* and took the time to share their memories and insights. Thanks especially to Harley Peyton, who generously wrote the foreword that opens this book, and to Michael Horse and Mary Reber, who welcomed me into their homes.

This book would look very different without the wisdom of both Rick Richter and Caroline Marsiglia, who helped wrangle my bottomless enthusiasm for all things *Twin Peaks* into a coherent book proposal.

As any writer knows, an editor has the power to make or break a book. I'm fortunate enough to have found a damn fine one in Randall Lotowycz, who believed in this project from our first meeting and improved every page of this book with his thoughtful notes. Thanks also to the rest of the remarkable team at Running Press: Amanda Richmond, Syarlin Syafruddin, Ana-Maria Bonner, Kara Thornton, Shannon Fabricant, and my cover artist Lorenzo Conti.

Anyone who writes about *Twin Peaks* is standing on the shoulders of giants. I'd like to extend a special thanks to John Thorne, Josh Eisenstadt, Brad Dukes, Steven Miller, Courtenay Stallings, and Scott Ryan for keeping the *Twin Peaks* torch lit and for sharing your insights with me.

I still have the six-cassette VHS box set my parents tracked down on eBay when it became clear this *Twin Peaks* obsession was going to stick. To Mom and Dad: Thanks, always, for your love and support (and for trusting us enough not to look *too* closely at what we were watching in middle school).

It would take more space than I have here to thank the many, many people who have gamely watched, discussed, and debated all things *Twin Peaks* with me over the years. I'm grateful to all of you—you know who you are—for your indulgence and your friendship. The next time we're together, coffee and pie are on me.

Jen: You, more than anyone, know what this book means to me, and what it took for it to come together. Thanks for walking through the woods with me.

Cora and Hildy: I love you. Don't watch *Twin Peaks* until you're older. (I'm not a hypocrite—middle school is fine.)

Finally: This book is dedicated to the memory of my brother Peter, who was right by my side, swapping thoughts and theories, the first time I watched this wonderful, strange TV series. Pete: If I ever get lost, I hope you're the one they send to find me.

Bibliography

Altman, Mark. Twin Peaks Behind the Scenes: An Unofficial Visitor's Guide to Twin Peaks. New York: Pioneer Books, 1990.

Bushman, David and Mark T. Givens. Murder at Teal's Pond: Hazel Drew and the Mystery That Inspired Twin Peaks. Seattle: Thomas & Mercer, 2022.

Dukes, Brad. Reflections: An Oral History of Twin Peaks. Nashville: Short/Tall Press, 2014.

Frost, Mark. The Secret History of Twin Peaks. New York: Flatiron Books, 2016.

Frost, Mark. Twin Peaks: The Final Dossier. New York: Flatiron Books, 2017.

Frost, Scott. The Autobiography of F.B.I. Special Agent Dale Cooper: My Life, My Tapes. New York: Pocket Books, 1991.

Iger, Bob. The Ride of a Lifetime: Lessons Learned from 15 Years as CEO of the Walt Disney Company. New York: Random House, 2019.

Lavery, David et al. Full of Secrets: Critical Approaches to Twin Peaks. Nebraska: Wayne State University Press, 1994.

Lynch, David. Catching the Big Fish: Meditation, Consciousness, and Creativity. New York: Tarcher, 2006.

Lynch, David and Kristine McKenna. Room to Dream. New York: Random House, 2019.

Lynch, Jennifer. The Secret Diary of Laura Palmer. New York: Gallery Books, 1990.

Nathan, Ian. David Lynch: A Retrospective. London: Palazzo Editions, 2023.

Rodley, Chris. Lynch on Lynch: Revised edition. New York: Farrar, Straus and Giroux, 2005.

Stahl, Jerry. Permanent Midnight: A Memoir. Los Angeles: Process, 1995.

Stallings, Courtenay. Laura's Ghost: Women Speak About Twin Peaks. New York/Columbus: Fayetteville Mafia Press, 2020.

Thorne, John. The Essential Wrapped in Plastic: Pathways to Twin Peaks. Dallas: John/Thorne, 2016.

Index